THE PAST TODAY

THE PAST TODAY
Historic Places
in New Zealand

EDITOR

John Wilson

Published for the
New Zealand Historic Places Trust
by Pacific Publishers
Auckland London

First published 1987

© 1987 New Zealand Historic Places Trust

Pacific Publishers
Auckland, New Zealand

ISBN 0 86479 001 5

Designed by Lindsay Cuthbertson.
Cover designed by Margaret Cochran
Maps by Jo Mayo

Typeset by Saba Graphics Ltd, Christchurch
Printed by Colorcraft Ltd, Hong Kong

Contents

Contents *continued*

Preface

IN recent years the New Zealand Historic Places Trust has published two major books on the historic buildings of New Zealand. These buildings, elegant or picturesque, were all both historically significant and photogenic, but they represented only one sector of the work of the Trust. In this volume we are taking a wider view of our historic places.

One kind of historic place is the traditional area of emotional and spiritual importance to the Maori people. This might be an urupa, an historic canoe landing, a landmark separating the territories of neighbouring tribes, or a sacred hill. A second kind of historic place is the archaeological site which is a testament, in many cases, to life in New Zealand before the advent of Europeans. There is also a more recent interest in the sites from which information about our early industrial life can be gained. These sites are the subject of study of industrial archaeology. The history of the work place is no less important than that of the home or the church. A third kind of historic place is a piece of land which has a direct association with an historic event or a notable person of the past. Examples would be the landing places of James Cook. Finally, a fourth kind of historic place is the built structure. Buildings are an important part of this class of historic place, but the class also includes bridges, stone walls, water races and features of the historic engineering of road and rail transport links. In this area, the Trust has cultivated a special interest in the restoration of Maori meeting houses.

In this book, Wynne Colgan, Chairman of the Editorial Advisory Committee, and John Wilson, our indefatigable editor, have depicted our heritage on this broader canvas. To do this they recruited local authors and historians from all parts of New Zealand and then fitted their contributions together into a national mosaic. It seems to me that the authors, the editor and those whose advice helped shape the book have achieved an admirable blend of different kinds of historic places set in the very different geographic circumstances of our long, narrow islands. The Trust is deeply indebted to them all.

As people come to see more clearly and appreciate better our colourful history, which stretches back for more than a thousand years, and as the stories of our historic places become more widely known, I am sure that all New Zealanders will strive to protect these places from thoughtless destruction so they will still be telling their stories to generations yet unborn.

Sir Neil Begg K.B.E.,
Chairman, New Zealand
Historic Places Trust.
Dunedin.

Editorial Notes

Because it was intended that this should be a popular book, the Editorial Advisory Committee accepted my decision not to include footnotes and full bibliographies for each chapter. The 'further reading' suggested at the end of each chapter lists only a few accessible items from which readers interested in specific places will be able to obtain more information than the book itself contains. In the 'Acknowledgments' at the end of the volume are the personal acknowledgments which certain authors wished to make publicly. The full references and complete bibliographies provided by most authors have been deposited in the New Zealand rooms at major public libraries and in the Auckland and Canterbury museums and Turnbull and Hocken libraries. There they are available to anyone who wishes to check the source of a particular quotation, to verify facts or to extend their reading beyond the few titles suggested at the end of each chapter.

Some usages presented me with problems. The term 'prehistory' is felt by many to be a slight on New Zealand's Maori past, though it has a strict and non-pejorative reference to the period before written records are available. But because Maori traditions and archaeology together provide reliable sources for a verified history, I have endeavoured to use the term 'prehistory' only where it is appropriate as a technical term. How to refer to the wars fought in New Zealand in the mid nineteenth century is a vexed question. I have a personal preference for the term 'Land Wars'

and have used it in most places in this book. Sheila Natusch wished to use the South Island dialectical forms for some Maori words in her chapter. I respected her wish rather than 'standardise' her spellings to those used elsewhere in the book. In line with current usage, Maori words in the text are not italicised. A glossary lists those words which may be unfamiliar to some readers. I left the final 's' off the plurals of Maori words, except where the 's' appeared in quotations.

All measurements in the authors' texts have been put into metric forms, except where amounts of money are quoted in £.s.d for which inflation has made modern equivalents misleading. Measurements in quotations have been left in the form in which they were originally written, with the metric equivalents given in brackets only where necessary for clarity. In quotations, spellings have been retained in their original forms and may differ from accepted modern spellings. This refers especially to the eighteenth-century spellings and abbreviations in quotations in the chapter on Captain Cook at Mercury Bay. In the chapter on Rangiaowhia this policy has resulted in variations in the spellings of some places and names within the chapter, but the sense is never obscured by these inconsistencies.

John Wilson,
Springston.

Introduction

IN *The Past Today* the New Zealand Historic Places Trust has prepared a volume to illustrate the great variety of sites, buildings and other remains which come under the broad heading of 'historic places'. The book is a successor to the Trust's earlier *Historic Buildings of New Zealand* volumes. The publication of those volumes — on the North Island in 1979 and on the South in 1983 — did much to foster an interest in and concern to preserve New Zealand's historic buildings. The volumes also, paradoxically, provoked concern that the belief might become current that the Trust understood the phrase 'historic places' to mean just buildings. Buildings are important relics from the past and several chapters in this volume too deal primarily with them. But the Trust also works to preserve many other sorts of relics and places from which we can gain an understanding of New Zealand's history, including Maori traditional sites, archaeological sites, the scenes of significant events and humble buildings that some might not think historic.

This book has been given a broader scope than the Trust's earlier volumes to embrace, particularly, the marks on the landscape which remain as evidence of the Maori occupation of New Zealand before the arrival of Europeans. As well, places devoid of any visible sign of the presence of people there in the past may have an atmosphere that makes them unequivocally historic places. Almost nothing at Mercury Bay recalls the visit of Captain Cook in 1769 about which Sir Neil Begg has written, but the bay is indubitably historic because, visiting it, we can recall that 'pivotal moment' in New Zealand's history about which Sir Neil has written. At Hairini, in the Waikato, only one building survives from the time the locality was Rangiaowhia, but the knowledge of what happened there presented in this book by Patricia Adams will equip visitors to Hairini today to recreate the past, even in the absence of much tangible to stimulate their imaginations.

One important result of shifting the focus of attention away from just buildings to, in particular, archaeological sites is renewed emphasis on the fact that New Zealand's human story began at least ten centuries ago. A growing awareness in New Zealand of the length and interest of the country's Maori past is already making it less necessary than it was even a few years ago to emphasise that although New Zealand was the world's last major land area to be settled by human beings, it has a history of respectable length and one replete with events and developments of significance and interest. The Trust hopes that no-one reading this volume will any longer countenance the suggestion that New Zealand is 'a land without a past' because we lack archaeological sites older than about a thousand years, 'ancient monuments' or mediaeval cathedrals and castles. The historic places described in this book, despite their youth compared with the historic places of most other countries, illustrate a story which is of interest and significance as part of world history.

II

The authors of chapters in this volume were asked not just to catalogue or describe the historic relics, buildings or other remains at the places they were writing about but to provide information which would help readers of the book to appreciate that on the sites or in the buildings with which the chapters dealt people lived, worked, fought, worshipped, took their leisure. They were asked to evoke the atmosphere of the past, to repeople the places. Different authors met this requirement in different ways, but the variety of approaches is a strength of the book, because the imaginations of different readers will be stimulated by different sorts of information. However it is done, to stimulate its readers' imaginations and so open doors onto the past is this book's main purpose.

Historic places are not important because they are quaint, picturesque or provoke nostalgia. They are important because they provide us with links back to past lives. When visiting historic places, by drawing on our knowledge and exercising our imaginations, we should be able to re-experience what people of the past did or even felt at those places and so reach beyond the restrictions imposed on us by our own social backgrounds and the times in which we live. Historic places help us to cross barriers of race and class into areas of human experience that would otherwise be closed to us. Many different sorts of historic places have been included in this book in an endeavour to put its readers in touch with a great variety of human experience.

Two opening chapters focus attention on Maori life in New Zealand before the advent of Europeans. Two following chapters describe the activities of two groups which first brought the races into contact — explorers and missionaries. The next chapter describes an incident in the wars fought between some Maori on one side and the settlers and British Army on the other. These wars were more significant events in New Zealand's history than many seem willing, even yet, to concede and this chapter has deliberately been brought towards the front of the book. After the chapter on the wars, the book backtracks in time to some extent with four chapters which include material on aspects of Maori life in New Zealand over the full span of New Zealand's history, from times remembered in mythology and tradition right through to the present. The chapter on Taumutu, by a Maori author who wishes to remain anonymous, illustrates the continuity of Maori life in New Zealand and is, appropriately, about a place in a province, Canterbury, which has tended to ignore its Maori past. Five following chapters discuss aspects of different industries in earlier and later European times and the community and political life based on people's experience in those industries. The concluding chapters focus on different aspects of town and city life in New Zealand in the nineteenth and twentieth centuries.

III

In developing this volume, the Historic Places Trust made a conscientious effort to include Maori historic places. The Trust felt it important to include such places in this book not just because of their intrinsic interest but also because the book would be read in a predominantly Pakeha New Zealand. Maori historic places alone put us in touch, in New Zealand, with a span of years far beyond that which can be retained in personal or family recollections. Janet Davidson writes about the fashioning of the volcanic cones of the Auckland isthmus over several hundred years and Beverley McCulloch about the lives of some of the earliest New Zealanders on the Kaikoura coast.

Besides providing us with paths back into the country's very distant past, Maori historic places can put Pakeha New Zealanders in touch with experiences in the more recent past markedly different from most Pakeha personal or family experiences — of cultural disruption, of defeat in war, of dispossession from their land and of a struggle against great odds to ensure that their culture survives. The two chapters by Maori contributors, on Manutuke and Taumutu, are, for this reason, among the more important chapters in the book.

In addition, some chapters on certain European historic places, Brian Wood's chapter on Blackball for example, touch on aspects of life in New Zealand since European colonisation which will be outside the personal or family experiences of many readers. Our understanding of New Zealand's past will be flawed if we confine our attention to sites or buildings associated with the famous, the powerful or the well-off. The dwellings described in Barbara Fill's chapter on some of New Zealand's first 'state houses' are as important to an accurate understanding of New Zealand's past as the grander Christchurch homes which appeared in the pages of *Historic Buildings of New Zealand: South Island*. The chapters on industrial buildings and sites have been included partly from a conviction that to become informed about the lives and conditions of work of the country's working people is essential to a dispelling of certain myths about the nature of New Zealand society.

IV

The selection of historic places in this book is fragmentary and incomplete. It would be impossible in a single volume of manageable size to weave in all the strands of New Zealand's history. But the selection is not arbitrary and care was taken to choose places that touched on many different aspects of life in New Zealand. Initially, the Trust's regional committees and staff were canvassed for suggestions. The Editorial Advisory Committee then whittled down the long list of candidate places which this canvass produced. Some 'accidents' influenced the final list of places included in the published book, but it is reasonably broad in scope nonetheless. Thematically, farming and rural life are badly under-represented, but farmhouses, homesteads and farm buildings did receive generous exposure in *Historic Buildings of New Zealand: South Island* and the Trust hopes, too, that it will have the opportunity to make good this and other omissions in subsequent volumes.

The book was not intended to serve as a guidebook, but the Trust hopes it will encourage readers to visit the historic places themselves. Sufficient information has been given, on maps if not in the text, to enable interested readers to find specific places mentioned in the book. Some of the sites and buildings described are privately owned. Permission was obtained from the owners to include those sites and buildings in this book, but this permission does not extend to readers visiting the sites or buildings concerned. Most owners should, however, willingly grant permission to view the sites or buildings they own to those who seek such permission out of genuine interest.

Finally, this book was not intended to press too obviously the cause of historic preservation, although the Trust hopes all its publications will, by fostering greater awareness of the value of historic places, arouse greater concern to see such places protected. While this book was in preparation, an important old brick house in Ashburton and the Borough Council lighting chimney in Timaru were demolished, making necessary last minute changes in the authors' texts. The book was almost to press when news came of the demolition of the United Friendly Societies Dispensary building in Napier, requiring further eleventh hour changes. The Trust will be well satisfied if the publication of this book saves any of the buildings or structures described in it from a similar fate.

V

In editing this volume I enjoyed generous support. Although she had no part in working on it, the volume I hope reflects the scrupulous standards and inspiration of Frances Porter, whose editing of the two *Historic Buildings* volumes set a high standard for me to match. The advice and encouragement of the members of the Editorial Advisory Committee, particularly of its chairman, Wynne Colgan, were invaluable. On the staff of the Trust, the publications officer, Margaret Long, handled a host of practical matters with expert ease and helped me over many obstacles with her unflagging confidence in my ability to produce a worthwhile book on time. The Trust's director, John Daniels, put his familiarity with the Trust and his diplomatic skills at my disposal when other problems arose. Frank O'Leary, an advisory officer, afforded unobtrusive but indispensable assistance with illustrations and the Trust's typists, under head typist Helen Aviss, made my task as editor much easier. Many of the contributors went beyond the strict letter of their agreement with the Trust to help me with illustrations and other matters concerning their chapters. Photographers and owners of old pictures in some cases provided their services at less than their usual rates or waived reproduction fees. In particular, Ron Murray of Cromwell made pictures of early Bannockburn available, Arthur Bates of Wanganui offered pictures taken in the Wanganui Valley, and Barry Brailsford supplied material on Kaikoura. The staff of many institutions went out of their ways to assist me, especially in gathering the illustrations. The institutions included the Alexander Turnbull Library, the National Museum, the Auckland Institute and Museum, the Auckland Public Library, the Auckland City Art Gallery, the Taranaki Museum, the Wanganui Regional Museum, the Hawke's Bay Museum, the Canterbury Museum, the Canterbury Public Library, the South Canterbury Historical Museum, the Forest Service (Hokitika), the Hocken Library, the Dunedin Public Library and the British Library, London.

John Wilson

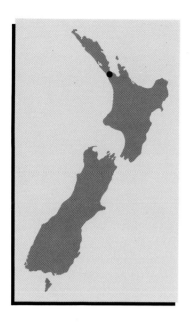

Marks on a Landscape: Auckland's Volcanic Cones

Janet Davidson

AUCKLAND is a city of volcanoes. The Auckland vol-
canic field stretching from
Takapuna in the north to Manu-
rewa in the south, covers an area
of approximately 500 sq km. Within this field, more than 50 separate
volcanoes have erupted during a
period of activity which began
more than 50,000 years ago and
continued to within a few hundred
years of the present. Some of these
volcanoes are represented principally by explosion craters, such as
the Orakei and Panmure basins.
The majority, however, take the
form of miniature mountains —
the so-called volcanic cones. Each
has a unique and usually complex
geological history. Each has spread
its products, in the form of ash, tuff,
scoria, or lava, over the surrounding land.

When the first Polynesian settlers arrived in Auckland, Rangitoto did not exist, at least not in
the form we know it today. It is
a sobering thought that so significant a natural feature in the
Auckland landscape could have
been formed within the period of
human occupation of the region.
The pioneering Polynesians found
the other volcanoes already extinct,
and settled on and around them.
In the nineteenth century, the
entire volcanic field could be seen
in all its beauty and diversity, the

geological features crowned by
marks of Polynesian occupation.
More recently, more than half the
volcanoes have been destroyed and
the remainder have almost all been
affected to some extent by processes
such as quarrying, roading and
reservoir construction.

The Auckland area offered many
attractions to prehistoric Polynesian settlers. The two harbours
provided ready access to seafoods
of various kinds and open gateways
to travel further afield. The short
distances separating the upper
reaches of the Waitemata and the
Manukau made direct access from
east to west coasts feasible. The
soils developed on the lava flows
and tuff fields surrounding the
volcanoes were suited to Polynesian gardening techniques, while
their stoniness was no serious
deterrent to a horticultural tradition which did not include the use
of the plough. The cones themselves offered ideal locations for
settlement and defence. Small
wonder that the settlers took advantage of these attractions, imposing
over the centuries their own impres-
·sions on a landscape already bearing the imprint of some 50,000
years of volcanic activity.

Maori oral traditions are silent
about the beginnings of occupation on the volcanic cones. Nor has
the earliest human settlement of the

Auckland region been well docu-
mented by archaeologists. Excavations on the volcanic cones have
been few and all have been undertaken in response to threats of
immediate destruction rather than
as research enquiries.

The earliest radiocarbon dates
come from Wiri Mountain, now
destroyed, at the southern limits of
the volcanic field. Here, clearance
of bush and construction of stone-
walled garden boundaries on the
lower slopes may have begun as
early as the thirteenth century.
Later, during the fifteenth or
sixteenth century, a living terrace
was built on the same spot. Earthworks had begun on Maungarei
(Mount Wellington) by the fifteenth century and storage pits
were constructed on the summit of
Puketapapa (Mount Roskill) at
about the same time or slightly
later. There is no reason to suppose
that these radiocarbon dates from
limited rescue excavations reflect
the earliest occupation of either
site.

By the seventeenth century,
various settlements on the volcanic
cones were occupied by members
of the Waiohua and Kawerau
tribes, principally the former, a
confederation that included several
related subtribes, the Nga Iwi, Nga
Oho and Nga Riki. To these people
can be attributed the bulk of the

▲
About 1845, the early Auckland painter John Guise Mitford painted two of the most prominent cones. 'Oawaraka' (Owairaka — Mt Albert) had been little modified by European activity when Mitford painted it, but it has since been badly mutilated and has been described as 'poor, pathetic, decapitated' Albert.

►
Another of Mitford's paintings depicts Maungawhau (Mt Eden).

great works which transformed the cones from smooth-sided hills to the terraced, sculpted monuments we see today. During the eighteenth century, the Waiohua and the Kawerau were defeated by incoming tribes. The Ngati Paoa and Ngati Maru moved up the Hauraki Gulf to settle in the vicinity of Panmure and on the North Shore and the Ngati Whatua moved down from Kaipara, eventually conquering the isthmus and possessing themselves of Maungakiekie (One Tree Hill), the greatest of all the volcanic cone settlements. Occupation of the cones finally ceased in the eighteenth century, for the incoming tribes did not make much use of them.

The present appearance of the surviving volcanic cones is the result of centuries of occupation and modification. The amount of earth that has been moved on the major cones such as Maungarei, Maungakiekie, or Maungawhau

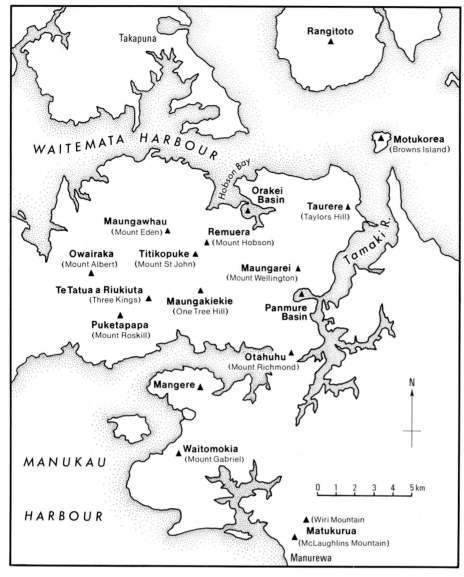

The main features of Auckland's volcanic field.

(Mount Eden) during successive occupations is almost unimaginable today, bearing in mind that it was done without metal tools or machines of any kind.

Apart from inhospitable Rangitoto, frequently visited by prehistoric Aucklanders but not permanently inhabited, the least modified cone is Motukorea (Browns Island). Here the slopes are for the most part smooth and natural. Terracing and defensive ditches are confined to a relatively small part of the crater rim and to a separate knoll to the north-west. This is probably how settlement began on all the cones, with the construction of terraces as flat surfaces for houses, cooking areas and storage pits and the digging of the storage pits themselves. The defensive ditches on Motukorea may be a relatively late feature; the other earthworks could have been constructed at any time during the history of occupation of the cones. The reasons for the relatively slight modification of Motukorea are probably several. Artefacts of early styles have been found on the island, showing that it was visited from the earliest times. However, water supply is limited, and not much land was available for gardening. There is indeed a small area of stone-walled fields on Motukorea, but this is miniscule compared with the vast

Motukorea (Browns Island) is the least modified, since the arrival of Europeans in the Auckland area, of all the volcanic cones. The rim of the crater is fortified with transverse ditches and terraces and there is a second area of terraces and pits on another knoll. Motukorea is not terraced as extensively as volcanoes on the mainland, probably because there was limited land for gardening and water on the island. The other cones would probably look much as Motukorea does today had they not been successively modified over many generations.

The pits still evident on the terraces of many of the cones mark the sites of kumara storage pits which would originally have been roofed over. Hugh Boscawen photographed these pits on Te Tatua a Riukiuta (Three Kings) at the end of last century.

acreage of prehistoric fields on the fertile soils surrounding some of the other cones.

Contrast Motukorea with Maungarei. Here, artificial terracing extends in an unbroken sweep from the rim to the base of the slope on the eastern side. These terraces are almost certainly not the result of a single massive phase of construction, but the end product of several hundred years of gradual modification. They were formed by cutting back into the slope and building out at the front with spoil won from behind. The rubbish of the settlement was thrown down the slopes, where it became mixed with more spoil from pit digging and similar activities, and accumulated in places to a considerable depth. The primary purpose of most of the terraces was residential, rather than defensive. Sleeping houses, storage pits, cooking areas and open spaces were found on them. Indeed on Maungarei, at least, the construction of storage pits was one of the main activities on the terraces. These pits were rectangular with vertical walls and a flat bottom and were covered with a pitched roof supported on wooden posts. They were normally entered from one end. They were used for storage of food, particularly the sweet potato or kumara crop grown in the surrounding fields.

Many splendid examples of pits belonging to the final phase of occupation can be seen today on the surface of the cones. However, many flat areas have also been used for pits, now entirely filled in. On Maungarei it was found that some terraces had been used for the digging and redigging of pits until it was impossible to dig any more pits on them. Scoria is a loose, friable material; once it has been disturbed and redeposited it does

not hold a vertical face. Prehistoric builders on Maungarei dealt with this problem, sometimes very successfully, by constructing stone facings and retaining walls around pits and against scarps. Even so, there came a point at which a terrace or flat area was so loose and disturbed that no more pits could be constructed. At this point the terrace probably had to be abandoned. The final response to this problem on Maungarei seems to have been to begin again by remodelling the top. The upper crater rim has far less evidence of repeated occupation than slightly lower areas and it appears that a major lowering and levelling of the rim took place shortly before the site was finally abandoned.

Each of the volcanic cones, then,

Larger pits on the terraces probably mark the sites of communal (rather than individual family) stores. This photograph in the Richardson Collection shows the remains of large pits near the summit of Maungarei (Mt Wellington) in the nineteenth century. These particular pits are still clearly visible today.

is to be seen as a vast sprawling settlement in which people lived, probably not continuously, but repeatedly over several centuries. Here they prepared food, cooked, ate, slept, rebuilt and refurbished their sleeping houses and storage pits, sorted and stored the produce of their gardens. Here also they sang songs and told tales. Here people were tattooed, tools and ornaments were made and repaired,

When the Rev. John Kinder photographed Mt Eden (Maungawhau) from near Newmarket in 1866, its terraces rose high above the humble wooden buildings of the infant city of Auckland. The terraces still remain as some of the largest and finest Maori earthworks anywhere in the country.

sacred rites were performed. But their way of life depended on the acquisition of food and for this they had to leave their settlements and descend to their gardens and to the harbours and estuaries.

The importance of gardening in the life of the people who dwelt on the cones is indicated by the size and number of the storage pits on the cones themselves, but even more by the extensive stone-walled fields that have survived until recently around some of the cones in rural south Auckland. Tragically, even these are now being engulfed by modern development.

The fields that once surrounded the better known cones have long since disappeared.

As we have already seen, gardening may have begun on the lower slopes of Wiri Mountain by the twelfth century. Major boundary walls radiate out from the twin cones of Matukurua (Wiri and McLaughlins Mountains) and probably reflect initial carving up of territory by the first settlers. Within the major divisions are many smaller garden plots, indicated by stone walls, sheltered basins in the uneven terrain of the lava field and 'mound gardens',

where the surface is dotted with small mounds of stones. Rubbish dumps and the sites of houses and shelters are scattered through the fields, indicating that people sometimes lived among their gardens. No doubt during certain seasons, and in times of peace, it was convenient to have a shelter at the garden site, perhaps in addition to a residence on a nearby cone. The gardens at Matukurua, like all the cones and their surroundings, were probably used intermittently for several hundred years. Their major period of use, however, appears to have been during the sixteenth and seventeenth centuries.

Apart from cultivated plants (which would have included taro, gourds, yams and a tropical form of cabbage tree as well as kumara), the cone dwellers probably made good use of the root of the bracken fern for food. Although there is as yet little evidence that bracken grew in fallow gardens at Matukurua, there is no doubt that it flourished on the Auckland isthmus in the nineteenth century. As the Polynesian settlers moved about the region from one cone to another, clearing gardens and leaving them to fallow, there would always have

Waitomokia (Mt Gabriel), towards the southern fringe of the Auckland volcanic field, was one of the most fascinating of the volcanoes before it became 'a sacrifice for the sewerage works' in 1956. Hugh Boscawen's photograph of the pa on the complex of three miniature cones nestling in the centre of a vast explosion crater illustrates the defensive potential of a very small cone surrounded by swamp.

This watercolour of 'the Three Kings volcanic crater' (Te Tatua a Riukiuta), with Maori earthworks evident, was painted in the nineteenth century by the Rev. John Kinder. Three Kings was the most complex of all the volcanoes. Only Big King remains, crowned by a water reservoir, its terraces largely obscured by vegetation.

been areas on which bracken could re-establish itself.

The other great food resource was seafood. Its importance is abundantly evident in the innumerable shells on the surface of the cones. The shells are predominantly those of the shores and estuaries — the pipi and cockles that still abound today. But other shells such as mussels, paua, scallops and tuatua, from rocky shores, harbour sand banks and ocean beaches, reflect a need for variety and at least occasional trips further

afield than the nearest estuary. Fish bones are also common, particularly those of snapper. Dogs, rats, and sometimes birds, provided an occasional change from the steady diet of seafood.

The modern main roads that traverse the Auckland region distract the eye from the direct routes between the cones and their nearest points of access to the sea. No cone is more than 3 km from the sea or its tributaries and many are much closer. Stand on Remuera (Mount Hobson) and imagine the well-worn tracks winding down to Hobson Bay; or, from the summit of Maungarei, visualise the quickest route to the Tamaki.

These, then, were the preoccupations of the cone dwellers — their gardens and their quest for seafood. Something of this is mentioned in traditions. The locations of settlements and gardens are often de-

scribed and events that sometimes occurred during fishing expeditions are highlighted — for such events sometimes led to war and war was an important factor in prehistoric Auckland life.

The prehistoric settlements on the volcanic cones have often been regarded primarily as fortifications. They have sometimes been imagined bristling with palisades from top to bottom and manned by huge numbers of warriors. Certainly their defensive possibilities were one of their attractions, but the manner in which they were defended was probably rather different from that outlined above. As we have seen, the terraces were constructed in the first instance to provide flat surfaces for occupation and some of them, at least, never carried palisades. For example, the two lowest terraces on the northern side of Maungarei, below the reservoir, which have now been cut by the road down the mountain, had no palisades, but had been intensively used as living areas.

Maungakiekie (One Tree Hill) is the greatest of all of Auckland's volcanic cone settlements. At the end of last century Hugh Boscawen photographed part of the Onehunga side of Maungakiekie on which some of the great terraces were evident. The original totara tree which once crowned the summit had long since been cut down and the tree on the summit is the pine, then an infant, now lofty, which marks the hill today.

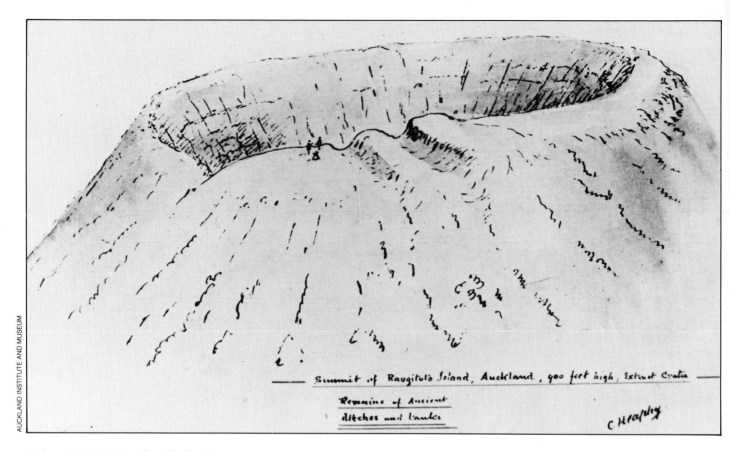

Summit of Rangitoto Island, Auckland, 900 feet high, Extinct Crater

Remains of Ancient ditches and banks

C Heaphy

When Charles Heaphy climbed to the summit of Rangitoto Island in the 1840s he found on the rim of the crater of this most recent of Auckland's volcanic cones 'remains of ancient ditches and banks'. No trace of these remains today.

The principal defended areas were the citadels or strong points on the summits and prominent knolls. Some of the more complex cones had several such points; others may have had only one and some may never have been fortified at all.

Evidence of a strong palisade at the edge of the summit of Puketapapa was discovered during rescue excavations in 1961. Two large post holes, probably part of a similar palisade, were observed at the summit of Maungakiekie when the monument was erected in 1940. There is little doubt that the steepness and height of the more prominent cones would be a defensive asset and the steepness of the scarps between terraces, even without palisades, would enhance this effect. Simulated 'attacks' on

Maungakiekie showed that even a fit warrior attacking by any route except that from the south would have difficulty quickly reaching the summit and still being fit to engage in fighting.

Most of the cones have no defensive ditches and banks. Defence relied entirely on height, natural steepness and artificial scarping, with palisading largely confined to strong points. Maungawhau, before it was modified by roads and reservoirs, probably had four such strong points. Puketapapa and Mangere probably had three and Taurere (Taylors Hill) two. There is, however, a group of cones on which defence was strengthened by the construction of defensive ditches and banks, usually placed across crater rims to impede access to the summits. Such ditches are found on Maungakiekie, Remuera, Titikopuke (Mount St John), Maungarei and Motukorea. These earthworks are a late feature, perhaps superimposed on earlier terraced sites during the eighteenth century conflicts between the Waiohua and the invading Ngati Paoa and Ngati Whatua. This late

addition of defensive ditches is particularly obvious on Remuera. It is interesting that even the recent, unstable, crater rim of Rangitoto was fortified at one time with transverse ditches, sketched by Charles Heaphy, of which no trace now remains.

The most complex defences are those of Maungakiekie, which has a major system of linear defences across the relatively easy southern approach and six strong points. One Maori tradition describes seven pa on Maungakiekie and may refer to these strong points. This complicated pattern is almost certainly the result of a number of separate episodes of fortification during which the various defences were constructed and modified. Such a complex history is not surprising in what was regarded, at least in the eighteenth century, as the principal site in the region. Needless to say, the various strong points need not all have been in use at the same time.

The least known aspect of life on the cones is that concerned with ritual, which would certainly have been a major preoccupation. Traditions give a few hints. There was an important shrine at the approach to Maungawhau from what is now Mt Eden Road and the main crater of this cone was dedicated to Mataoho, god of volcanoes. A sacred totara grew on the summit of Maungakiekie, giving rise to an alternative name for the hill, Te Totara i Ahua. This totara, cut down by vandals in the mid nineteenth century, was the original tree which gave the hill its English name.

The most obvious indication of ritual behaviour by the cone dwellers is their use of the crevices and caves of the surrounding lava fields as burial places for their dead. There must have been many sacred places of this kind in the landscape which are no longer remembered. Rangitoto, too, was much used as a burial ground, presumably by the people who lived on the neighbouring islands.

The number of people who lived on each cone can only be guessed. Earlier writers numbered them in thousands, but this may have been unrealistic. A recent study was based on the number of terraces, thought to have supported family groups, and the number of pits required to feed them. Assuming that an entire site was occupied at the time (which need not have been the case) the following figures are suggested by counting the terraces: Maungakiekie 1074, Maungarei 710, Maungawhau 570, Titikopuke 198. Figures based on numbers of pits are slightly lower. For the three larger sites, the numbers should be increased by 100-200 to compensate for recent damage which has destroyed an unknown number of terraces and pits.

Maori traditions about the Auckland region describe a fluid society of shifting alliances. Families and hapu banded together at times and squabbled amongst themselves at

WHITES AVIATION

other times. Groups moved fairly frequently and could be found residing at one cone at one time and elsewhere at another time. Each site was the scene of unique events, only a few of which have been remembered. In broad terms, each site tells the same story, of an endless round of clearing, using and abandoning gardens, constant fishing and shellfish gathering, the minutiae of daily life in prehistoric Auckland. Yet each site has its own character, its own unique variation on the universal theme, its own setting and charm. The sheer size and grandeur of Maungawhau, Maungakiekie, Mangere and Maungarei must impress, but the smaller, less well-known cones also have much to offer the visitor. Taurere, Titikopuke, Remuera and Otahuhu (Mount Richmond) all have special charms. All the surviving cones have something to contribute not only to Auckland's present beauty, but to the story of its past.

On Maungakiekie (One Tree Hill) the results of centuries of fashioning and shaping are still evident in the form of terraces on the cone's steep outer slopes, the sides of the horseshoe-shaped breached craters and even the inner slopes of the craters which are still intact.

Further reading

Fox, A. *Maungakiekie. The Maori Pa on One Tree Hill* (Auckland 1978)

Fox, A. *Pa of the Auckland Isthmus: an archaeological analysis* (Offprint from *Records of the Auckland Institute and Museum* 14: 1-24)

Mount Wellington Borough Council *Maungarei (Mount Wellington)* (Auckland 1975)

Searle, E. J. and Davidson, J. *A Picture Guide to the Volcanic Cones of Auckland showing Geological and Archaeological Features* (Auckland 1975)

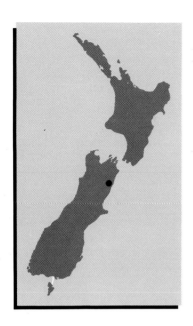

New Zealand's First-comers: The Maori at Kaikoura

Beverley McCulloch

THE Kaikoura district has been a popular place for people to live since the earliest human occupation of New Zealand. The wealth of historic and prehistoric sites in the area is evidence of this. The abundance of this evidence of early occupation, particularly of Polynesian origin, extends from the Conway River, 30 km south of Kaikoura Peninsula, to Mangamaunu, 13 km to the north. Another important concentration of Maori sites occurs at the mouth of the Clarence River, 20 km further north. Every one of these sites is of interest, but it would not be possible to do justice to all the fascinating places within this extended area in a single, short chapter; I have therefore chosen to confine 'Kaikoura' to the peninsula and its fairly immediate environs.

When visiting sites, particularly those which date back well into prehistory, it is important to remember that the environment in which they exist today may not be the environment of the time the site was occupied. When the earliest humans arrived in the Kaikoura

Maori occupation sites: Kaikoura district.

An excavation through one of the garden walls on the Fyffe moa hunter site, made during archaeological investigation of the site.

A large flake 'butchering knife' from the earliest level of human occupation on the Fyffe site. It is made from flint obtained locally.

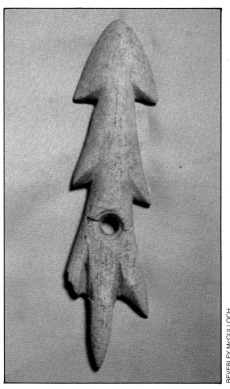

This unique harpoon head made from moa bone excavated from the Fyffe site shows marked similarities to harpoon heads of similar age from the Marquesas Islands.

area, probably somewhere between 800 and 1000 years ago, the forest was possibly all around, very close to what is now the township (although there is no evidence of forest growing on the peninsula itself). Animal life too was, initially quite different with many species of birds living locally which are now extinct, or confined to habitats far from Kaikoura.

Knowledge of these and other changes which have occurred can help the visitor to visualise what a particular place may have been like to live in, and help in recapturing the atmosphere of an abandoned site. Where such information on the past is available for the Kaikoura area it is included with the general description of the human activity which took place there. Both prehistory and history should be a great deal more than simply people and objects. So some 'human ecology' is added so that

the historic places of Kaikoura which we are to visit may be better appreciated.

The earliest site of human occupation that we know of in Kaikoura is at Avoca Point. It is commonly referred to as the 'Fyffe' moa hunter site because these early people lived upon and adjacent to the land where, centuries later, the whaler George Fyffe was to make his home. All we know of the Fyffe moa hunter site has been learned by archaeological excavations, plus some fortuitous discoveries made by people digging here for other reasons, such as house construction. But from this evidence we can imagine what it was like when the

A close up of the excavation of the garden wall on the Fyffe site, showing the structure of the wall with the build up of rubble beneath. The sandy beach exposed at the bottom of the trench marks the level of the earliest human occupation of the Fyffe site.

first people lived here about 1000 years ago.

The land adjacent to and to the west of the Fyffe cottage, now grassed and divided into building sections, must be visualised with all the grass and the thin layer of soil stripped away, together with about half a metre of limestone rubble. Underlying this is a beach of golden sand containing large quantities of microscopic shells and bryozoa, quite unlike anything found in Kaikoura at present. Stacks and spurs of flaggy white limestone jut out of the sand in places, especially at the foot of the mudstone hill at the back. The hill is still there today although in those early times both it and the raised beach terraces beyond were probably covered with scrub.

Between eight and ten centuries ago the first Polynesians in Kaikoura lived on this sandy beach. Here, they experimented with local rocks for making tools and manufactured harpoons and fish-hooks from bone, much as they or their ancestors had done in their Pacific Island homeland. They had no knowledge of greenstone, but had brought with them obsidian (volcanic glass) from the North Island. Their main foods were birds — moas, kiwis and several smaller forest species, various seabirds, including penguins, and ducks. They also ate rats, dogs, seals, tuataras and numerous kinds of fish and shellfish in which the area abounded.

We know little else of their lifestyle and habits; no indications of their clothing, what sort of houses they may have had, or whether they included vegetable foods in their diet have been preserved for the archaeologist to discover. But they buried their dead with some ceremony — and this we look at later in the chapter.

It seems likely, however, that they did not stay very long; there is no great depth of occupational material at this very lowest level. We do know that not long after they arrived, limestone rubble began to cover that desirable golden beach, and that man made little use of the

The eastern coastline of the Kaikoura Peninsula, in the vicinity of the Whalers Bay cave, used by the early Maori inhabitants of the peninsula.

cove again until centuries later when the descendants of these early visitors practised agriculture in the first thin soil to form on the site, protecting it with stone walls that can still be seen today. Later still, the first Europeans settled on the same land, but this, too, we will discover later in the chapter. But once people had arrived in Kaikoura they were there to stay, even if not always on the Fyffe site. Evidence of their occupation of this very pleasant area in which to live is abundant everywhere.

One of the more popular pastimes for the more active visitor is to follow the walkway from the carpark at the end of the seal colony road up the hill and along the cliff tops. This walk leads to another fairly early site of human activities. Whalers Bay, signposted from the track, is reached by a steep but relatively easy scramble down a cliff track. (At low tide you can walk to it along the shore platform.) In the foot of the cliff,

behind a clump of bush, is a quite large cave occupied by the Maori people about 400 years ago. The original floor deposit indicated that their particular activity here was the manufacture of fish-hooks out of very large green mussel shells, although the cave has long since been dug out by 'treasure hunters' in a search for artefacts. This concentration on manufacturing fish-hooks suggests that seafoods — especially fish — may have become a very much more important part of the people's diet at this time and possibly indicates that some bird species, including the moa, had become scarce. Of equal interest is the fact that the green mussel, *Perna canaliculus*, is only rarely found around Kaikoura Peninsula today, and then only

BEVERLEY McCULLOCH

Fish hooks made of green mussel shell, showing various stages of manufacture. They were excavated from the Whalers Bay cave and indicate that the people who used the cave relied on the sea for some at least of their diet.

very small specimens, which may mean that some sort of environmental change has occurred since Whalers Bay cave was utilised.

The Fyffe moa hunter site and Whalers Bay cave are the two most easily accessible places of early human occupation around the Kaikoura Peninsula. Even more common and easily recognised are the later Maori sites, principally pa, which can be found on the peninsula and on the terrace above the township.

Pa, which are sites that were prepared for defence, are characteristic of the later or 'classic' period of Maori occupation of the area. Pa sites are often most easily recognised by 'earthworks', usually an earthen wall and associated ditch which was originally used in conjunction with palisading. Some hilltop pa show, as well, terracing

and pits, indicative of housing and storage.

On the Kaikoura Peninsula lies what is almost certainly the largest pa site in the South Island, with extensive earthworks, pits and terraces. It is extremely impressive but it has no traditional history, no known name (being referred to archaeologically as 'Pa 39'), and shows no visible sign of actual occupation. It is worthy of note solely for its size and magnificent state of preservation, but, being on private land, is not easy to visit.

Also on top of the peninsula, accessible and signposted, is the pa called 'Nga Niho'. It appears spectacular to the visitor, but the 'history' associated with it — which is widely believed — is largely incorrect.

The name 'Nga Niho' (The Teeth), is not a traditional one. It was associated with this particular site for the first time in 1950 by W. J. Elvy, who gives no source for the name. It refers to a battle known as Niho Manga or the 'barracouta tooth'. This was a revenge battle in which the North Island Ngati Toa chief Te Rauparaha attacked

and slew or captured most of the inhabitants of a Ngai Tahu pa at Kaikoura about 1830. However, historic accounts clearly place this battle as taking place at Omihi Pa, 20 km south of Kaikoura. There is no genuine traditional history attached to the pa popularly called 'Nga Niho' and certainly no evidence that it was ever involved in Te Rauparaha's raids on the area. The earthworks visible today are also known to have been deliberately modified by Europeans to make them more apparent. This pa is perhaps the most frequently visited in the South Island, so it is important that the true facts about it become better known.

A pa with a genuine history, for which supportive evidence is provided by archaeological investigation, is Takahanga (or Takahaka in South Island dialect). Takahanga is situated on the terrace above the Kaikoura Domain and Garden of Memories. A modern marae for the Maori people of Kaikoura has been built on this traditional site. Like Pa 39 and 'Nga Niho', it is enclosed by defensive earthworks, except on the

BARRY BRAILSFORD

Pa 39 on the Kaikoura Peninsula is one of the largest in the South Island. Its defences were based on a steep terrace edge and two flanking gullies. Three distinct defensible areas have been identified, numbered 1, 2 and 3 on the photo. Each would have been defended by ditches, banks and palisades.

eastern side where the defence is the steep, natural scarp of the terrace.

The site was occupied for some time prior to the construction of the pa, by the Ngati Mamoe people who preceded Ngai Tahu in the South Island. The pa was handed over peaceably to the Ngati Kuri branch of Ngai Tahu and it is not clear which tribe actually constructed the earthworks. Certainly Ngai Tahu people would have been resident when James Cook sailed past Kaikoura Peninsula in 1770, naming it 'Lookers On' for the Maori people who watched him, and later when whalers first worked the bays around New Zealand. But by the time of the first European shore settlement in Kaikoura, Takahanga had been

destroyed, with only a few dilapidated whares still occupied below the terrace.

Takahanga Pa was one of the true casualties of Te Rauparaha's raid on the area in May 1830. Immediately after the 'barracouta tooth' battle and the destruction of Omihi Pa, Te Rauparaha sent several of his chiefs south to Kaiapohia Pa where they were killed by the Ngai Tahu residents. On his return through Kaikoura, Te Rauparaha and his Ngati Toa warriors attacked and sacked Takahanga Pa before heading back to their stronghold on Kapiti.

Archaeological investigations made at Takahanga in 1982 confirmed the authenticity of a raid on the pa. A defended gateway had been burnt out, as had the associated palisading on the earthworks. The presence of a musket ball was evidence that the attack had indeed occurred within European times.

Takahanga Pa, one of the most important in Kaikoura, has had reserve status since the earliest days of European settlement, although

this has not prevented a certain amount of unauthorised damage being done to the massive encircling and subdividing earthworks.

Mrs Becky Clayton holds a broken greenstone adze head which was excavated during archaeological investigations at Takahanga.

The final excavation of the gateway at Takahanga Pa, outlined by burnt stakes and showing the 'hooked' modification to the entrance passage, a probable response to the threat of musket attack.

BEVERLEY McCULLOCH

An artist's reconstruction of the defended gateway and house at Takahanga Pa, based on the results of archaeological excavation of the area.

AUTHOR'S COLLECTION

The enclosing main wall of this pa at South Bay (Pa 42) on the Kaikoura Peninsula was built at a right angle. The children are standing on top of the wall at the angle. The pa was strongly protected by additional ditch and wall defences outside the main wall.

BARRY BRAILSFORD

George Fyffe's house today. A pencil drawing by Bernard Clark. The house is now owned by the Historic Places Trust and is open to the public.

Now, having reverted to the care of the traditional Maori owners, it is to be hoped that it will be preserved for all time as a monument to Kaikoura's original people.

Within a few years of the sacking of Omihi and Takahanga, the first European settlers were beginning to stake their claims in the district. They found a much depleted Maori population — reported in 1849 to be between 40 and 60 persons. Probably the first European settler on Kaikoura Peninsula was Robert Fyffe who set up a shore whaling station, Waiopuka, in 1843. This was situated where the small stream runs into the sea at what is now Armers Beach. No visible surface trace of it remains today, although blackened whale bones can still be found washed out from the creek banks after high seas. In 1853 Robert was joined by his younger cousin, George Fyffe, who took over the whaling station on Robert's death in 1854. It was George who, about 1859, commenced building a house at Avoca Point on the now grassed land

beneath which lies the early moa hunter site.

During excavations on this land 2 years earlier, in 1857, George had uncovered a moa hunter burial — the first ever found in New Zealand — a relic of those first-comers many centuries before. Along with a skeleton were several stone adze heads and an enormous, whole moa egg, neatly perforated at one end and probably intended for use as a water bottle. This egg is still the largest ever found; it was sent to England some years later but eventually, in the late 1960s, was returned to New Zealand and placed in the safe keeping of the National Museum in Wellington.

George's house — or rather cottage — still stands. Owned now by the Historic Places Trust, it looks much the same today as it did last century with its weatherboards and hand forged nails. The original pink hue (derived from its first painting with a mixture of whale oil and red and white lead) has been retained, as have the whale vertebrae used for piles under one section.

The Fyffe cottage represents the beginning of the end of the prehistoric era in Kaikoura and it seems somehow appropriate that it stands on the earliest known site of human occupation of the Kai-

koura area. Within a few years of the setting up of Waiopuka whaling station other Europeans — farmers (often squatters), shopkeepers and traders, as well as other whalers — began to settle all around Kaikoura and the peninsula. Their arrival marked the real end of the prehistoric era in the district and a further decline of the Maori population, already depleted by Te Rauparaha's raids.

James Mackay made the 'Kaikoura Purchase' on 29 March 1859. Sites such as Takahanga Pa (Native Reserve E) were included in the 2250 ha of land left in Maori hands. However, over the next decades much of this land — including Takahanga — became European property. It is a sad but true commentary on the times that the early white settlers did not want the 'natives' living among them, or even in close proximity to their growing little township. Most of the Maori people seem to have moved to Mangamaunu, 13 km north up the coast. It is nice to be able to record that they have now come home to Takahanga.

The prehistoric and early historic sites around Kaikoura described in this chapter are only a few of those known. They have been chosen largely for their interest and accessibility. There are

From the surviving earthworks of 'Nga Niho' Pa, on the Kaikoura Peninsula, can be glimpsed part of the modern town of Kaikoura. The conjunction of Maori pa and European town testifies to the long history of the Kaikoura area.

WARREN JACOBS

many, many more, all important and all deserving our interest and protection. When you visit Kaikoura, remember you are at the end of a long line of people who have come to the place, enjoyed its climate and scenery and made use of its resources. People have enjoyed Kaikoura and lived on its resources for about 1000 years.

Make sure you do nothing to spoil the enjoyment of those who will follow you.

Further Reading

Davidson, J. *The Prehistory of New Zealand* (Auckland 1984)

McCulloch, B. and Trotter, M. 'Investigations at Takahanga Pa, Kaikoura, 1980, 1982' *Records of the Canterbury Museum* Vol. 9, no. 10: 387-421

Trotter, M. 'Canterbury and Marlborough' In *The First Thousand Years: Regional Perspectives in Archaeology* (N. Prickett ed.) (Palmerston North 1982)

Trotter, M. and McCulloch, B. *Prehistory at Clarence Bridge* (Kaikoura 1979)

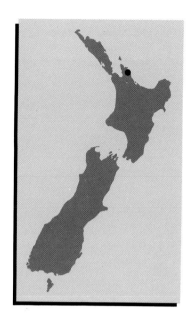

The Two Races Together: James Cook at Mercury Bay

Neil Begg

AT 4 p.m. on 4 November 1769 the *Endeavour*'s anchor splashed into the quiet waters of Mercury Bay. James Cook was anxious to set up a landbased observatory so that his scientists could observe the transit of Mercury, due to take place on 9 November. 'If we should be so fortunate as to Obtain this Observation,' he wrote, 'the longitude of this place and country will therby be very accurately determined.'

As the ship lay at anchor, Herman Sporing completed two sketches of the coastline of the bay. Looking south he drew the mouth of the Oyster River, or Purangi, and the beach, now known as Cooks Beach, from which Mr Green took his observations. Pickersgill recorded that the scientists worked at a point some 280 m from the western bank of the river. And looking northwards Sporing sketched the sweep of Wharekaho Beach (now Simpsons Beach) from the western headland of Wharetaewa Pa to the pa on the arched rock shown as 'Sporing's Grotto'. From these sketches and the careful map drawn by Cook we not only know the precise anchorage of the *Endeavour* but can also follow the routes followed by Cook and his men to the watering place, the two pa and the observation point.

As ever, Cook's first duty was to secure fresh food for his officers and crew. Though they did not have much success with their nets, dressed and dried fish and 'Cockles, Clams and Mussels' from the Maori people added to their supplies.

The 9th dawned clear and the observation party went ashore as planned. Unfortunately their results were unsatisfactory. The scientists checked the time of the transit but, according to Mr Green, 'unfortunately for the Seamen their lookout was on the wrong side of the Sun'. Cook was too busy taking the sun's altitude to ascertain the exact time and missed the transit observations. However, he recorded the longitude of the beach as 184° 4' west from the meridian of Greenwich. To make matters worse, during the period of observation five canoes approached the *Endeavour* and began trading. Lieutenant Gore, in charge during Cook's absence, shot a Maori who had bilked payment for a piece of cloth. It was a harsh retribution which, Cook wrote, 'did not meet with my approbation'.

Having completed his astronomical studies, Cook determined to explore the river at the head of the bay. On 10 November Cook and Banks and the other gentlemen took two boats up the river to a distance of 7 or 8 km. The mangrove trees, the river birds and the

shellfish were noted and Cook suggested that the river would provide a safe and commodious anchorage up to 5 fathoms in depth. The seamen were impressed by a fortified village which had been sited on a peninsula just inside the river mouth, on the east side. Accessible only from the land side, it was there protected by a ditch and a wall which measured 6.7 m from the top of the wall to the depths of the ditch. 'It is strong by nature,' wrote Cook, 'and made more so by Art.' It had been taken and burnt even before Cook's visit, although as Pa Point it remains an impressive sight today.

While the *Endeavour* was coasting up the Bay of Plenty shore, those aboard had speculated about the function of the palisades or fences which surrounded some of the hill villages. Tupaia considered they had a religious significance. Cook had a more practical view: 'I rather think they are places of retreat or Stronghold where they defend themselves against the Attack of an Enimy.' From the deck of the *Endeavour* at anchor, the top of the fighting stages of the Wharetaewa Pa, spelled Wharretoowa by Banks and Wharretouwa by Sporing, could be seen and Cook noted, 'I intend to see the whole'.

The opportunity to do so came on 12 November when, accompan-

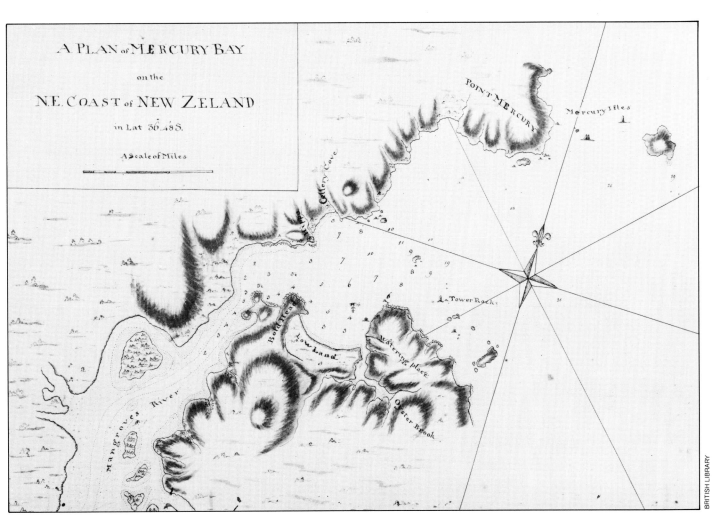

Cook's chart of Mercury Bay.

ied by Banks and Solander, Cook took the pinnace and the yawl to the north side of the bay. First they visited 'Sporing's Grotto', which stirred Bank's imagination. He saw it as 'the most beautifuly romantick thing I ever saw'. The pa was sited on an arched rock 'not less than 20 yards perpendicular above the water' and was detached from the mainland. Pictures of the pa, Te Puta o Paretauhinau — The Hole of Paretauhinau, remain though now only the pillars stand as the rest has collapsed into the sea.

The party moved westwards to examine the larger pa at the other end of Wharekaho Beach, named Cellery Cove by Cook and now

The waters of Mercury Bay, on which Cook brought the Endeavour *to anchor on 4 November 1769.*

A modern aerial view of Mercury Bay. Some of the places mentioned in Cook's account of his stay in the bay and some modern features or places are: 1. 'Sporing's Grotto'; 2. Wharekaho (Simpsons) Beach; 3. Whare-taewa Pa; 4. Whitianga; 5. Cooks Beach; 6. Purangi (Oyster) River; 7. Watering place.

known as Simpsons Beach. They landed about a mile short of the pa 'and were met by the Inhabitants in our way thether who with a great deal of good nature and friendship conducted us into the place and shewed us every thing that was there'.

Banks and Cook described Whare-taewa Pa in great detail, marvelling at the defences, admiring the weapons and the skill and speed of two warriors who staged a mock battle. Cook wrote: 'They handle all their arms with great Agility particularly their long Pikes or Lances, against which we have no weapon that is an equal match except a loaded Musquet.' Perhaps the best description of the pa came from Joseph Banks:

It was calld Wharretoowa and was situate on the end of a hill where it Jutted out into the sea which washd two sides of it, there were sufficiently steep but not absolutely inaccessible; up one of the land sides which was also steep went the road, the other was flat and open to the side of the hill. The whole was

The defensive ditch of Whare-taewa Pa in which James Cook, Joseph Banks and their party walked on the day they visited the pa. The ditch was then much deeper than it is now.

Many versions exist of the 'Indian fortification built upon an Arched Rock in Mercury Bay' which was called 'Sporing's Grotto' by the English. This is Cook's own sketch, close to one Sporing drew at about the same time.

The central arch of the small pa which Cook's party called 'Sporing's Grotto' collapsed into the sea some time in the late nineteenth century, but the two pillars of the arched rock are still standing.

inclosd by a pallisade about 10 feet high made of strong pales bound together with withs; the weak side next the hill had also a ditch the face of which next the pallisade we measured to be 20½ feet in depth. Besides this over the pallisade was built a fighting stage which they call Porava, which is a flat stage coverd with boughs of trees upon which they stand to throw darts or stones at their assilants out of

danger of their weapons. The dimensions of it were thus: the hight from the ground 20½ feet, breadth 6 ft 6, the length 43 feet. Upon it were laid bundles of darts and heaps of stones ready in case of an attack.

James Cook was impressed with the pa and wrote that he saw it as 'a very strong and well choose post and where a small number of resolute men might defend them-

selves a long time against a vast superior force'. He noted, however, that the besieged might suffer from a shortage of water as the nearest supply was 'a brook which runs close under the foot of the hill' — the Tohetea Stream. To complete what was the first European description of a Maori pa, Cook gave a detailed picture of the fighting stages and an account of the

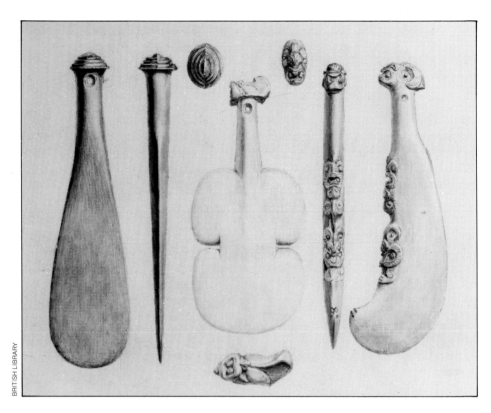

Patu made of stone, wood and bone, drawn probably by Herman Sporing. Observations made by Cook's party at Mercury Bay of Maori artefacts and customs were some of the earliest European impressions of Maori life and customs.

▼ *A pleasure craft curves its wake in the waters off Cooks Beach, Mercury Bay. It was on the far end of the beach that Cook and his party observed the transit of Mercury on 9 November 1769.*

weapons used by the Maori warriors. These were sketched, probably by Sporing, finished in London by J. F. Miller, and remain in the British Museum as a record of stone, bone and wood patu of pre-European times. There are also drawings of spears, or huata, a staff, or taiaha, the pouwhenua, the axe, or tewhatewha, and darts, or pere. The records make Whare-taewa Pa a place of great significance to all of us but it is held in special veneration by its owners, the Ngati Hei, who see it as ancestral land with memories and traditions reaching back far beyond the advent of the Europeans.

Another feature of Cook's visit to Whare-taewa Pa was the goodwill and friendship which was offered by the Maori people and gratefully accepted and returned by the visitors. The meeting certainly showed the hospitality of the Ngati Hei which may have been prompted in part by qualities they saw in James Cook. Perhaps this meeting was in the mind of Dr John Beaglehole when he wrote: 'We are fortunate in being able to look back to James Cook, and not to one of lesser quality of mind, as the man who first brought the two races of our nation together.'

It was time for the *Endeavour* to continue her voyage and Cook took green vegetables, fresh fish, water and wood on board. The watering place was shown on Cook's map and was only a short distance from the anchorage. Here a little stream tumbles down from the hills to enter the bay about 200 m from the mouth of the Purangi River. The Admiralty had been explicit in its instructions to Cook and he remembered 'You are also with the Consent of the Natives to take possession of Convenient Situations in the Country in the name of the King of Great Britain.' For the first time Cook had felt at ease with his Maori hosts and thought he might assume 'the Consent of the Natives' so, almost as an afterthought, he wrote in his journal: 'Before we left this Bay we cut upon one of the trees near the watering place, the Ships Name, date &c[a] and after displaying the English colours I took formal posession of the place in the name of His Majesty.'

This was the first such ceremony since the *Endeavour* arrived in New Zealand and so has historic significance. Taking possession in the name of His Majesty may now be part of an outmoded colonialism but we could also remember the instructions given to Cook before he left England. He was advised by James Douglas, Earl of Morton and President of the Royal Society, that he should with patience and forbearance do his best to make friends with the native people who might be encountered on the voyage. It should be remembered, Douglas wrote, that these people had the right to occupy any part of their country and it was natural and just that they should attempt to repel invaders. They should be treated with 'distinguished humanity'. For his part, James Cook developed a high regard for the Maori people: 'I have allways found them of a Brave, Noble, Open and benevolent disposition, but they are a people who will never put up with an insult.' Te Horeta te Taniwha visited the *Endeavour* with some of his young friends as she lay in Mercury Bay. Many years later he remembered James Cook: 'He was a very good man, and came to us — the children — and patted our cheeks, and gently touched our heads.' He recalled that his companions said: 'This is the leader of the ship, which is proved by his kindness to us; and also he is so very fond of children. A noble man — a rangatira — cannot be lost in the crowd.' There was much respect and goodwill between New Zealand's two races at their first real contact at Mercury Bay.

On the morning of 17 November the *Endeavour* sailed away past 'the North head of Mercury Bay or *Point Mercury*', tacked and stood to the northward. Her people had left us a precise and accurate account of a pivotal moment in the history of our nation.

Further Reading

Beaglehole, J. C. *The Endeavour Journal of Joseph Banks* (2 vols, Sydney 1962)

Beaglehole, J. C. *The Journals of Captain James Cook* (Vol. 1, Cambridge 1968)

Begg, A. C. and Begg, N. C. *James Cook and New Zealand* (Wellington 1969)

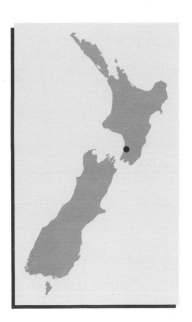

'For the Salvation of the Maoris': The Catholic Mission of Pukekaraka

Patricia Adams

THE Catholic community of Otaki dates its foundation from the first visit to the area in 1844 of a young French missionary, Father Jean Baptiste Comte. Bishop Pompallier had appointed him to 'this mission of Port Nicholson...to aid the Irishman Fr. O'Reily and work especially for the salvation of the Maoris whose language Father O'Reily did not know'. The mission of Port Nicholson covered a vast territory on both sides of Cook Strait and at first, when not travelling, Comte lived in Wellington. At what date he shifted his headquarters to Otaki is not certain but the evidence inclines one to think it was in mid 1846.

For 5 years before Comte appeared in Otaki, an Anglican missionary, Rev. Octavius Hadfield, had worked among the Maori of the Kapiti Coast. Some communities, however, had remained aloof from him and Comte chose (or was chosen by) one of these to live among in Otaki. They were the Ngati Kapumanawawhiti, a hapu of Ngati Raukawa. Their territory stretched northward from Otaki to the Forest Lakes and included a settlement on and about the sandhill Pukekaraka, just inside their southern boundary. On this hill Father Comte built his house and church, on ground given by the

Father Jean Baptiste Comte S.M. (Pa Kometa) who founded the Otaki mission in 1844 and served it for 10 years.

Chief Tonihi, who himself lived there. The church was probably built in 1845 for in October of that year Rev. Richard Taylor observed 'a Popish chapel on the high ground at the back of the pa, on the most conspicuous site that could be settled'.

It was a temporary building of raupo and within a few years

timber was sawn for a replacement. Due to lack of funds construction had not been started when, in May 1854, Comte left Otaki. He seems to have left for the sake of his peace of mind. A man of great energy and practical ability, he had thrown himself into the material as well as the spiritual life of his flock, helping them to improve agriculture, get a mill to grind grain and a ropewalk to process flax, a shop, even a schooner to carry surplus produce to Wellington. As a result he found himself acting as treasurer for the community and though this role did not enrich him personally, he felt it was incompatible with the life of poverty to which he was vowed as a member of the Society of Mary. At the same time he was under pressure from his family to return to France and disenchanted by strife and social disorders which he was unable to suppress. In 1853 or 1854 he moved from Pukekaraka to Kareti, then in May 1854, left Otaki altogether. Having obtained from Bishop Viard a dispensation from his vows to the Marist order, he went home to spend the rest of his life as a diocesan priest. With him travelled 15-year-old Francis Redwood, going to France to study for the priesthood, eventually to return as Viard's successor.

Comte's abilities must have been greatly missed in Otaki in the years

FRANK O'LEARY

The statue on Pukekaraka of St Peter was unveiled in 1907. The house Ohaki erected in 1894 marks the site of Fr Comte's first presbytery on the hill. In the enclosure on the summit of the hill, between the pine trees and the memorial which marks the site of the original raupo church, are the graves of some of the fathers, brothers and nuns who served the parish.

that followed. As the market for flax collapsed and that for grain fluctuated, the ropewalk, mill and shop went out of business. The ship ran aground on the Otaki bar and was not repaired. Typhus and other diseases devastated the Maori people. As for their spiritual life, the Otaki Catholics, like others in small settlements, saw priests only at intervals when they were able to itinerate from the larger towns.

In early 1858 one such priest, J. A. J. Séon S.M., on a journey between Wellington and Wanga-nui, collected subscriptions for a new church at Otaki, the original one having by then burned down. It seems that the church was finished, or at least sufficiently finished to be used, in the following year. This is the church which still serves Otaki, the oldest Catholic church in New Zealand. Its survival is remarkable, considering the 'improving' instincts which in this century have swept away many of its contemporary churches, and considering, too, the turbulence of its surroundings during its earliest years.

In the 1860s the Maori King movement had a strong following at Otaki and particularly at Puke-karaka. Kingite flags were flown, armed men drilled and patrolled, and large meetings debated options which alarmed Pakeha settlers. The Maori, too, lived in constant tension from the threat of armed intervention by the Government. In the mid sixties other notable politico-religious ideas were introduced by preachers of the Pai Marire (Hauhau) faith. Between the attractions of Pai Marire and lack of instruction in Catholicism, the flock built up by Comte had greatly diminished by the time the next resident priest, Delphine Moreau S.M., arrived. As he recorded:

> When I returned to Otaki in September, 1871, to make it my headquarters, I found that not only the children but also the young men and women did not know a word of the 'Prayer' or of the Catechism and had very little wish to be taught them.

Moreau's district extended up to the Rangitikei River and when the Pakeha population built up following the founding of towns in the Manawatu he apparently found Otaki less suitable as a headquarters. From 1876 he lived at Feilding. The real revival of Pukekaraka as a religious centre began after the

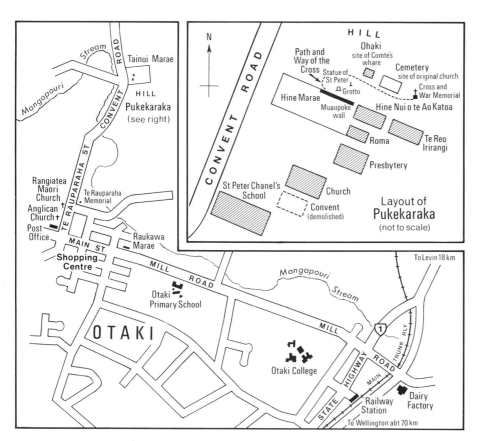

Father François Melu S.M. (Pa Werahiko) who was appointed to the Otaki mission in 1885 and served it for 50 years. He died on 27 October 1938 and is buried on Pukekaraka.

Pukekaraka and its location in Otaki.

▼ *The Wellington photographic firm of Wrigglesworth and Binns took this view of 'Otaki Looking South' possibly as early as 1874 but probably somewhat later. The cottage behind the church is probably the presbytery built by Father Pertius, a priest who made periodic visits to Otaki in 1868-70. It was rented out to lay tenants from about 1876 to 1891.*

appointment in 1885 of Father François Marie Melu — Pa Werahiko — 'little in size but big in zeal', as his colleague Father Claude Cognet S.M. described him.

Apart from the present school building and the church, everything which now meets the eye as

one steps through the gates at Pukekaraka was built during the 50 years that Melu served there. In front one sees the usual pairing of presbytery and church and, to the right, the school, built in the 1950s. A few feet to the left of the presbytery stands the marae with its two meeting houses and fringe of old trees and beyond that is the hill, the puke itself, now bereft of karaka trees but with a few pines at the summit. Winding up the hill one sees an outdoor way of the cross, accessible by a path. Climbing this, one passes by the Blessed Virgin sheltering in her little grotto and St Peter braving the elements on his pedestal, and reaches a whare whakairo, a little carved house which marks the site of Comte's dwelling. Just before reaching the crucifix, which rises from the memorial to the school's war dead, one finds the marked site of the original church and the graves of Melu and Cognet, of one of the Marist brothers and of half a dozen of the Sisters of St Joseph who worked in the parish. Round about are the unmarked graves of other dead, mostly early converts of the mission. Also unmarked is the site of the marae on which Tonihi lived and Comte had a garden. Turning towards the north the visitor looks down on Tainui, the present marae of Ngati Kapumanawawhiti, and the burial ground separating it from the hill.

The Church

'The Church at Otaki begun by Fr. Séon was finished by Fr. Moreau in 1859,' noted Antoine Garin S.M. and though he was writing in the 1870s or 1880s he was a good recorder and probably got it right. The building was certainly part-built by 29 April 1859 when Bishop Viard wrote Moreau a letter regretting that his own financial troubles prevented him from paying for its completion and suggesting that he 'Tell the natives that if they can continue the works of the Church they will draw down on their families the blessings of the Lord.' Then, in a rather desperate effort to be practical, he added:

MARIST ARCHIVES

St Mary's Church, Otaki, as it appeared when it was constructed in 1858-59. For a few years towards the end of the century the church had a square room behind the side porch and a veranda along this room and the whole length of the back wall. The church was lengthened at the east end (furthest from the camera) in 1901. The tower was later removed and a porch built at the west end.

P.S. If the natives want to employ Mr Seymour who is asking 40£ to finish what is started I undertake to contribute 5 pounds sterling which I shall deduct from the boarding school fees of Mr Seymour's daughter.

How Seymour and the natives reacted to this suggestion is not known but the church got built. In a report dated 1861 it is called *'une jolie chapelle'*, no doubt referring to its outward appearance rather than the unlined and practically empty interior. Nothing further seems to have been done about it until one Sunday in May 1886 when Melu was approached by some Otaki Maori. 'They want to see their church finished,' he wrote 'and propose doing the work themselves which will simplify the financial problem. The carpenter proposes making the seats for 1£, furnishing the wood himself.'

St Mary's Church today, without its original tower and with a new porch on its front.

On 24 April 1887, having been duly lined (apart from the ceiling), repainted and provided with seats, altar and a statue of Christ, the church was blessed by Archbishop Redwood and reopened amidst much rejoicing. It was at this time that it got its name, St Mary's. The next year Father Braxmeier, a teacher from St Patrick's College

The interior of St Mary's today. The statues, from the left, are: The Virgin Mary, a statue made in France which was given to the mission by Fr Melu's sisters and arrived in Otaki in 1888; St Peter Chanel, a statue of unknown origin which has been in St Mary's since about 1903; St Joseph, also given by Fr Melu's sisters in the late 1880s; and the Sacred Heart, a statue which appears in photographs of the interior taken before the 1901 extensions but the early history of which is unknown. The windows behind the altar, unveiled in 1905, depict the Virgin Mary and St Peter Chanel. The painting behind the crucifix depicts the view from Pukekaraka and was done in 1974.

in Wellington, came up during the Christmas holidays to decorate the interior in a manner described in the *Manawatu Standard* of 10 September 1889:

The corners of the altar space are beautifully painted in a green imitation of a growing creeper single vine, and the floor and altar [steps] are painted in carpet like colours, making a pleasing illusion of a real carpet. There is on each side of the figure of our Saviour, a very life-like figure of Joseph leading a child by the hand, and also of the Virgin Mary with a child in her arms on the opposite side, all being superior works of art executed in France... At the western end and opposite the altar is a choir gallery, containing an American organ.

By 1901 it had become necessary to expand the church but first the building was slewed round slightly, to make it face in the same direction as the presbytery and convent which had by then been built on either side of it. It then underwent improvements which Melu drew to the attention of his flock on Sunday 28 July:

Today you notice some changes in the porch and in the gallery... Ask the members of the choir and they will tell you their feelings with regard to the difference in the size of the gallery and in the stairs which now are easy and safe. Not only the gallery but also the porch has been enlarged by exactly one third and this no doubt will be well received by you.
    A confessional far more decent and more comfortable to priest and to the penitent has replaced the rudimentary and shabby one which had been in use for years. The Baptismal font at its proper place is another improvement and a most important one. From now the priest will be saved a great deal of trouble and the sponsors some waiting as everything required for the Sacrament will be in readiness.
    The only ones who perhaps will be displeased at first with the changes are our young men. I must say that it has been really pleasing to see a very fair number of them coming at all the services but they

FRANK O'LEARY

St Mary's has a number of fine stained glass windows. The windows behind the altar (visible also in the picture on the opposite page) depict the Virgin Mary and St Peter Chanel. They were unveiled by Archbishop Redwood on 7 December 1905. The windows in the body of the church are all memorials to the dead and were installed in 1942.

seemed to like very much the stair corner, entering from the side door. Now they will have to make an effort to find a place in front of the font or in front of the confessional without leaning upon them ....
    A momentary disadvantage of the improvements is that the seating accommodation in the body of the Church is reduced a little. But as a sanctuary will soon be added to the Church the inconvenience will be only for a time. Moreover most of the children could be accommodated in the gallery.

The new sanctuary was duly added later that year and in 1905 decorated with stained glass windows. The other stained glass in the church, memorials to the dead, was not added until 1942. Other changes

have included the erection of small side altars in 1902 and, perhaps in the twenties, the loss of the little tower which appears in even the earliest pictures.
    Ironically, the features which emphasise the native roots of the parish are all, apart from a Maori dedication on one of the stained glass windows, among the most recent additions. In the enlarged entrance porch built in the 1970s are kowhaiwhai patterns. The original tabernacle has been replaced by a small carved pataka, the work of John Gardner of Ngati Wehiwehi, who also carved a lamp holder. Behind the altar a painting by A. Keller depicts the view from the top of Pukekaraka where the first church once stood.

The School and Convent

For a brief period in the 1850s when Comte had several Marist colleagues at the mission station, Otaki had a Catholic school of 36 Maori pupils taught by one of the priests. The present school, named after the Marist martyr, St Peter Chanel, dates from 1894. It opened without a school building, the pupils being accommodated in the church and elsewhere on the premises. A convent for the teachers, Sisters of St Joseph, was opened that same year. This pleasant, two-storeyed, wooden building stood until comparatively recent times, complementing in size and design the still surviving presbytery building on the opposite side of the church.

The school building, when achieved in 1895, was described by the *West Coast Mail* as 'a very nice little structure, reflecting great credit on the contractor Mr Chas Nees'. There were two rooms capable of seating about 100, the infants' room being partitioned off by folding doors. It stood at the foot of Pukekaraka until 1905 when it was moved nearer the convent. The present school building, further to the south, replaced it in the 1950s.

The Presbytery

Comte's whare on Pukekaraka, like his church, burned down after his departure. Priests on pastoral visits stayed in another whare until one of them put up a rough wooden house. Moreau apparently used this 'wretched place' but later it was rented out, there being no resident priest and money being badly needed. When Melu took over the mission there was difficulty about getting it back and it was August 1891, he recorded, before

> …we were able after much trouble to take possession of the old little cottage. 'Katahi koe he tangata' You are now a man, said our young chief. When the new presbytery was built in 1897 'Katahi koe he rangatira' Now you are a gentleman, said the young man.

The 1897 presbytery still stands, repaired and extended, but still

Processions were a popular form of religious devotion at Pukekaraka in the early years of the twentieth century. The position of the school, the building on the right, establishes that this procession took place in 1905 or later. The school building shown in this picture has been replaced by a new building. Beside the church is the two-storeyed convent which has been demolished and not replaced.

▼ *Children of St Mary's Parish pose on their first communion day in front of the school. The year is 1898 and the priests are Fathers Delach and Melu. The man in the top hat is probably Hakaria Rangikura, a prominent layman frequently mentioned in parish records.*

presenting a gentlemanly outward appearance and a fitting visual link between the marae and church

The Hill

On 30 December 1894 the Otaki Catholics, by then predominantly Pakeha, and Archbishop Redwood celebrated the 50th anniversary of the mission. Father Comte was still living and sent from France a donation towards the totara cross erected on the hill as part of the celebrations. Erected there also was a small carved house, since called Ohaki, to mark the site of his whare. On this was displayed a photo of the venerable missionary, brought back from France by Cognet who noted that Maori passing before it paused to perform *le "tangi" le plus respectueux'*.

The cross stood for about 60 years before it collapsed and was replaced by the present steel one, the base of which is a memorial to ex-pupils of St Peter Chanel's School killed in two world wars. Between the cross and the whare whakairo lie a number of graves, the earliest that of Cognet — Pa Koneta — who died in 1912. Melu is buried there. He died on 27 October 1938, the last of the French priests connected with Otaki.

Two statues stand on the hill. The lower one representing the Virgin Mary stands in a grotto which is a tiny antipodean offshoot of the great shrine of the Immaculate Conception at Lourdes. The statue has stood on Pukekaraka since 1901 and of the grotto Melu recorded, 'When I came to Otaki for good, with the help of our boy William Bevan I had a rustic one built on the side of the hill. Later on a concrete one was built.' Though the present grotto, dating from 1905, has the appearance of a lined cave, early photos indicate it began as a freestanding concrete shell and earth was then packed round it and secured by a stone wall which is now invisible under vegetation.

Higher up is the metal statue of St Peter. Unveiled on 10 February 1907, it originally rested on the simple pedestal which now sup-

FRANK O'LEARY

Looking down from Pukekaraka onto the buildings of the marae and church. The red roofs in the foreground are those of the meeting houses Roma and Hine Nui o te Ao Katoa. Beyond them are the presbytery, the church and St Peter Chanel's School. Otaki town lies to the south. The church in the middle distance, beside two large Norfolk Island pines, is Rangiatea, erected by the rival Anglican mission a few years before the Catholic mission built St Mary's.

▼ *Pukekaraka about 1910. The buildings are, from left to right: the meeting houses, Hine Nui o te Ao Katoa and Roma; the presbytery; St Mary's Church, after the extensions of 1901; the convent, now demolished; and Blessed (later St) Peter Chanel's School, since replaced by another building.*

MARIST ARCHIVES

The exteriors of the two meeting houses, photographed in 1906 but appearing much as they do today. The name of the larger house, Hine Nui o te Ao Katoa, means 'Queen of all the World', a title for the Virgin Mary. The apex has a koruru in the form of a globe, cross and letter M for Mary. The smaller house, Roma, built in 1904 a year before the other, also has an appropriate koruru in the form of papal keys.

The two meeting houses, Roma and Hine Nui o te Ao Katoa, today, looking much as they did when they were built in 1904 and 1905 except for the addition of carved amo to Hine Nui. These carvings were formerly attached to a meeting house at Manakau called Te Uawhaki.

ports the statue in the grotto. Its present elaborate base was presented in 1913 by Herena Te Ara o Rehua, a chieftainess who announced her conversion to Catholicism by the apt statement that she had 'crossed the Mangapouri', that being the creek which separates Catholic Pukekaraka from Anglican Rangiatea.

The most recent addition to the hill, a mere 60 years old, is its way of the cross. All Catholic churches contain a series of 14 pictures or sculptures which serve as an aid to meditation on the passion of Christ, but an outdoor way of the cross is a feature of Catholic Europe which is very rare indeed in New Zealand. Otaki's one was blessed on 7 May 1925 by Archbishop Redwood.

The Marae

Among the various priests who worked with Melu the name of Joseph Delach — Pa Hohepa — is a particularly honoured one. Reputedly a French aristocrat, he was a writer of Maori hymns and prose (he produced a periodical *Whare Kura*) and an inspired organiser of things and events. The big hui which brought Catholic Maori together early this century (and which since 1946 have been revived in the Hui Aranga at various centres) were largely Delach's projects.

However, the one held in 1904 was initiated by the local Maori people. Ngati Kapu, Ngati Huia, Ngati Awa, Ngati Wehiwehi, Ngati Karehe and Ngati Tewatewa all participated in the preparations which included the building of a small meeting house. In this the leading chiefs stayed while other visitors were accommodated in tents and marquees in the paddock behind the presbytery. At Delach's suggestion the house was called Roma. It must surely be the only one ever to have the papal keys as a koruru at the roof apex. The following year another larger house was built alongside it and Herena Te Ara o Rehua and another woman gave it the name 'Te Hine Nui o te Ao Katoa' — a Maori title for the Virgin Mary.

No carvings were made for either house, but Hine has since acquired the amo of Te Uawhaki, a house which formerly stood at Manakau. Hine has also been adapted internally, but Roma seems to have changed little in 80-odd years. Pukekaraka has yet another meeting place, a very large one, — the hall Te Reo Irirangi which stands behind Hine and Roma and was built in the 1950s, replacing an earlier building.

The meeting houses line one side of the marae, which is fringed on two other sides by mature trees. On the fourth side is the hill which once covered much of the marae's flat space and is now held back by a concrete wall. 'Na Muaupoko tenei parepare i hanga 1910' says the inscription on it — 'Muaupoko built this wall 1910'. Muaupoko are a tribe displaced from much of their land on the Kapiti Coast when Ngati Raukawa and others moved into the area last century. Though the marae stands on land seized by a Ngati Raukawa chief, Te Uhi, Muaupoko are equally at home there for it is a Catholic, not a tribal, marae which is reflected by its name, Hine. Though this is probably accepted by most as meaning the Virgin Mary it also carries a reference to tribal reconciliation. It recalls that a breach between Ngati Raukawa and Ngati Maniapoto was healed after a daughter was born of a Ngati Raukawa-Ngati Maniapoto marriage and a meeting place was created in Waikato which was called Hine, Daughter, after the child.

Further Reading

Faith, L. C. *Otaki Parish and Convent School Jubilee 22nd, 23rd and 24th November 1974* (Otaki 1974)

Ramsden, G. E. *Rangiatea: The Story of the Otaki Church, its First Pastor and its People* (Wellington 1951)

Simcox, F. S. *Otaki, the Town and District* (Wellington 1952)

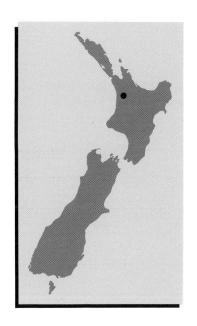

'The Choicest Part of Waikato': The Sacking of Rangiaowhia

Patricia Adams

In this redrawn version of an early pencil sketch of part of Rangiaowhia, the 'English Church', which has survived as St Paul's, Hairini, is to the right.

▼ In this second sketch, also redrawn, the Roman Catholic Church at Rangiaowhia, which has not survived, is in the left of the picture.

IN November 1864, a few months after the Waikato War had ended, Major William Jackson of the Forest Rangers wrote to the Hon. Thomas Russell, Minister for Colonial Defence, to make a claim for land in the conquered territory. He referred to a meeting he had had with Russell and Governor Grey on 6 August 1863, when they had discussed the possibility of his raising a force of colonial irregulars to pursue the Maori in the bush where it was difficult for British soldiers to operate. He had pointed out, he said, that by 'following up the Natives' he ran a great risk of being killed and it was not pay nor anxiety to 'get a name' that would induce him to do so. Rather, he had told them, 'if I get through I shall expect a lump of good land'. To this, said Jackson, Grey had replied: 'We do not wish to bind ourselves too tight, but I will give you not merely a lump, but a large slice of the choicest part of Waikato; I will settle you down in Rangiawhia.' 'And on the strength of these words,' wrote Jackson, 'I raised the Forest Rangers.'

Rangiaowhia, 'the choicest part of Waikato', was, of course, neither Grey's nor his Government's. Many years previously it had been given by Waharoa of Ngati Haua to Ngati Apakura as utu for the

JOHN WILSON

Through old trees near St Paul's, Hairini, can be seen lush Waikato pastures. There is no sign now of the village, the wheat fields, the water mill, or the peach and other fruit trees of the largest settlement in the Waikato, one of the King Movement's bread baskets.

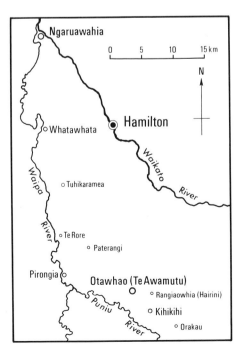

killing of a chieftainess, Rangianewa, during the capture of Kaipaka Pa. Ngati Apakura had established cultivations at Rangiaowhia around a pa called Ngauhuruhuru. As more peaceful times developed they began to live among their plantations without defences and the pa was virtually deserted. In 1844 the subtribe Ngati Hinetu, having also abandoned a pa at Rarowera, came to join their Ngati Apakura relatives at Rangiaowhia.

From 1841 Rangiaowhia received visits from both Anglican and Catholic missionaries. The latter established a mission there in 1844 while the former had headquarters at Otawhao (now called Te Awamutu) about 7 km distant. In general, Ngati Apakura inclined to Anglicanism and Ngati Hinetu to Catholicism. This divergence resulted in much theological debate and some rivalry in the matter of church building. By 1856 the little settlement had two substan-

tial weatherboard churches only a few hundred metres apart.

The Anglican missionary, John Morgan, introduced wheat into the district. Finding it impossible to get a regular supply of flour from the coast, he decided to plant wheat on the missionary property. After his first harvest he presented a few quarts of seed to the chief Pungarehu and he in turn planted at Rangiaowhia. In his second year Pungarehu had a good-sized field and his success touched off a revolution that within a few years changed the Rangiaowhia landscape. The area planted in wheat rose steadily. About 325 ha were recorded in 1852, perhaps the year of peak production. By that time the people had erected a mill to process their crop (another was built later) and were supplying a substantial part of the flour sold on the Auckland market. A visitor calculated that, even assuming a return of no more than five shill-

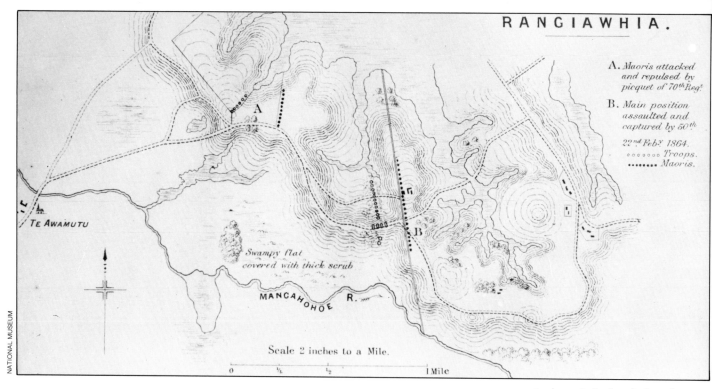

RANGIAWHIA.

A. *Maoris attacked and repulsed by picquet of 70th Reg.*

B. *Main position assaulted and captured by 50th*

22nd Feby 1864.

ooooo *Troops.*

•••••• *Maoris.*

TE AWAMUTU

Swampy flat covered with thick scrub

MANGAHOHOE R.

Scale 2 inches to a Mile.

0   ¼   ½   1 Mile

A plan of the battle fought at Rangiaowhia in February 1864.

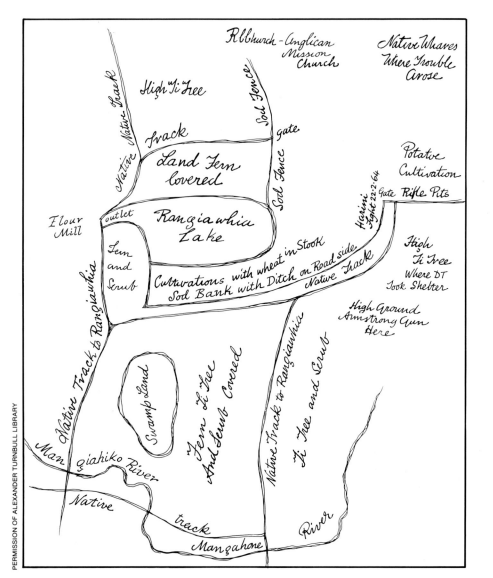

Rd Church - Anglican Mission Church

Native Wharves Where Trouble Arose

High Ti Tree

Native Native Track

Track

Sod Fence

gate

Sod Fence

Land Fern covered

Rangiawhia Lake

Potative Cultivation

Harini Fight 22-2-64

Gate Rifle Pits

Flour Mill

outlet

Fern and Scrub

Cultivations with wheat in Stook
Sod Bank with Ditch on Road side.

Native Track

High Ti Tree Where DT Took Shelter

Native Track to Rangiawhia

High Ground Armstrong Gun Here

Native Track to Rangiawhia

Swamp Land

Fern Ti Tree And Scrub Covered

Native Track to Rangiawhia

Ti Tree and Scrub

Mangiahiko River

Native

track

Mangahone

River

Rangiaowhia, 1864. Facsimile of a page from the diary of Edward Mellon.

ings a bushel, wheatgrowing at Rangiaowhia was almost as profitable as gold digging in the neighbouring colonies. The Maori farmers also produced potatoes, maize, barley and oats and many varieties of fruit, peaches being particularly successful. Their surplus was taken by cart to Te Rore, then by canoe down the Waipa and Waikato Rivers and along the Awaroa to Waiuku, then loaded onto a cutter for Onehunga and finally carted across the isthmus to Auckland. Back by the same route came sugar, tobacco, clothing and sometimes rum.

Some of the profits, however, were reinvested in farming equipment and livestock. Morgan recorded in 1849: 'The value of the flour sent down this year from Rangiawhia and now ready for the Auckland market may be estimated at about £330 — of this sum upward of £240 has or will be spent in the purchase of horses, a dray and ploughs.' In 1851 he recorded: 'The Rangiaowhia natives have about 15

Few pictures of Rangiaowhia before or during the attack on the settlement in February 1864 have survived. This watercolour by J.A. Wilson is titled 'The Fight at Rangiawahia (February 21 1864) for the recovery of McHale's body' and depicts an incident during the British attack on the Maori village.

carts, 17 ploughs and they have also purchased harness and several more cart horses.' Official approval and encouragement of all this enterprise was expressed from time to time by grants of goods and technical aid and even by the gift of two royal portraits dispatched by Queen Victoria after Grey had encouraged the villagers to send her samples of their flour.

Though other adjacent areas were also expanding their agriculture in this period, Rangiaowhia in particular took the eye of visitors. The Austrian scientist Dr Ferdinand von Hochstetter, who saw it on 18 May 1859, was one of several who left descriptions of it:

At 5 p.m. we reached Rangiawhia situated in the fertile plain between the Waikato and Waipa. Extensive wheat, maize and potatoe-plantings surround the place, broad carriage-roads run in different directions, numerous horses and herds of well-fed cattle bear testimony to the wealthy condition of the natives, and the huts scattered over a large area are entirely concealed among fruit-trees. A separate race-course is laid out; here is a court-house, there a store; further on a mill on a mill-pond, and high above the luxuriant fruit-trees rise the tapering spires of the catholic and protestant churches. I was surprised on entering the latter sanctuary at beholding a beautifully painted glass window reflecting its mellow tints into my wondering eyes. Such is Rangia-whia — the only Maori settlement, among those I have seen, which might be called a town — a place which by its central position in the most fertile district of the North Island, and as the central point of the corn-trade bids fair to rise ere long to the rank and size of a flourishing staple-town.

In fact, Rangiaowhia had probably passed the peak of its prosperity by the time von Hochstetter was writing. Continual cropping had depleted the fertility of the soil and prices were less attractive than a few years earlier. Though the villagers were still interested in European-style development of their lands — in 1857 they had taken steps towards individualising titles for instance — their attention was now directed to political change to protect and advance their status. Governor Thomas Gore Browne, visiting Rangiaowhia in April 1857, dined with three of its principal chiefs at the house of the Catholic missionary, Father Garavel. A meeting had recently been held in the kainga to discuss the proposal to elect a Maori king and the chiefs were anxious to obtain the Governor's views on the matter and also to expound their own.

Gore Browne subsequently explained the latter in a letter to the Hon. H. Labouchere:

It was, however, clear that they did not understand the term 'King' in the sense we use it; but though they constantly professed loyalty to the Queen, attachment to myself, and a desire for the amalgamation of the

▲ *After the sacking of Rangiaowhia in February 1864, the occupying troops built a redoubt, known as Blewitt's Redoubt. Here it is seen in a watercolour painting by J.O. Hamley (1820-1911) in the mid 1860s, standing between the two churches of the settlement.*

◄

Troops at Rangiaowhia, 1864.

races, they did mean to maintain their separate nationality and desired to have a Chief of their own election, who should protect them from any possible encroachment on their rights and uphold such of their customs as they were disinclined to relinquish.

Two months after this was written, Gore Browne received a letter from Rangiaowhia written by the Ngati Hinetu chief Hoani Papita and others gathered there. The writers announced their intention to appoint a king and magistrates to 'carry out the principles of Christianity, that we may be one flesh'. In justification they instanced the practice of civilised nations both

ancient and modern and cited scripture and the writings of St Paul. The letter also stated that conflict between the King and the British Crown was not intended and urged co-operation to avoid strife.

This meeting at Rangiaowhia was only one of a number which took place in the Waikato in 1857 and 1858 and eventuated in the choice of the Ngati Mahuta chief Te Wherowhero, also called Potatau, as the first Maori King. At one of the early meetings at Paetai in May 1857, there was a general reconciliation of all feuds dividing potential adherents of the King in the Waikato. To cement good

relations between Ngati Haua and Ngati Apakura, who had been estranged over the killing of Rangianewa, the daughter of the Ngati Haua chief Wiremu Tamehana Tarapipipi was brought by her father to Rangiaowhia and given to the people there. This gesture seems to have assisted Potatau, who was the grandson of Rangianewa's sister, to settle some of his qualms about accepting the position of King. He visited Rangiaowhia and was ceremoniously proclaimed King by the assembled people led by Tapihana, signifying his acceptance of the role by throwing down his white hat.

In 1860 war broke out in Taranaki as a result of the Government's attempt to purchase the Waitara block against the wishes of Wiremu Kingi te Rangitake. As the latter's Te Atiawa tribe were adherents of the King and their lands under his mana, the question arose as to what help the Waikato Kingites should render them. Opinion at Rangiaowhia was divided. Hori te Waru, the Ngati Apakura chief, was firmly against a Taranaki expedition whereas his Ngati Hinetu colleague, Hoani Papita, was sympathetic to the idea but decided to remain 'to watch the Waikato' as Morgan put it, that is, to be prepared for any move the Governor might make to attack Waikato while its fighting force was engaged in Taranaki. Nevertheless, some men from both the Rangiaowhia tribes joined the forces which marched to the aid of Wiremu Kingi and his allies.

It was 3 years before the spread of hostilities to Waikato anticipated by Hoani Papita eventuated. In the interval King Potatau died and was succeeded by Tawhiao, his son. A sort of semi-professional King's army developed, consisting of small units raised by the various Maori settlements, who took turns acting as bodyguard to the King at Ngaruawahia. Rangiaowhia had one such squad which consisted of 50 men out of a population that probably numbered about 1000. They drilled regularly and on Sundays marched to church in their plaid uniforms.

Europeans naturally became uneasy at sights like this and at signs of Maori determination to reassert control over local affairs such as conveyance of mail — which was entrusted to the King's soldiers — and impounding of cattle. European women and children began to leave the area and by the time war broke out in 1863 the men too had left.

During the summer of 1863-64, British troops and colonial forces led by General Duncan Cameron pushed down the Waikato from the north fighting skirmishes and besieging pa where the inhabitants offered resistance. As they neared the great granary of the Waikato — the region around Otawhao (Te Awamutu), Kihikihi, Orakau and Rangiaowhia — on which the Kingite forces relied for sustenance, four great bastions were erected across the access routes to block their passage. Only one of these has left its name on modern maps — Paterangi, which was about 1 km west of the modern settlement of that name. The men from Rangiaowhia were stationed at a more northerly pa called Pikopiko or Puketoki which stood beside the present Te Awamutu — Meadways Road, to block the track which then ran up to Ngaruawahia via Tuhikaramea and Whatawhata.

On 28 January 1864 the invading army reached Pikopiko and for an hour its columns stood massed before the pa while the defenders shouted challenges at them. They then swung away westward and encamped at Te Rore, a short distance from Paterangi. During the next 3 weeks the guns of the British advance position directed occasional shells towards the pa, there were exchanges of long-range sniping and at least one skirmish at some distance from the defence works, but no assault was launched. Cameron was building up a strong depot from which to supply his next onward push.

Then, early in the morning of Sunday 21 February, his army suddenly appeared before Rangiaowhia. At 11 o'clock the previous night, while clouds covered the moon, Cameron had marched over 1200 of his men out of the camp at Te Rore. Carrying no lights and observing a disciplined silence they had passed Paterangi without alerting the watch. By dawn they were at Otawhao — henceforward to be known as Te Awamutu — where to their surprise they found the mission premises undamaged. Bishop Selwyn, who had accompanied the column, stayed behind to ensure the continued protection of the buildings by putting up white flags and the army pressed on to the still unsuspecting Rangiaowhia.

No defences had been erected against an attack which was completely unexpected and many of the men of fighting age were absent. About 20 hastily turned out to fire from the shelter of a patch of bush as the 65th Regiment and Colonial Defence Force came in to attack. They were soon driven back into the path of the mounted Royal Artillery and Forest Rangers who rode in from the east. Those who escaped capture took shelter in buildings from which the villagers fired on the attackers. The latter presently became concentrated around a large building, presumably the wharepuni, whose occupants kept up a particularly vigorous defence, driving back those who attempted to rush the door. The building was then set on fire. The *Daily Southern Cross*, 4 days later, gave this account of the end of the affair:

... As the smoke and flames forced the rebels from their retreat, they were at once shot down and fell amidst the flames, suffering a most horrid death...

...The whare was about eight yards in length, but not until six yards at least had been burnt, and a number of volleys fired into the place, did the last of the Maoris make a dart for the purpose of escaping. He had not advanced two paces before he fell on his hands and knees, amidst the burning embers of the portion of the roof already fallen in. From the intense heat of the flame it was impossible to save him and he died and was burned where he fell. This was the last victim. When the fire had burned itself out the embers of the whare were examined to discover the body of Private McHale of the Defence Force, who had been shot down when the rush was made at the door, and had fallen inside. The charred remains were found and duly taken care of. The bodies of the Maoris were likewise discovered, frightfully scorched and burned with the skin peeling off...The killed and wounded having been placed on stretchers the order was given for the troops to retire, and this was done slowly on Te Awamutu.

Thirty-three prisoners, including 15 women and four children, accompanied the column but a group of villagers in the Catholic church who displayed a white flag were left unmolested on the General's orders. Next day the men among them joined with those who hurried down from the now useless fortresses to the north in throwing up fortifications at Hairini, between Te Awamutu and Rangiaowhia, in a desperate attempt to keep the invaders from taking permanent possession of the latter. Cameron's army drove them out and proceeded to the plunder of Rangiaowhia, carrying off 'pigs, poultry, rabbits, and succulent vegetables, spears, mats, long and short-handled tomahawks, greenstones, guns, cartouche boxes, cooking utensils, clothing, etc.' A few days later they returned to clean out the potato pits to supply the kitchens of their camp at Te Awamutu.

According to John Morgan, writing to ex-Governor Gore Browne on 30 May 1864:

Hori te Waru and Taati and Hoani Papeta and others strongly advocated laying down their arms after Rangiaowhia was taken but Wm. Thompson [Wiremu Tamehana] as strongly opposed it saying they would not make peace at Taranaki and he would not make peace then.

Others who were of similar mind assembled at Orakau, 7 km from Rangiaowhia, where the last battle of the Waikato Wars was fought from 31 March to 2 April ending with a final rush of the last defenders of the pa through the encircling lines of attacking troops.

The Imperial forces erected redoubts at Rangiaowhia and for 2 years provided a garrison to watch over the district while the Forest Rangers settled onto farms laid out on the confiscated lands of Ngati Apakura and Ngati Hinetu. In mid 1866 the British departed and defence rested mainly with the settlers. The Government built them a three-roomed blockhouse early in 1867 as a refuge in time of danger, and mounted patrols under the command of Major Jackson continued until well into the 1870s.

But no counter-invasion ever came. Ngati Apakura had gone to

Taupo, the home of their eponymous ancestress Apakura. Ngati Hinetu had also left, probably for the Pirongia area from which they had come originally. Some of the half-caste children remained in the school still conducted at the Catholic mission station and no doubt enjoyed an exciting day on 21 March 1865 when the soldiers of the 65th Regiment rushed from the nearby redoubt to save their school while the priest's house burned to the ground. The school building, however, was of raupo

The only building to survive at Hairini from the times when the district was known as Rangiaowhia and the scene of a flourishing Maori village is St Paul's Anglican Church. The church came into use in 1856 as the chapel of the Anglican mission at Rangiaowhia. The church of the rival Catholic mission has not survived.

and probably disappeared before too long, like the other Maori buildings of Rangiaowhia. This is how an item in the *Daily Southern Cross* described the settlement in December 1865:

Around St Paul's Hairini are the graves of a tranquil country churchyard, interspersed with clumps of delicate snowdrops. Almost nothing about the church and its churchyard today recalls the building's origin as a mission church, built in the middle of a thriving Maori settlement.

JOHN WILSON

Since the men have settled down Rangiaowhia has changed in a remarkable degree and if the future should prove as successful as the past, there can be no doubt that the above-named place will carry off the palm as being the garden of the Waikato. Little now remains to show where its late occupants had been, the two churches standing in close proximity being the last remnants of Maoridom.

The Catholic church has long since gone but the Anglican one, now known as St Paul's, survives in good order. Sadly, the name Rangiaowhia does not, for in 1912 the Post Office did away with it. Any traveller nowadays who wants to see where the events related above occurred must look for the peaceful hamlet which the road signs call Hairini.

Further Reading

Cowan, J. *The New Zealand Wars* (2 vols, reprinted Wellington 1983)

Gorst, J. E. *The Maori King* (London 1864, reprinted 1974)

von Hochstetter, F. *New Zealand* (Stuttgart 1867)

Kelly, L. G. *Tainui* (Wellington 1949, reprinted 1980)

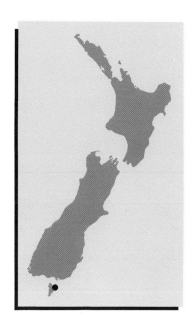

One Foot at Sea, One on Shore: Foveaux Strait and Paterson Inlet

Sheila Natusch

STEWART ISLAND has two deep harbours, Port Pegasus to the south, and, over the hill from the township at the head of Half Moon Bay, the spacious waters of Paterson Inlet. Paterson *River*, it used to be called; and indeed it does continue the course of the Freshwater River that flows into the head of the inlet (which began as a down-faulted valley invaded by the sea). Its entrance is guarded by Native Island and, to the east, by a former island, now a peninsula known as The Neck. In sandy places on both island and near-island, and in other parts of the inlet, are found signs of very old Polynesian camps or settlements, shown by excavation to go back to the period when the moa was hunted. Frail bones of birds, fishes and mammals, and heaped shells that crumble at a touch, lie about in hollows among the dunes of Ringaringa, The Old Neck and Native Island, with bits of worked stone here and there; later comers have left chips of glass and fragments of clay pipes. Generations of those old Polynesians must have collected kits of mussels and other shellfish just as Islanders do to this day. The bleached shells of small subfossil land snails among the sandhills of Native Island suggest that old fires, accidental or deliberate, must at times have spread

into the bush; and that columns of sand must have been sent flying on many a gale before wiry coprosma and muehlenbeckia, golden sand sedge (pikao), pink-flowered convolvulus and other sand-fixing plants established themselves.

Legendary Maui, known all over the Pacific as a fisher-up of islands, baited his hook for his New Zealand catch well out of sight of other land. His canoe was the South Island; his anchor Stewart Island: Te Puka o te Waka a Maui. Legend peoples the far south, successively, with the giant Kahui Tipua, the Rapuwai and the Waitaha. The latter emerge from the mists of prehistory as the tribal ancestors of some present southerners. (Colac Bay, according to Naina Russell, was a Waitaha settlement site.) There are shadowy figures of great size, shaggy aspect and voracious habits, referred to by some informants, significantly, as 'wildfowl', belonging — it seems — to a borderland on the edge of memory where moa met moa hunter.

Late in the sixteenth century (or thereabouts), the Waitaha, who were then numerous, found themselves beset by invaders from the north, the Kati Mamoe. These people (some of whose descendants pronounce the name Katchi Mamoe, suggesting affiliations with the Chatham Moriori) had been

elbowed south by territorial rivalry. Their own turn came next century when the Kai Tahu bore down upon them. They were not exterminated, but (in Tuhawaiki's words) 'the Kati Mamoe to the south of us were slaves.'

Te Wera, who had both Kai Tahu and Kati Mamoe relatives (for the tribes mingled by intermarriage), was Kai Tahu chief at Waikouaiti during this period. His name is associated with a place name, Hekia, suggesting the Freshwater River (O Hekia), as well as with The Neck, where he is said to have got his famous fright. Touchy even for those days in matters of utu, he was for ever stirring up strife, taunting, killing, eating and casting makutu, then moving on just ahead of trouble. Having eaten the defenders of Pukekura Pa 'from top to toe' he was soon off again because 'Toronga had said somewhat against him'. Not only warriors but their womenfolk, not excepting some from his own pa, were knocked down as casually by Te Wera as they themselves prised paua off the rocks.

There are several versions of Te Wera's moment of truth at The Neck. White's *Ancient History of the Maori* features amphibious whales (attracted ashore by the aroma of cooked greens) as well as

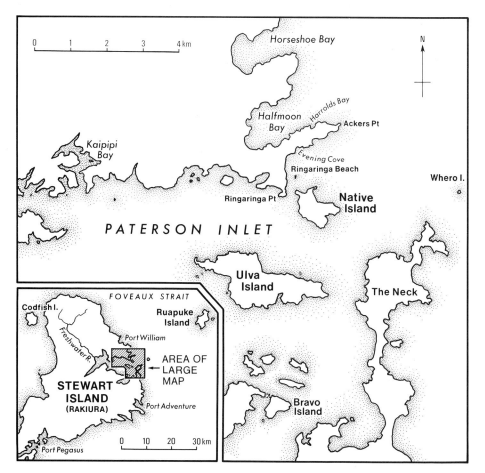

The entrance to Paterson Inlet, Stewart Island.

An aerial view over the entrance to Paterson Inlet, Stewart Island, with several of the places mentioned in this chapter identified by number. Tiny Whero Island, off the tip of The Neck, was the scene of important ornithological studies undertaken earlier this century by Dr Lance Richdale. 1. Halfmoon Bay 2. Oban 3. Ringaringa Point 4. Paterson Inlet 5. Native Island 6. The Neck 7. Ringaringa Beach 8. Evening Cove 9. Whero Island.

sea lions — but anyone who has suddenly been confronted by a burly bull whakaha (sea lion) would agree that alone would be enough. Meditating a short while (or so White says), Te Wera remarked: 'I did not dread the point of a spear; but for once I have felt a dread, and that of a whakaha.' He withdrew. If the meditation preceded the withdrawal, it must have been a brief pause for reflection! It seems the chief in his latter days had forsaken kai takata for kai moana, though he did not relish the diet of retirement. Stale blubber

The mission house on windswept Ruapuke Island. This house was built long after the Rev. J.F.H. Wohlers first arrived on Ruapuke. On the ground today, very little remains of the mission house or of the church/schoolhouse which can be seen in the background of this Burton Bros picture, just to the right of the mission house.

A portrait of the Rev. J.F.H. Wohlers, the missionary who first landed on Ruapuke in 1844 and spent the rest of his life on the shores of Foveaux Strait, dying on The Neck, Stewart Island, some 40 years on. The photographer was W. Dougall.

from stranded whales did not compare favourably with freshly killed humanity. As he lay dying, perhaps from malnutrition, perhaps from food poisoning, Te Wera cautioned his up-and-coming warriors to seek a proper resting place in the umu of the foe: 'It is good to be eaten by man.' He was a product of his time and of the old school.

The next threat to the south came from the fighting chief Te Rauparaha of the Ngati Toa, who had himself been driven out of Kawhia. By now the musket had been added to the Maori arsenal. The Maori in the far south had traded land for muskets. Te Rauparaha, having sacked several pa about Banks Peninsula and further north, did not chance his arm against Tuhawaiki, ariki nui in the far south, who had carried war into territory held by Te Rauparaha with noticeable success. Instead, an ambitious associate, Te Puoho, undertook to subdue the south. His march down from Nelson, via the rugged West Coast, Haast Pass, Wanaka, Crown Range and Kawarau and Mataura rivers is comparable to Hannibal's alpine crossing. At the Mataura-Waikaia forks his war party surprised an eeling party and it was easy to capture the pa of Tuturau, occupied by children, old people and some women. It was, however, a mistake to relax and sleep off the resulting feast without precau-tions. Tuhawaiki and others, having got wind of the invasion, armed themselves, crept up the Mataura River, and by a surprise attack recaptured Tuturau. There was very little blood-letting (though Te Puoho himself was shot dead by Teone Topi Patuki and his head taken to Ruapuke). No further trouble from ambitious north-erners, either!

The moko of Tuhawaiki, resident of Ruapuke and one of the para-mount chiefs of Ngai Tahu at the time of the first sustained interac-tion between Europeans and the Maori of southern New Zealand. Tuhawaiki was drowned off the South Canterbury coast in 1844, the year Wohlers landed on Rua-puke. The authenticity of this moko has been questioned in a recent book.

In the mid 1890s, Elizabeth Mary Hocken (1848-1933) painted the simple wooden building on Ruapuke Island which the Rev. J.F.H. Wohlers had used as schoolhouse and church.

Mrs Hocken also painted the ruins of Wohlers's house. Today on Ruapuke almost no trace remains of church or mission houses in which Wohlers conducted his ministry.

Tuhawaiki had mixed with many Europeans; he was an intelligent, adaptable man, with a cool head for business. When the Wesleyan pioneer missionary James Watkin settled at Waikouaiti, Tuhawaiki was one of his early converts. He was anxious for a missionary of his own, on Ruapuke — not a native teacher, he hastened to assure Watkin, but 'a missionary full-grown'. John Jones, head of the whaling station at Waikouaiti, had realised the value of 'a bit o' the fear o' God' and given Watkin every encouragement (though an embargo on Sunday whaling came as a drawback). Tuhawaiki, chief on Ruapuke, no doubt sought to improve the tone of his local community, as well as enhance his own mana. Whaling manners were not those of the missionaries, who frowned on swearing, rum and old-fashioned ways of dealing with runaway slaves. There was another matter for concern: more insidious ravages than even Te Rauparaha's were at work on the southern Maori population in the form of bacteria and viruses — 'plagues unknown to our fathers' — which wiped out whole families. Tuhawaiki's own predecessor, the handsome 'Tarboca' of Boultbee's journal, had been one of many swept away by an epidemic of measles, brought in, unwittingly, by the European. The common cold and influenza, with their debilitating symptoms, reinforced the dread of the ngikongiko (or kikokiko), man-eating spirits that hovered over houses of death, waiting for new victims to hollow out. There was no word for 'hope'.

It was at this juncture that Tuhawaiki met the German-born pastor Wohlers, who had come south with

From the 1830s on, The Neck, an extended, low peninsula on the southern side of the entrance to Paterson Inlet, was settled by whalers, many of whom had Maori wives. The families of The Neck gardened and raised poultry, cattle and sheep for their sustenance. This early scene of the kaik on The Neck, from Richard Taylor's Sketchbook, shows the rough conditions of the settlement's early days. Later settlement on Stewart Island concentrated at Halfmoon Bay and The Neck is now deserted.

the *Deborah*. Edwin Palmer, who piloted the little brigantine in southern waters, also put his oar in — there was clearly a vacancy for a well-qualified missionary in the Foveaux Strait area, based on Ruapuke. Consequently, as the vessel stood off Ruapuke, a boat put ashore, taking Mr Wohlers and his few goods and chattels — he loved to travel light — and delivering him into the hands of his future congregation. 'And there I was,' he reported back to Germany, 'whether they liked it or not.'

His letters and reports over the next 41 years make light of the discomforts of his days. His pious and formidable English wife, Eliza, tackled community health problems with soap, sweeping brooms and the medicine chest, while her husband saw to spiritual health and hygiene. He was not the kind of man who would have expected to be remembered a hundred years later (he died in 1885), though he would have liked to think his work went on.

The *Deborah* had not come down in 1844 just to land Wohlers on Ruapuke; he was incidental to her voyage. What she was looking for was a site for a settlement of Scots. It had been planned originally that she examine the whole coast of the Middle Island (as it was then known) from Port Cooper to the West Coast Sounds. In the event, Paterson's River was her southern limit. From there she pointed her jib-boom back up the coast toward the future Dunedin.

At the time of her arrival (and Wohlers's) in Foveaux Strait, relations between Maori and European were cordial. Early settlers on Codfish Island — seamen who had settled down with Maori womenfolk, rather than spend their whole lives at sea — grew a few vegetables, caught fish for the pot and did a bit of sealing and whaling in season. Understanding and trust having been established between the races, there was no need to continue living by the sometimes hazardous roadstead of Sealers Bay on Codfish Island and the families began drifting off to more sheltered resorts. These included some remote bays along the north-west shore of Stewart Island, as well as Port William and its neighbourhood, the Horseshoe Bay/Half Moon Bay area and The Neck. With the decline of whaling, many families from Ruapuke also moved to The Neck.

In 1846 Wohlers, paying one of his visits to The Neck, was welcomed by a shy young Maori woman who said her husband was Ko te Kata (Carter), 'a clever boatbuilder and makes all the boats for the Maoris'. Dr Monro in 1844

Later a sturdy 'Native School' was built on The Neck for the education of its many children of mixed origin.

The missionary Wohlers, his wife and their daughter are all buried on Ringaringa Point, on the northern side of the entrance to Paterson Inlet. This early picture of Ringaringa Point shows the graves standing unsheltered except for the new picket fence around them. The graves today shelter under huge macrocarpas and there are no traces left of the yards and other buildings erected on the low neck of land leading out to Ringaringa Point by the Traill family, the Wohlers's daughter, Gretchen, having married A.W. Traill Sr and made her home at Ringaringa.

▲ *The Wohlers and Traill graves on Ringaringa Point are enclosed by a lichen-covered wooden picket fence and sheltered by huge old macrocarpas. In her biography of Wohlers, the author of this chapter wrote of the graves and their location: 'On that narrow neck of wind-swept tussocky headland, the old graveyard is quiet and cool below soughing macrocarpa trees; they seem to echo the sea sounds drifting up from the beaches on either side. Here J.F.H. Wohlers, forty-one years a missionary in the south of New Zealand and on Ruapuke, rests from his labours; also Eliza, his beloved wife; a grandson and a great-grandson, both drowned in Foveaux Strait, are here remembered. Gretchen (Kerekini), who loved the Maori people, lies here too, and her husband Arthur William, born at Rousay, Orkney. If we turn and face the sea, looking out to the north-east, we can in clear weather discern the outlines of Ruapuke, "lying low on the sea, and coloured blue like distant mountains".'*

▼ *Ringaringa Point today, with only the graves and their guardian macrocarpas remaining on the low neck of the land. To the left of the picture is one end of Native Island and beyond to the right one end of Ulva Island. Part of The Neck can be seen in the far distance.*

▲ *The cove at Ulva Island, painted in 1876 by an anonymous hand. The building there at that time, which served as the home of Charles Traill and a post office and store, is no longer standing.*

◄

A group outside the Post Office on Ulva Island which served all of Stewart Island's settlers for many years. An island of great natural beauty, Ulva has been a favourite place for excursions for several generations.

had found the Stewart Islanders living 'in a tolerably comfortable manner, without much sweat of the brow', in good substantial houses kept tidy by their Maori helpmeets. There seemed to be plenty to eat: pork, poultry, potatoes and muttonbirds. Ko te Kata's contribution, the whaleboat, was greatly valued: 'the natives are great travellers, and are well provided with capital large boats, in which they jaunt about in pursuit of profit and amusement.'

Wohlers, who also did his jaunting about in whaleboats, did not always find the experience so amusing:

The waves reached an awful height, and the air was darkened by spindrift torn from the waves and whipped about. We took in sail as much as we could; two men slacked off and reefed according to the

— label at right edge of image:

In 1937 Emily Moffett, the grand-mother of the author of this chapter, painted this view of Evening Cove, looking across the waters at the entrance of Paterson Inlet to The Neck. These are the waters mentioned by Wohlers in the passage which concludes this chapter.

strength of the gusts while the steersman was obliged to give his whole attention to finding the most favourable position in between the waves. Others bailed.... It is an unsettling spectacle when close to the boat a steep sea tops up higher than the masthead.

There was nothing the missionary could do about it, so he settled down to a philosophical nap, disturbed now and then by a sloshing sea that came aboard to drench him to the skin.

Many documents give the flavour of Foveaux Strait life in the 1840s. Bishop Selwyn breezed through the settlements, christen-

ing, marrying, preaching disapproving sermons against bigamy and other time-hallowed local customs, writing vivid little notes in his visitation diary and rushing off to catch the tide. Letters from the whaling men who had settled in places like The Neck are full of salty gossip about round-starned brigs, the state of the schooner on the stocks, complaints about Yankees who were 'eyes out' after other people's whales, and requests for oakum, cows and other needs of the moment. The survey ship *Acheron* called a few years later.

When Stewart Island was bought in 1864 from the Maori chiefs and people of the Kati Mamoe and Kai Tahu tribes, a good part of The Neck, as well as several other tracts of land, remained in reserve for half-caste families, as did the muttonbird islands. Ruapuke Island was not part of the deal; it remains in the hands of descend-

ants of those who had decided to 'sell and convey... the whole of the island Rakiura' (Stewart Island). The 1860s also saw the opening of two sawmills at Kaipipi in Paterson Inlet. A fish-curing station was set up in Port William and good deep-water oysterbeds discovered at Port Adventure and off Port William.

Ulva, the largest island in Paterson Inlet, was originally Coupar's Island. Charles Traill bought property on the island, calling his estate 'Ulva' (a name now applied to the whole place). A keen naturalist and gardener, he also established the first post office, remains of which can still be seen at Ulva Landing. He is said to have been in on the first discovery of oysterbeds in Island waters, but these may have meant more to the conchologist in him than the businessman. He kept a little trading store, collecting provisions,

ASH SPICE

One building on Stewart Island has survived from the days of the early shore whalers and their Maori wives. Ackers Cottage, already standing when Wohlers first landed on Ruapuke, was built at Harrolds Bay in the 1830s (possibly 1834) by a whaler and his Maori wife who were visited there by Wohlers in 1846. It looks out onto Foveaux Strait.

oars, ropes, fishing-tackle and other needed commodities in his cutter *Ulva*, which also carried mail and was subsidised by the government. 'He is the only honest storekeeper I ever met in the colonies,' declared Robert Paulin. 'His articles are what he says they are, and his prices such as I am sure must leave but a small profit.' His Danish-born wife, Henriette Jessie Bucholz, was described by Paulin as a pleasant, intellectual, welcoming hostess, so untiring in her efforts to make her guests at home that it almost shamed them. She was to be remembered with affection for her 'efforts on behalf of the natives at The Neck and Bravo Island'.

Two families lived on Bravo, the Goomes (or Gomez, properly) and the Smiths. Manuel Goomes and Denison ('Yankee') Smith were shipbuilders who had married two part-Maori sisters and raised large families. They ran sheep, cattle, pigs and poultry and the children

drove the cattle across the gravel-spit at low water to forage among the grasses on the south shore of the Inlet. One of the girls, Alice Goomes, won a certificate of bravery for saving her father: seeing his dinghy drifting about, she rushed into the sea fully clad, swam out and found him unconscious in the bottom of the boat. She got him ashore but could not bring him round, so not stopping for a dry change, she set off to pull to The Neck for help. Manuel recovered, but Alice caught a bad chill and never really recovered from its effects. She died at 21.

The Neck settlement had its own school, the first schoolmaster being A. W. Traill (a half-brother of Charles) who had married a daughter of Wohlers, Gretchen. If anyone was smacked for speaking Maori, one does not hear of it; on the contrary, Mr Traill's daughter Etta remembered bilingual lessons: 'd-o-g, kuri! c-a-t, naki!' and so on. There was a certain amount of

truancy in fine weather when boys and girls alike were tempted to put to sea, but the addition of navigation lessons to the curriculum seems to have put that to rights. Eventually Mr and Mrs Traill moved to Ringaringa, where their old house still stands, tucked away out of sight.

Just over a hundred years ago, old Mr Wohlers visited his daughter and son-in-law, who were still living at The Neck. They had been waiting for a break in the weather to let them pull round to Half Moon Bay so that Mr Wohlers could hold a service. To cross from The Neck to the opposite shore, a couple of miles of water open on one side to the straits, is a long haul that nobody would dream of making now under oars. Instead of keeping on round Ackers Point (where the lighthouse is now), the party decided to haul their boat ashore in a snug corner, most likely Evening Cove, and walk through the bush to Half Moon Bay. Wohlers wrote:

When the gathering was over it had grown dark. One of the men there would not have it that an old man like me should go through the dark bush — it was a pitch-black night — especially on such a rough track. He pressed us to come with him in his boat; he was going to pull round to where we had left ours. I felt tired and cold in the boat, but kept thinking all the time we were coasting along in the still water between the two promontories, what a delightful trip this would be for some of the younger people in Germany living far from the sea! It was a still...clear evening; the sickle moon, still slender and young, stood only a little way above

In 1928 Dorothea Traill, the mother of the author of this chapter, painted the view from R.H. Traill's house across to The Neck. The vessel entering Paterson Inlet is the Sir James Clark Ross, *heading for the whaling base further up the inlet.*

the landscape, and the trees threw wonderful and strangely shaped shadows across the surface of the water. While the two men, my son-in-law and the other man, were rowing, my daughter and three little girls who had come with us sang lovely English songs.

The Stewart Island community, one foot still at sea and one on shore, polyglot, hardy, humorous, at times strongly opinionated, still does credit to the adaptable Tuhawaiki, the whalers and their tidy Maori wives, and the missionary

who died 100 years ago hoping that he left Foveaux Strait no worse than he found it.

Further Reading

Howard, B. *Rakiura* (Wellington 1940)

Natusch, S. *Brother Wohlers* (Christchurch 1969)

Natusch, S. *Southward Ho!* (Invercargill 1985)

Sansom, O. *The Stewart Islanders* (Wellington 1970)

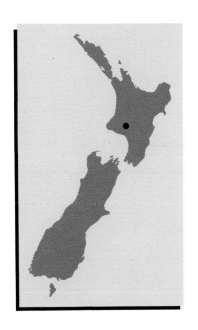

A River's Flow of History: Jerusalem to Pipiriki

Ian Church

IN Maori tradition the people of the Wanganui River have the three children of Tamakehu and Ruaka as their guardians: Hinengakau, their daughter, protects the upper reaches above Retaruke; Tamaupoko, the elder son, guards the middle reaches between Retaruke and Ranana; and Tupoho, the younger son, looks after the lower reaches from Matahiwi to Putiki. They are portrayed in a modern carving in the grounds of the Wanganui Public Library. Jerusalem and Pipiriki lie in Tamaupoko's domain and these settlements preserve a little of the history of this great river. Though the scenic beauties of the landscape can be preserved for future generations, time is not kind to the relics of the passage of man.

The Ati Haunui a Paparangi people of the river are an amalgam of the tangata whenua — the original Polynesian settlers — the Nga Paerangi who ventured overland from the east coast and the descendants of the complement of the Aotea canoe which Turi led to the west coast. The valley was populated over several centuries and the boundaries of each hapu settled by inter-tribal fighting.

The influence of the arrival of Europeans in New Zealand was first felt in the early 1800s when pigs and potatoes were obtained from the Ngati Ruanui people of Patea. Mysterious illnesses, known as rewharewha, took their toll of a people with no immunity to cholera, measles and influenza. In the 1820s and 1830s the musket arrived in the hands of Nga Puhi and Waikato invaders and the river tribes began to congregate in very large hilltop pa, such as Pukehika, opposite Jerusalem, to defend themselves. John Nicol, 'Scotch Jock', was the first trader to ascend the river, reaching Pipiriki in 1834.

Relative peace came with Christianity which was first brought by Maori evangelists, notably Wiremu Eruera Tauri, in the late 1830s. In December 1839 the Rev. Henry Williams of the Anglican Church Missionary Society stayed a night at Pukehika and was roused by 'the pleasing sound' of three bells for morning prayers in the 'different hamlets in the neighbourhood'. The Wanganui missionaries, John Mason and Richard Taylor, regularly held services in the riverside villages and it was the Rev. Taylor who gave the name Jerusalem to Patiarero in the 1850s. Hiruharama, the Maori equivalent, has never enjoyed the currency of other Maori versions of Biblical and European names such as Atene (Athens), Koriniti (Corinth) and Ranana (London).

The original name, Patiarero, probably derived from the saying 'Haere ki patiarero' meaning 'Then go and put yourself in danger'. The village was settled when the relative peace brought by Christianity enabled people to disperse from Pukehika which, until the early 1850s, had a population of over 1000. A chapel was built in which Anglican services

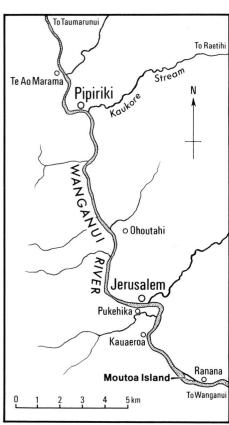

Jerusalem to Pipiriki.

were held but the people had a strong wish for a missionary of their own. When the Catholic Father John Lampila S.M. moved up from Kaiwhaiki, on the lower reaches, to Kauaeroa below Jerusalem on the opposite bank, his teachings found a ready reception. He also had the advantage that, being French, he was not linked to hostility to the actions of the British Government.

Father Lampila built three churches in succession at Kauaeroa, trained catechists such as Tai Whati, Te Opotini, Wheraiko and Poma to help spread his faith and planted grapevines on the slopes. Between 1852 and 1866 he baptised 1006 followers along the river. His mission ended in April 1866 when the spread of warfare in the area demoralised the people. Some of his catechists were killed in the battles of Moutoa Island on 14 May 1864 and at Ohoutahi in mid February 1865. A plaque in St Joseph's Church commemorates Brother Euloge (Antoine Chabany) and Te Hiwitahi Kereti, catechist at Kauaeroa, who were killed at Moutoa Island. Kereti was the leader of 400 men from Putiki to Karatia who prevented a party of 140 Hau Hau warriors from descending the river to threaten Wanganui. Their leader, Matene Rangitauira of Taumarunui, and about 50 of his followers were killed.

In the grounds of the Jerusalem convent are two trees planted to mark the centennial of the reopening of the Catholic mission by Father Christopher Soulas in June 1883. One of his notable assistants was Ruhe Keremeneta. A church built on the present site was burnt down, it is said as the result of a quarrel among members of a shearing gang. Fundraising enabled the St Joseph's Church to be erected in 1892.

Jerusalem will always be associated with Mother Mary Aubert, who commenced her religious, nursing and educational work there in 1883. Later she set up an orphanage providing a refuge for abandoned children. To support this work her community of nuns farmed 285 ha

ARTHUR BATES

The Wanganui River in the deep trench between rugged hills through which it flows between Pipiriki and Jerusalem.

in the hills above the village. This included a cherry orchard which, in later years, was a popular venue for New Years Day picnics. Mother Aubert used her knowledge of herbs and Maori remedies to produce medicines and ointments which sold for 2/6 a bottle: 'Marupa' for influenza and whooping cough, 'Paramo' for liver complaints, 'Romino' for sprains and rheumatics, 'Hapete' for tumours and sores and 'Wanena' for superficial injuries. Samples of her medicines were

sent to the Pasteur Institute in Paris and to French troops serving in Madagascar. The Sisters of Compassion built up a wonderful tradition of service to the people of the area which continues today.

At the turn of the century Jerusalem had a population of 200 and a mail service twice a week, the post

PETER MORATH

Its oft-photographed church is the most dominant of the many interesting old buildings at Jerusalem, originally Patiarero. The Catholic mission was first established in the area in the 1850s and reopened in 1883.

office being at the mission. There was a large hall known as the Parliament Building, a billiard hall and a dining room which was pulled down after a typhoid epidemic about 1920. The men worked in their crops of oats, maize, potatoes and tobacco while the women made flax mats, kits, piupiu and taniko weaving. The Dominion Museum ethnographic team of Johannes Andersen, Elsdon Best and James McDonald filmed the people at their crafts and recorded

NATIONAL MUSEUM

An expedition from the Dominion Museum visited the Wanganui Valley in 1921 to record information on the crafts, activities and tribal lore of the area. At Jerusalem, this party posed for the photographer James McDonald to demonstrate some of their foods and how they were prepared — bread, meat, potatoes and tea in a large enamel pot.

One of the local crafts photographed by James McDonald on the 1921 Dominion Museum expedition to the Wanganui Valley was the making of hinaki in Jerusalem for the taking of eel from the river.

NATIONAL MUSEUM

Eel weirs were still a common sight on the Wanganui River at the time of the 1921 Dominion Museum expedition. They were built to facilitate the taking of large quantities of eel, the weirs guiding the eel into hinaki suspended on them.

NATIONAL MUSEUM

their tribal lore in 1921. Surviving sections of the film have been restored by the New Zealand Film Archive.

One of the village characters was Joe Symon, a Syrian, who ran a store in a pataka at the northern end of the pa. Another was the Ratana policewoman Miriama who kept spectators off the rugby field by striding up and down with her cane. A notable resident was Utamate Tauri, Mrs Waetford, whose singing raised funds for the

soldiers of World War I throughout the North Island. Afterwards she toured America with a concert party.

The Jerusalem hall was the venue for many concerts and dances and the Morikau Football Team trained two nights a week in a wharepuni, after running round outside, with the elders and women sitting round the walls, smoking their strong local tobacco while they watched the exercises. The Upokotauaki Meeting House was

used by Tamatea Te Kooru, one of several tohunga, to meet his patients. Sports meetings, welcomes to distinguished visitors, tangi, concerts and dances brought the people together in a manner seldom seen today since most of the residents have drifted away to urban centres. One of the last notable occasions was the welcome to Cardinal Tom Williams when the centenary of the re-opening of the Catholic mission was celebrated in 1983.

▲ *The original settlement at Pipiriki was on the opposite side of the river from today's township. Very old marae were located in the vicinity of 'old' Pipiriki village. When Alfred Burton took this photograph in 1885, wheat was being grown around the village.*

◄

On his 1885 trip up the Wanganui Valley, Alfred Burton took many photographs of great ethnographical interest today. This group in 'old' Pipiriki may look posed, but the photograph reveals a wealth of information about the buildings, clothes, paddles and other items of everyday use of the times.

Pipiriki has suffered a similar urban drift but recently some families have returned. One meaning of its name is 'bush wren' but T. W. Downes in *Old Whanganui* records the story of an old chief, Tukai-ora, who was dying at this place and requested some pipiriki — small shellfish. A swift canoe

was sent away to the coast for the desired delicacy but the chief died before it returned. The story does not say what name, if any, the locality had before this incident.

When the Rev. John Mason first visited old Pipiriki, opposite the present township, in November 1840, he found the chief Hori

Patene Ngakai ministering to the religious needs of its 140 residents. Mason described him as 'an intelligent and well-disposed man' able to read a little. The Rev. Richard Taylor was so impressed with the situation of Pipiriki that he had a house built where he took his wife and family for summer holidays.

An early photo taken in Pipiriki which shows the flourmill erected in 1854 on the banks of the Kaukore Stream. The mill building survived long enough to be converted to an early power house, but only fragments now remain of it. The photograph shows it was similar in appearance to the restored Kawana Mill at Matahiwi.

A succession of catechists — Richard Matthews, William Ronaldson, William Telford and James Booth — lived intermittently at Pipiriki. A Wesleyan missionary, the Rev. William Kirk, resided at Te Ao Marama, the next village up the river.

The progress in the village was recorded in a letter the teacher Hamuera wrote to William Ronaldson in February 1852. A large new church was being built of rammed earth with a planked floor, sawn timber rafters and a shingle roof. The people had acquired 40 sheep and ten cows, were growing wheat and were considering the construction of a water-powered flourmill. This was built in the next 2 years on the bank of the Kaukore Stream where a few remains may still be found. Old photographs and the restored Kawana Mill near Matahiwi show what the mill was like. Richard Booth, James's brother, was the miller and sacks of flour and wheat were taken to Wanganui for trade. The flour was described as 'beautifully white and in every respect of the best quality'. The mill survived the fighting of the 1860s and 40 years later it was rebuilt to generate power for Pipiriki House.

James Coutts Crawford describes Pipiriki in 1861 in his *Travels in New Zealand and Australia*. His party passed the deserted Pukehika, an unfinished church 'embowered in a lovely grove of karaka trees' and Father Lampila's residence and vineyard. Crawford was taken by the beauty of Pipiriki with its whare set among karaka, peach, cherry and other fruit trees. He noticed the large church and the

weatherboard house belonging to Richard Booth, the trader. The chief settlement was still on the right bank but there were 'extensive cultivations and many dwelling houses' where the present village is. The movement of canoes up,

The only surviving mill on the Wanganui River is the Kawana Mill at Matahiwi, built in 1854 and reconstructed 1978-80. Of the similar mill at Pipiriki on the Kaukore Stream only a few boards, half covered by second-growth bush, remain.

Canoes were used by Maori on the Wanganui River long before the advent of European riverboats. They continued in use until well into this century. This scene of a canoe being shaped on the banks of the river, probably early this century, was reproduced as a postcard.

down or across the river went on all day long.

After having Christmas dinner with Richard Booth, the party crossed over to visit Hori Patene whose house Crawford described as 'a wretched slab hovel'. 'He was a civil and pragmatical old gentleman of rather good profile and pleasing expression and made no end of excuses for his poverty and inability to supply us with food.'

(Three years later Hori Patene was killed fighting in Taranaki.) The flourmill was out of order — a common state of Maori-owned mills according to Crawford. The travellers were able to purchase a pig for 12 shillings and 'backshish' of two sticks of tobacco. With stews, fries of beef, ducks, and pigeons they lived 'luxuriously'.

War between Maori and European came twice to the Wanganui

River. In 1847 Pukehika and Patiarero were the centres of opposition to the New Zealand Company's 1840 purchase of Wanganui, with the result that their progress was held in abeyance and their cultivations and churches neglected. In the 1860s Pipiriki was drawn into the Hauhau movement and its men fought at Moutoa Island and Ohoutahi as well as in Taranaki. James and Richard Booth and their families were driven away in May 1864. To ensure the safety of Wanganui, British and colonial troops were garrisoned in three redoubts built round the prominent hill Te Rangiahua, opposite the Pipiriki boat-landing, in March-April 1865. While the European forces were engaged at Weraroa, Waitotara, in July 1865 Major Brassey's garrison was besieged at Pipiriki and became short of supplies and ammunition. Messages were sent away to Wanganui by several ingenious means, including requests for assistance written in Latin to foil any interceptors. After Weraroa fell the Government forces moved on Pipiriki in August and the Hauhau supporters withdrew up the river.

Pipiriki was all but deserted, a few people gradually returning over the next 10 years to cultivate their land. Some returned to Christianity under the leadership of the Rev. Eruera te Ngara of Te Ao

The Pipiriki landing, 1905. The riverboats Waiora *and* Wairua *are moored to the coal hulk which was stationed at the landing. These were the years when Pipiriki was at the height of its popularity as a tourist destination, the new Pipiriki House having just been opened.*

The Wanganui River Trust was established in 1891 to clear and maintain navigable channels in the river. By 1903 the channel had been cleared right up Taumarunui. The Trust was disestablished in 1940, but evidence of its work, like these training walls in the river near Matahiwi, remains.

ARTHUR BATES

The Ongarue worked the river for more than half a century, from 1904 to 1959. Today it stands on dry land at Pipiriki as a memorial to the riverboat era on the Wanganui River. It was dedicated as such in 1984.

ARTHUR BATES

The letterhead which was in use by Wanganui River Services in the 1940s, when the riverboat era on the river was beginning to draw to a close.

OPERATING ON NEW ZEALAND'S WONDERFUL WATERWAY

P.O.BOX 388
TELEPHONES 5050 TOURIST OFFICE
2661 OFFICE

WANGANUI RIVER
SERVICES LTD

TAUPO QUAY
WANGANUI, N.Z.

Marama (ordained on 1 November 1886) and his son Henare Keremeneta, brother of Ruhe of Jerusalem. Mission work in the villages along the river was also conducted by the Salvation Army and the Presbyterian Church.

With the planning of the construction of the Main Trunk Railway in the 1880s and the opening up of the Waimarino country, Pipiriki took on a new importance. The river was opened up for shipping by the clearance of snags and the blasting of rapids, providing a convenient route for men and materials to Pipiriki from where a track led off to the future townships of Raetihi and Ohakune. The steamer *Tuhua* was put on the river and in July 1886 it took up a gang of men to commence work on the Pipiriki-Raetihi road. Huts were built for the Public Works Department staff, S. H. Manson opened a store and in 1891 Arthur E. Huddle opened the first accommodation house for visitors.

Alexander Hatrick, an Australian-born Wanganui entrepreneur, put his first river steamer, the *Wairere* into service in December 1891. His service prospered and Pipiriki became an important township with its store and post office, goods sheds, tourist houses and European homes built well above the river to avoid floods. Under the guidance of Hori Pukehika, Native Sanitary Inspector for Wanganui, old-style Maori whare along the river were replaced by better homes. The house occupied by Reone Te Maungaroa is now the Colonial House Museum and Information Centre. Reone was chairman of the school committee, the school being opened in October 1896 with 18 pupils. Night classes were held for adults.

Alongside the Information Centre is the site of Pipiriki House, once an important stage in the North Island tourist route from Auckland, through Rotorua and Taupo to Wellington. The Wanganui River Trust cleared the river through to Taumarunui, allowing tourists to be brought down in motorised canoes and shallow-

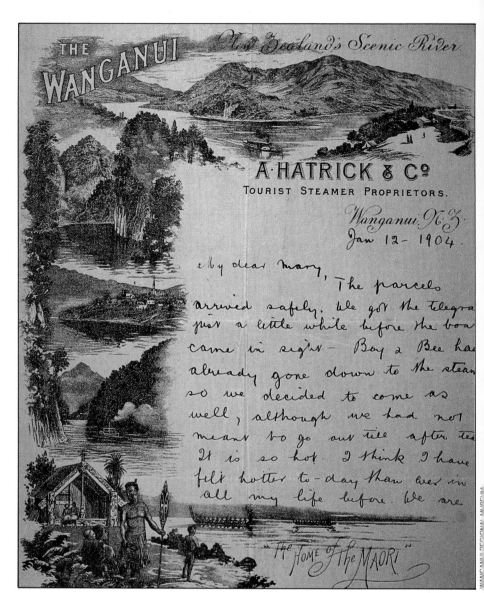

This letterhead, in use by A. Hatrick and Co. in the early years of this century, depicted scenes on the river which could be seen from the tourist steamers which the company had just begun to run on the river.

draught launches, to the overnight stay at the houseboat, moored at the mouth of the Ohura River. The larger boats took them on to Pipiriki where Alexander Hatrick had purchased Huddle's Accommodation House in 1899 and added a two-storeyed wing. In 1903 the original part of the building was replaced by a two-storeyed hotel with a long veranda giving panoramic views of the river and the Te Poti Marae on the opposite bank.

Pipiriki House was destroyed by fire on 10 March 1909 and the double-decked steamer *Manuwai* was hastily converted to a houseboat to provide overnight accommodation. The new Pipiriki House was built in similar style, with gables and veranda, rooms for 120 guests and an indoor winter

garden. At that time the river was being promoted as 'The Rhine of Maoriland'.

The tourists were entertained by the local Maori concert parties with haka, poi displays and songs. As at Jerusalem there was a strong community life and in 1906-7 Potango Waiata of Pipiriki was one of the leaders of the river people who took their skills to the New Zealand Exhibition in Christchurch. A model pa was constructed in Hagley Park, Christ-

NATIONAL MUSEUM

▲ *By the early years of this century most activity in the Pipiriki area was firmly established on the present site of the township, on the opposite side of the river from the old Maori kainga. This Muir and Moodie photograph of 'new' Pipiriki was taken in 1905.*

►

The Colonial House Museum and Information Centre at Pipiriki was built some time before 1885. One of its owners, in the 1890s when Pipiriki began to flourish as a river town, was Reone Te Maungaroa. The house was handed over to the Wanganui River Scenic Board in 1976 and reopened in its new role in December 1977.

JOHN WILSON

church, by Gregor McGregor of Morikau Station and his team who took down some of their old houses as well as carving new ones. Six canoes were fitted with new topstrakes and Potango and Turei were the captains and time-givers (kai-hau-tu) of the canoe *Taheretikitiki* in which the Governor-General, Lord Plunket, was taken round the Victoria lakelet in Hagley Park. Potango Waiata was described as 'one of the most energetic of the Wanganui Maoris in the pa' and he led the party in old chants and haka.

After World War I and the influenza epidemic, the Ratana faith gained many adherents among the Wanganui River Maori. Lewis Eastman, Anglican mis-

The original Pipiriki House as it appeared probably in the mid 1890s. By the late 1890s, a two-storeyed wing with a balcony had been added to the original building. The photograph was taken by Alfred Willis.

In 1903, Alexander Hatrick, of riverboat fame, took over Pipiriki House, demolished the original single-storeyed wing and built a large, two-storeyed wing. The hotel then had 65 double rooms and eight parlours. This building burned down in 1909.

In 1910 a new, slightly smaller, Pipiriki House was built. It survived until 1959, when it too burned down.

sioner and layreader at Pipiriki, became the first European 'apostle' of Ratana in 1925. He lived at Raetihi but continued to hold services at Pipiriki. From this time families began to move away from the river.

Pipiriki House — 'the house' to the locals — became the social centre for the soldier settlers in the remote river valleys such as the Mangapurua. There they could relax for a short time from the rigours of carving farmland out of the forest. Tourist numbers never reached the pre-war figures and in the 1930s the depression and alternative forms of transport led to a decline in the riverboat service. Once the Chateau Tongariro closed as a wartime measure in 1939, the boats ceased to run except for local trips out of Pipiriki. 'The House' became a dreary place and good meals were prepared only for the infrequent tourists. Liquor was sold at the back door.

The riverboat era in the middle reaches came to an end in 1958 when Capt. Andy Anderson drowned in the river, as his father had done in 1897. Together, father and son had worked on the river for almost 70 years. Pipiriki House burnt down on 23 May 1959 and this time it was not replaced. In January 1984 the restored riverboat *Ongarue* was dedicated at Pipiriki as a memorial to the riverboat era. She had worked the upper section of the river from 1904 to 1939 and the middle reaches to 1959.

Pipiriki, Jerusalem and the river have provided inspiration for several writers. Sylvia Ashton-Warner taught with her husband at the old Pipiriki School from 1942 to 1945. Her experiences were distilled in

On the site of Pipiriki House today are a few concrete slabs and old steps, all that now remain after the fire which destroyed the building in May 1959.

three novels — *Myself, Greenstone* and *Rangatira* — as well as several short stories and an interesting section of her autobiography *I Passed This Way*. The river called to poet James K. Baxter in 1969 and his 2-year residence in his Jerusalem commune resulted in his *Jerusalem Sonnets*. When he died in Auckland his body was taken back to Jerusalem and buried on 25 October 1972. His grave is on private property and not readily accessible.

In recent years there has been a revival of tourist interest in the Wanganui River. Parties of canoeists now relive the experiences of earlier travellers and a new riverboat *Wakapai* takes passengers from Taumarunui to Wanganui, with overnight stays in camps and marae. Road access from Wanganui and Raetihi is being upgraded and forest industries are making it possible for families to return to Pipiriki and build new homes. With the creation of the Wanganui River National Park, new life will be breathed into Pipiriki and Jerusalem.

Further Reading

Ashton-Warner, S. *I Passed This Way* (Wellington 1979)

Bates, A. P. *The Bridge to Nowhere* (Wanganui 1981)

Bates, A. P. *A Pictorial History of the Wanganui River* (Wanganui, 1985)

Downes, T. W. *Old Whanganui* (Hawera 1915, reprinted 1976)

Wanganui River Reserves Board *The Wanganui River* (Pipiriki n.d.)

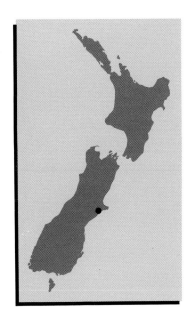

'The Food Basket of Rakaihautu': Taumutu

Dedicated to Riki Ellison

Ko te pae tawhiti, whaia kia tata.
Ko te pae tata, whakamua kia tata.

Seek out the distant horizon and
cherish those you attain.

LAKE ELLESMERE, the large
body of shallow water which
laps against the south-
western flank of Banks Peninsula,
is known to the Maori as Te
Waihora, 'water spread out'. On
the southern edge of the lake, near
where for several hundred years it
has periodically been opened to the
sea at the narrowest point of
Kaitorete, the spit which separates
it from the sea, is the small settlement of Taumutu, a place long of
importance in the history of Te
Waipounamu. The name Tau-
mutu comes from one of the names
of the original pa in the area, Te
Taumutu, also known as Te Pa o
te Ika Mutu. Its site has been lost
to coastal erosion.

Two older traditional names for
Te Waihora are Te Kete Ika o
Rakaihautu and Te Kete Ika o
Tutekawa, 'the foodbasket of Rakai-
hautu' and 'the foodbasket of
Tutekawa'. Rakaihautu was the
commander of the Uruao canoe
which sailed down the east coast
of the South Island about A.D. 900.
Tutekawa was the father of Te
Rangitamau, one of the first Ngai
Tahu chiefs to make his base at
Taumutu.

These traditional names indicate
Te Waihora's importance as one of
the South Island's greatest mahingakai. Traditionally, and into modern times, Taumutu has gained its
standing from the access people
living there have to the abundant
food resources of the lake. In or on
the waters of the lake itself were
tuna (eel), patiki (flounder), awa
(mullet) and water birds. Tuna
were specially abundant and more
than 33 names identified different
types of tuna according to the
different ways they could be preserved. The tuna were taken in
hinaki or, in huge numbers, by
lowering the level of the lake.
Stories of eeling practices of the
past are preserved in old waiata,
oriori and pao. Flounder were
taken by digging trenches into the
shingle of Kaitorete. Duck and
other water birds were taken in
great drives when they were moult-
ing and unable to fly. From streams
which flow into the lake were taken
uaua (whitebait), inanga (a type of
whitebait), kanakana or piharau
(the lamprey eel) and koura (freshwater crayfish). Many of these foods
were dried and stored for winter,
including uaua, inanga and tuna.
The tuna were dried on whata,
large wooden frames erected on the
lakeside. Besides these resources of
food, raupo, wiwi and harakeke
grew in abundance in the swamps

on the lake margin and on the
sandy spit were large areas of
pingao, a native sedge used for
traditional crafts. A special black
mud (paruparu) was used to dye
fibres.

A lake as important for its food
and other resources as Te Waihora
had to have a guardian. Te Waihora's was Tuterakihaunoa, who
lived in a cave at Whakamatakiuru
(Fishermens Point), Taumutu.
Tuterakihaunoa was a protective
taniwha who preserved the lake as
a source of food and any breach
of respect by any of the tribes
occupying land around the lake
was fatal.

To the area's natural resources,
the Maori added the important
crop kumara. At Taumutu are the
remains of some of the southern-
most kumara gardens in New
Zealand.

In traditional times there was a
well organised round of food-
gathering from the pa and kainga
of Taumutu which kept the local
communities supplied and provided commodities for exchange
with, or presentation to, other
communities in Te Waipounamu.

Before the arrival of Europeans,
the spit, Kaitorete, was a major
route south from populous Banks
Peninsula and points further north
(Kaiapohia and Kaikoura) south
towards Murihuku. This route

avoided the swamps around Te Waihora, then much more extensive than they are today. The many middens to be found on Kaitorete are evidence of its importance as a route of travel. Taumutu, at Kaitorete's southern end, was a strategic point on this 'southern highway' of earlier times. Because it also had access west across the Canterbury Plains and over passes of the Southern Alps to the Poutini Coast (Westland) it was a centre of greenstone working, probably second only to Kaiapohia, north of the Waimakariri River, which enjoyed more direct access to easier passes across the Southern Alps.

Being a place of such importance in traditional times, it is not surprising that many archaeological remains — ovens, middens and burials — dating from moa hunter times are to be found at and near Taumutu today. The first 'archaeological' investigation of Taumutu was made in 1868 by Julius von Haast. He recognised that Taumutu was a place of long occupation. Modern archaeological investigations of a moa hunter midden at the Rakaia River mouth, just south of Taumutu, have dated occupation of the area to, conservatively, 550-600 years ago.

The traditional history of Taumutu begins at the time the Ngati Mamoe kainga there became caught up in the Ngai Tahu 'conquest' of the South Island. (There was intermarriage as well as conquest during the Ngai Tahu occupation of the South Island and many South Island Maori to this day proudly claim Ngati Mamoe as well as Ngai Tahu descent.) The pa of three Ngai Tahu heroes, Te Rangitamau, Te Ruahikihiki and Moki II, were established at Taumutu. Members of the local hapu to this day refer to themselves as Ngati Ruahikihiki or Ngati Moki.

Te Rangitamau, one of the earliest Ngai Tahu chiefs to make his headquarters at Taumutu, crossed Brownings Pass and by defeating Ngati Wairangi in battle at Lake Kaniere, took the Poutini Coast, and its greenstone, for Ngai Tahu. Te Rangitamau's pa has

WARREN JACOBS

▲ *Te Waihora (Lake Ellesmere) is a prominent feature in this aerial photograph looking north along the length of the spit Kaitorete towards Banks Peninsula. Taumutu occupies the point of land bottom left between the lake and a small lagoon. The huts on Fishermens Point and the Hone Wetere Church are visible.*

▼ *These pits, which extend in a long line across a paddock behind Awhitu House, are believed to be borrow pits from which the Maori who lived at Taumutu before the arrival of the European took sand and gravel to create soils nearby suitable for growing kumara.*

BEVERLEY McCULLOCH

Maori huts on the shore of Lake Ellesmere at Taumutu, sketched in 1874 by Eliot Whately.

The remaining buildings of the old pa at Taumutu at the turn of the century. The old kainga at Taumutu were already in decline when this picture was taken and the site today is open paddock.

The lakeside at Taumutu early this century, showing the craft and fishing gear of the fishermen who settled on 'The Point' in the last quarter of the nineteenth century.

been washed away by coastal erosion affecting the shore south of Kaitorete. (The remains of burials uncovered by this erosion have been respectfully reinterred in the graveyard of the Hone Wetere Church.) The pa of Te Ruahikihiki and of Moki II remain, their surviving earthworks guarding the Hone Wetere Church and the Ngati Moki runanga hall. The low earth walls of the old pa rise today out of dry land, but at the time the pa were built the lake's high-water level was more than 2 m higher than the level at which the lake is opened to the sea today. The pa, when built, would have occupied tongues of dry land surrounded by swamp and open water and so been easy to defend.

In the early nineteenth century, Taumutu was involved in the Kai Huanga feud, a bitter dispute within Ngai Tahu, and its population was much depleted by the time Europeans first began arriving in Canterbury. The land of Canterbury passed into European hands with the Kemp Purchase of 1848. Reserves were set aside at Taumutu, but they were relatively small areas of poorer land, close to the lake edge and so subject to flooding. The Taumutu Native Commonage Act of 1883 added some 283 ha to reserves in the Taumutu area to support the native residents of the vicinity, but already by then the pressure on the Maori community from European farmers occupying the surrounding land and from European fishermen congregating at Fishermens Point was strong. Kainga remained at Taumutu through the late nineteenth century and turn of the century photographs show parts of the old pa and kainga at Taumutu still occupied.

But by then the largest settlement in the Taumutu district was at Fishermens Point, a fishing community of up to 250 people of very varied nationalities. In the last quarter of the nineteenth century a substantial commercial fishery developed on Te Waihora. The fishermen caught eel, flounder and 'herrings' (yellow-eyed mullet).

Hori Kerei Taiaroa, his wife Tini Kerei and two of their grandchildren, Tini Wiwi and Ria Mohiko. This is a hand-coloured version, with a new background painted in, of a photograph taken in front of Awhitu House, Taumutu, a short time before Hori Kerei's death in 1905.

They built their huts on a landing reserve which had been gazetted by Canterbury's Provincial Government in 1867. (The status of this land is still a source of ill-feeling among local Maori, who feel it should be returned to the commonage of which it was part.)

The community at Fishermens Point flourished and in the early twentieth century, Taumutu's New Year's Day regattas, held at the point, drew crowds of people from all through the Ellesmere district.

But as European farmers prospered on the farmlands of Ellesmere and as European fishermen exploited the rich resources of Te Kete Ika o Rakaihautu, the Maori kainga declined. Many Taumutu Maori drifted away, to work on local farms, to Southbridge, Leeston and even further away. Today the sites of the nineteenth-century kainga are bare paddocks, although their locations remain known to those Maori in the Ellesmere district who trace their descent from those who lived in the kainga.

It was at this time of decline, for the Maori people as a whole as well as for the Maori community at

Taumutu, that a Maori of national standing and influence entered Taumutu's history. Hori Kerei Taiaroa, Member of the House of Representatives for Southern Maori 1871-78 and 1881-85 and Member of the Legislative Council 1879-80 and 1885-1905, decided, in the late 1870s, to move to Taumutu. H. K. Taiaroa was a member of the influential Maori 'gentry' which emerged in the late nineteenth century and which played an important role in straddling the divide between the still more or less separate Maori and Pakeha worlds. Taiaroa is a key figure in the story of Maori adjustments during the difficult years of the colonisation of New Zealand by Europeans.

H. K. Taiaroa's father was Matenga Taiaroa, a Ngai Tahu chief who had participated in the Kai Huanga feud and in the wars

The front lawn of Awhitu House has been the scene of many important gatherings. On this occasion, in 1962, members of the Doyle family were handing back to the Taiaroa family an heirloom which had been presented to the Doyles many years before. On such occasions, the Lindauer portraits of Hori Kerei and Tini Kerei Taiaroa hanging in Awhitu House are customarily brought out onto the lawn.

The Hone Wetere Church, Taumutu, a photograph taken after the original shingle roof had been covered with corrugated iron but before the attractive open belfry on its western gable was removed.

between Ngai Tahu and Te Rauparaha's Ngati Toa. By the time he died in 1863, Matenga Taiaroa had accepted Christianity and the need for the Maori to adopt and use Pakeha knowledge and technology. His son, Hori Kerei, fully exemplified this willingness to adjust to the European presence. He underwent a Pakeha education and advocated the use of European medicines and the adoption of European agricultural methods. But his goal was always to maintain the 'mana Maori' of Ngai Tahu and a major part of his life's work was to seek resolution of 'Te Kerema' ('the claim'), the Ngai Tahu insistence that the Government should fulfil the promises made to them at the time of the Kemp Purchase and subsequently disregarded. ('Te Kerema', partly settled at the time of the first Labour Government, is still being pursued by Ngai Tahu.)

H. K. Taiaroa had large land holdings at Otakou (near to the head which bears his family name) and he and his father are both buried in the urupa above the church at Otakou, but he also had ancestral ties to Taumutu, one of his lines going back to Te Ruahikihiki, one of the Ngai Tahu heroes of Taumutu. One reason for his decision to settle at Taumutu, where some of his ancestors of high rank were buried in the spring Te Waiwhakaheketupapaku, was to be closer to Wellington, where he was obliged to spend much of his time. The Taiaroa family home at Taumutu, Awhitu House, designed by the Christchurch architect T. S. Lambert, was built in 1879-80. By 1884, Taiaroa had completed the transfer of his family to their new home. Though he spent much time in Wellington and also had a town house in Christchurch, Awhitu House has, since Hori Kerei's time, been the papakainga of the Taiaroa family. It is younger and less grand than many old Canterbury farmhouses, but unique in having remained since it was built in the hands of a family whose ties to the land on which it stands long predate the acquisition of any parts of Canterbury by even its longest established European families.

Two other buildings at Taumutu, the Hone Wetere (John Wesley) Church and the runanga hall Ngati Moki, date from the years immediately after H. K. Taiaroa's move to the district. Christianity had come to Taumutu in advance of the first European missionaries. When Bishop Selwyn passed through Taumutu in January 1844 he found some of the Maori living there conversant with the scriptures and catechism, brought to them by Maori converts. In 1865 Taumutu became part of the wide circuit of the Maori Methodist clergyman, Te Koti Te Rato, who was based at Rapaki on Lyttelton Harbour. In the early 1880s, having completed Awhitu House for his family, H. K. Taiaroa, moved by a 'great love of the church', began to raise funds to erect a church building at Taumutu. Money flowed in from Maori and Pakeha in the Ellesmere district and from Maori of other Canterbury kainga. The site chosen for the church was that of the pa of Te Ruahikihiki, called Orariki, a site of spiritual significance which stands in a special relationship to the hills of Banks Peninsula, the mountains of the Southern Alps and the waters of Te Waihora. The church, also designed by T. S. Lambert, was opened on Easter Tuesday, 7 April 1885.

Over the years many denominations have used the church, which has served the Pakeha as well as Maori families of the Taumutu district. Iron has replaced shingles on the roof and the church has lost the belfry which once crowned the peak of the western gable but it remains a picturesque building in its open setting, the graves in the churchyard sheltered by the low wall of the ancient pa.

A few years later Taumutu also acquired the runanga hall which was built on the site of the pa of Moki II and named after him. It was opened on 7 May 1891, replacing an earlier structure on the same

▲ *This crowd gathered at the Hone Wetere Church, Taumutu, for the tangi, at the end of last century, of one of the sons of Hori Kerei and Tini Kerei Taiaroa who had died on the Chatham Islands.*

▼ *Visitors to the Hone Wetere Church, Taumutu, pause to pay respect at the grave of Riki Te Mairaki Taiaroa Ellison, at the northern end of the church. The church stands on the site of an ancient pa, Orariki.*

Until his death in 1984, Awhitu House was the home of the Ngai Tahu paramount chief Riki Te Mairaki Taiaroa Ellison. Here Mr Ellison stands with Mrs Ruku Arahanga, his cousin who kept house for him after the death of her own husband, with the portraits of their great-grandparents, Hori Kerei and Tini Kerei Taiaroa, which hang in Awhitu House.

site. Modern 'improvements' to Ngati Moki have increased its size and reflect the resurgence of the Maori in Ellesmere in the 1980s, but have sadly diminished its historical character. It is now, however, better able to serve as the main marae of the Ellesmere district.

H. K. Taiaroa died in 1905. His wife Tini Kerei, who was born in Moeraki, lived until 1934, making her home in Awhitu House. One of her sons, Riki Te Mairaki Taiaroa, became acknowledged as the paramount chief of Ngai Tahu. Widowed early in his life, he lived at Awhitu House until his own death in 1954. Riki Te Mairaki Taiaroa adopted his grandnephew, a great-grandson of Hori Kerei and Tini Kerei, Riki Te Mairaki Taiaroa Ellison, who was brought up in Awhitu House by his great-grandmother and grand-uncle. Riki Ellison lived in Awhitu House all his life, except for a period of service overseas during World War II. A warm, humble man, he enjoyed great mana throughout the South Island and New Zealand. His standing gave Awhitu House importance in country-wide Maori affairs. When he died in 1984, thousands gathered at Taumutu for the largest tangi seen in the South Island for many years. He was buried in a simple grave close to the western end of the humble

church he had loved and cared for all his life and which he called his 'cathedral'.

Awhitu House has been important as the papakainga of the Taiaroa family and as the residence of successive paramount chiefs of Ngai Tahu. It has also played a significant part in the life of the wider Taumutu-Sedgemere community. Until it was closed in the 1960s, the Sedgemere school held its annual picnic on the lawn of Awhitu House. The picnics were great events for all locals, Maori and Pakeha, young and old. Maori and Pakeha alike joined too in such community customs as first footing at New Year. The doors of the hall Ngati Moki and the Hone Wetere Church have always been open to all members of the local community, regardless of race. The interaction between the Maori of Taumutu and the European settler families of the Taumutu and Sedgemere districts would, written about in detail, tell much about the accommodation between the races in Canterbury.

The accommodation has mostly been happy, but not without friction, and the lake — the foodbasket of Rakaihautu — has been a main and continuing source of friction. Concern for Te Waihora — Uncle Riki's lake to some young people who are frequent visitors to Awhitu

House — is a major preoccupation of the Maori of Taumutu and the depletion of its resources of food a cause for bitterness. The Maori people of Taumutu have placed great store on being able to sustain and entertain visitors with the traditional foods of tuna and flounder for which the lake has been renowned since Maori first settled on its shores hundreds of years ago. The choicest tuna were those taken in Muriwai, a lagoon just south of Taumutu, and Muriwai tuna were reserved for use in special feasts for manuhiri. It is culturally important to Maori that locals be seen to cater more than adequately for guests and that people travelling to gatherings elsewhere take ample supplies of the particular food or foods which their local community enjoys in abundance. The decline in the number of tuna in Te Waihora is, therefore, of burning importance to the people of Ngati Ruahikihiki/Ngati Moki. So is the mining of sand on Kaitorete, which threatens the destruction not only of middens but also of some of the now restricted stands of pingao. But it is the depletion of the lake's resources that is felt particularly keenly. Already the memory is fading of the time when those in other South Island Maori communities would say confidently that 'Taumutu will bring eel'. The practice of people from Taumutu taking tuna, often in large quantities, to hui continued well into living memory, but is a practice the local Maori now find it more difficult to maintain. The specially preserved form of tuna pawhara was a particular delicacy which Taumutu used to contribute to gatherings at other South Island marae and even to conferences in the North Island.

Efforts over many years to get at least part of Te Waihora reserved from commercial fishing for traditional Maori cultural uses have not been successful. Taumutu first emerged as a place of importance, hundreds of years ago, because of the resources of its foodbasket. To see those resources exploited heedlessly and threatened is to see Taumutu's long Maori history treated with disrespect.

Today on the road to Taumutu from Leeston or Southbridge, the tarseal ends just short of Taumutu itself. The shingle road passes close to the earth rampart of the pa of Moki II on which stands the recently extended runanga hall. Further off, the Hone Wetere Church stands lonely in its open landscape, but protected by the ramparts and moat of Te Ruahikihiki's pa Orariki. A short distance further on, on the other side of the road, Awhitu House is

Maringirangi Tamou, great-great-great-granddaughter of Hori Kerei and Tini Taiaroa, displays pieces of roughly worked greenstone found in the Taumutu district. Behind her is part of Awhitu House, built for her great-great-great-grandparents more than 100 years ago.

almost hidden by trees and a huge macrocarpa hedge. In the background is the sound of the sea, close but invisible behind the shingle bank that is the southern end of Kaitorete. From the rather ramshackle cluster of huts on Fishermens Point, Banks Peninsula, across the broad waters of Te Waihora, looks like the island it was in far distant times.

The scene is peaceful, a change from the days when a Kaikoura party, passing in friendship

through Taumutu to see friends at Moeraki, were ambushed and slain, all for some distant slight. Retribution came from Moeraki and during the fray a warrior Kuwhare was taken prisoner by Korako to be used as sacrifice to Mua. He broke away and, being a celebrated runner, outdistanced his pursuers around the shores of Te Waihora and reached safety with friends at Kaiapohia. Taumutu is a place of many memories.

Maori people of many tribes, now resident in Canterbury, look to Taumutu for parts of the traditions, heritage and culture of their race. Groups, Pakeha and Maori, staying in the hall Ngati Moki study the local scene of a place with a long, rich history. The Maori people of Taumutu have been much changed by their long association with European culture, but the changes have not altered their recognition of their ancestral traditions.

Further Reading

Andersen, J. C. *Place Names of Banks Peninsula* (Wellington 1927, reprinted 1976)

Graham, G. W. and Chapple, L. J. B. *Ellesmere County* (Christchurch 1965)

Taylor, W. A. *Waihora: Maori Associations with Lake Ellesmere* (Leeston n.d.)

The Work of a Master: Manutuke

Darcy Ria

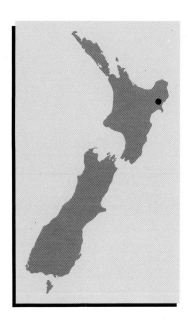

IN the small township of Manutuke, about 10 km southwest of Gisborne, are buildings which illustrate significant developments in the history of Maori carving and painting in the nineteenth century. In particular there are in Manutuke two of the most splendid carved and painted meeting houses in New Zealand, important because of their age and their association with a carver after whom one of the houses is named, Raharuhi Rukupo (1800-73).

Modern carved meeting houses are a feature of Maori life today. Their origins lie in the eighteenth century, in the houses of the chiefs and temporary guest houses, and in the early nineteenth century, in the missionary church. They owe their present forms mainly to the work of the artist chief Raharuhi Rukupo of the Rongowhakaata and Ngai Tamanuhiri tribes of the Turanga district. At a time when carving was in decline in many parts of the country, the Turanga school of Poverty Bay was at its zenith under the leadership of Raharuhi Rukupo, one of the greatest of all Maori carvers.

It was he who added a new dimension to Maori art by fully carving the first meeting house Te Hau Ki Turanga at Manutuke in 1842 with the help of Ngati Kaipoho, his subtribe of Rongowha-

kaata. This house, which now stands in the National Museum in Wellington, was built as a monument to the memory of Te Waaka Mangere, the elder brother of Raharuhi Rukupo, who at the time of its erection was chief of the tribe. Sir Apirana Ngata described Te Hau Ki Turanga as 'the finest flowering of Maori art'.

It is probable that Rukupo began carving with stone tools, but he quickly mastered the new technology that came with the traders and all his extant works have been carved with metal tools. With a full set of steel carving chisels he produced high relief and fine line decoration. Rukupo's carving style is strong, his figures very alive.

Rukupo and his pupils were some of the main carvers of their time who carved houses all over New Zealand. Today houses are still being carved in the style of Rukupo and the Turanga school, more than 100 years after his death. The brothers Pine and John Taiapa, renowned for their own work, were followers of the Rukupo style of carving.

Rukupo, who was born at Orakaiapu, an area of land on which the Mormon church now stands at Manutuke, was first heard of as a canoe carver in the 1830s. In the late 1830s, he and Te Waaka Perahuka, another Rongowhakaata

chief, are credited with carving the decorations on the celebrated war canoe *Te Toki-a-Tapiri* which is now in the Auckland Museum.

Rukupo was known to be hostile towards European authority, though he never took up arms against Europeans. He came to believe that the missionaries came to clear the way for the soldiers who in turn cleared the way for the land grabbers. Rukupo was one of the most uncompromising opponents of the Pakeha. He openly defied Governor Gore Browne to fly the Queen's flag over his land; his people were free and independent, he claimed.

Christianity was introduced into the Poverty Bay area in the late 1830s and had early successes there. A trading economy replaced the traditional subsistence cultivation and gathering. The decade of the 1840s was remarkably tranquil in Poverty Bay. Rukupo himself was an early convert to Christianity. He also became chief of Ngati Kaipoho on his brother's death, although there was little to excite political activity. Rukupo attended to his duties, both at the mission where he was a teacher from 1843, and among his people whom he led by example.

Poverty Bay's remoteness from the centres of European settlement meant that at first there was rel-

Three buildings stand in line on the Manutuke Marae. They are, from the right, Epeha Meeting House (partly visible), the Maori Battalion Dining Hall (centre) and Te Poho o Rukupo Meeting House (in the background).

atively little pressure from settlers for land, but this was not to last. Events during the 1860s led to the development of a strong nationalistic sentiment among the Poverty Bay chiefs and culminated in some of them, including Rukupo, converting to Hauhauism in 1865. Later that year the Hauhau resistance in the area collapsed after the siege at Waerenga-a-Hika. Rukupo died in 1873 and is buried at Pakirikiri. At a tribal wananga held at Whakato Marae in 1984 it was agreed unanimously that Raharuhi's whakapapa makes him a direct descendant of Rongowhakaata and Ngai Tamanuhiri.

The meeting house Te Poho o Rukupo is Raharuhi Rukupo's memorial in his home district of Manutuke. The house, one of the oldest in Poverty Bay, was first erected at Pakirikiri, some 5 km from Manutuke near the mouth of the Waipaoa River in 1887. It was moved to its present site in Manutuke some time in 1913. A unique feature of the house is the artistry and beauty of the kowhaiwhai patterns and designs painted on the roof heke and poupou of the building. Strange as it seems, these kowhaiwhai designs were painted over by a simpler design when the building was re-erected. It was only by chance, when he paid a casual visit to the house, that Sandy Adsett, Arts Advisor with the Education Department, noticed that this had been done. His visit took place in 1976 and set in motion a series of events that has seen the original kowhaiwhai recovered and restored. First Les Lloyd, then Director of the Dunedin Art Gallery and an expert in restoration work, visited the house. Following him came officers of the Historic Places Trust who felt the restoration of the house was worthy

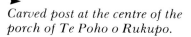
Te Poho o Rukupo Meeting House, on the Manutuke Marae, is the main memorial in the Manutuke district to the master carver Raharuhi Rukupo.

Carved post at the centre of the porch of Te Poho o Rukupo.

The interior of Te Poho o Rukupo showing some of the finely painted decorative work before restoration.

At work on the restoration of the painted surfaces of the interior of Te Poho o Rukupo.

Detail of part of a painted panel inside Te Poho o Rukupo before restoration.

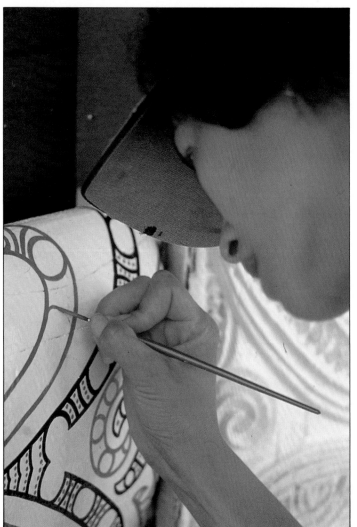

of their support as it was a very historic building. The local people are thankful to the Trust for their monetary aid and, in particular, for providing training for local young people to do the restoration work. They enjoyed working with Cliff Whiting and his team from the time the work started to its completion in 1984. As a result of the sterling efforts of these groups, of workers on government employment schemes and many others, the Rongowhakaata people are justly proud to have now a jewel of a meeting house — Te Poho o Rukupo.

Te Poho o Rukupo is the most important of the buildings on the marae at Manutuke, but it shares the marae with three other buildings of interest, the Epeha Meeting House, the Maori Battalion Dining Hall and a Pakeha-style house used by Kohanga Reo.

Until the late 1920s, the area on which these buildings stand was under four different titles. When a consolidation of land scheme was introduced into the area, the opportunity was taken to merge the four titles into one, and a new title, about 2.25 ha in area, was created. In September 1927, the marae was set aside as a Maori reservation and the following year a committee of management of seven people was appointed. One of the first committee members was Heni Materoa, who was the wife of Sir James Carroll.

Included in the new title of the Manutuke Marae was an area of adjoining land of about 0.1 ha, known as Epeha B, on which the Epeha Meeting House originally stood. The house is owned by the Whaitiri family. When large gatherings were held on the marae, the Whaitiri family would occupy the house. In the consolidation proceedings of the 1920s, one of the family, Tamatea (Bob) Whaitiri, sought permission to have the Epeha B block vested in the marae. This was agreed to and the block now forms part of the marae reserve, vested in the trustees for and on behalf of the members of the Rongowhakaata hapu. The house

▲ *The Maori Battalion Dining Hall, Manutuke Marae.*

▼ *The amo and raparapa and part of the porch of the Epeha Meeting House, Manutuke Marae. The carvings on this house differ from those of the Rukupo style on other Manutuke buildings.*

FRANK O'LEARY

was subsequently moved to its present position alongside the Maori Battalion Dining Hall. It is said that the carvings on the Epeha Meeting House are not from the Manutuke area and could be from Te Arawa or further north. They are definitely not of the Rukupo style of carving.

The Maori Battalion Dining Hall, which stands beside the Epeha Meeting House, was originally called Te Poho o Hinehou. It is understood that it has also, like Te Poho o Rukupo, been moved to Manutuke from Pakirikiri. The main function of this building on the marae has been as a dining room. In the days before World War II, the cooking was done in a kauta adjacent to the house, the cooked food being carried into the house by hand. This was very unsatisfactory to the local people, so fundraising was commenced and additions made to the house which included cooking facilities, storerooms, vegetable and meat rooms. These additions were completed in the early days of World War II and the house was renamed the Maori Battalion. On the house is a carved tekoteko holding a taiaha on the koruru in the veranda portion of the building and the maihi and amo are other carved features on this house. The dining room caters for some 400 guests.

More recently, the buildings on the marae gained a further companion. A five-roomed former New Zealand Railways house from Awapuni Road, Gisborne, was purchased at a reasonably low cost through the Maori Affairs Department and transported onto the marae. It was renovated and repainted by government employment and work skills programme workers and is now in occupation by Kohanga Reo.

The other important meeting house in Manutuke stands on Whakato Marae. The carvings on Te Mana o Turanga, which was opened in 1883, depict ancestors and constitute a visual recording and illustration of oral traditions. In them can be seen an assertion of pride in Maori culture and

FRANK O'LEARY

▲ *The latest building to be placed on the Manutuke Marae is a former Railways house from Gisborne which was moved to the marae and is being renovated for use by Kohanga Reo. Its presence alongside the buildings which have stood far longer on the marae is evidence of the continued vitality of the Maori culture and of the marae as a focal point of that culture.*

▼ *Te Mana o Turanga, a meeting house on which the master carver Raharuhi Rukupo and other carvers of the Turanga school worked, is the most important building on the Whakato Marae, Manutuke. The house was opened in 1883 but many of the carvings incorporated in it were completed before that date.*

FRANK O'LEARY

FRANK O'LEARY

A poupou in the porch of Te Mana o Turanga.

FRANK O'LEARY

One of the amo of Te Mana o Turanga.

FRANK O'LEARY

The korupe (window lintel) of the main porch window of Te Mana o Turanga.

FRANK O'LEARY

The pare (door lintel) of Te Mana o Turanga.

HISTORIC PLACES TRUST COLLECTION

Work under way on the restoration of Te Mana o Turanga.

A hand-coloured wood engraving of the interior of the first Manutuke church as it was expected to look when completed. The engraving is based on a drawing by a Maori artist, 1852.

tradition *vis-à-vis* the Pakeha. Some of the carvings of Te Mana o Turanga were carved prior to 1865, for earlier houses or for houses which were never completed. These carvings were worked on in Raharuhi Rukupo's lifetime either by him or under his supervision. Most of the carvings from the period 1865-73 were completed after the project of building the meeting house had been taken over by Karepa Ruatapu. These carvings are more representational and less traditional. The house was shifted to a new site in 1942 and re-erected and modernised. Along with Te Hau Ki Turanga and the canoe *Te Toki-a-Tapiri,* Te Mana

o Turanga is counted among the most important of Raharuhi Rukupo's surviving work.

Manutuke's historic interest today centres on the two carved meeting houses, Te Poho o Rukupo and Te Mana o Turanga, which have association with Raharuhi Rukupo. But Manutuke is also of interest as having been the site of an early mission station, with a surviving church, opened in 1913, as a reminder of early missionary endeavours among Rongowhakaata. The mission occupied three sites in the first 20 years of its existence and today's church is the last of a series of churches built in Manutuke.

The mission at Manutuke was first established as the Kaupapa mission station by the Rev. William Williams in 1840, in the vicinity of several Rongowhakaata pa which housed several thousand

inhabitants. In 1842, the original site being affected by flooding, the mission station was shifted, the new site being given the name Whakato, 'to plant'. This is still the name of the marae on which Te Mana o Turanga stands. In 1856 the mission was moved again, from Whakato to Waerenga-a-Hika. The history of the various churches built at Manutuke casts further light on the importance of the district as a centre of Maori carving. The first church in the area was commenced at Kaupapa in 1840 but was still unfinished, though in use for services, when blown down in a storm on 22 November 1844. James Stack visited the church as a young boy in 1842:

The large church erected by the Maoris was the most striking object about the place. It was the loftiest building I had yet met with. It had a strange appearance, for though

The interior of the second Manutuke church in 1889, while it was under construction. Many of the carvings being incorporated in the new building were recovered from the previous church. The photographer was W.F. Crawford. This was the church which burned down in 1910.

the thatched roof and boarded floor were completed, the sides were left uncovered and the totara slabs supporting the roof afforded the only protection from the weather for the congregation.

This church had been built as an enlarged version of a traditional house with a longitudinal ridge-pole supported on large posts at each end and rafters running down to wide totara timber wall panels (poupou) set in the ground with equal spaces between them to be filled later by raupo walls. There were no carvings. Bishop Selwyn, who arrived at Kaupapa just 3 days after the church had been blown down, noted that 'it was a noble building for native work, capable of containing one thousand persons, and frequently filled'. On the following Sunday, Selwyn preached to a congregation of about 1000 Maori standing within the ruins of their church.

Between 1842 and 1863, services were held in a large meeting house called Hamokorau at Orakaiapu Pa, built in 1841 for the reception of visitors and offered for the use of the mission when the church was destroyed. Though not a carved house, Hamokorau may have had kowhaiwhai decorations. A new church was commenced in 1849 to replace the one destroyed, this time at Whakato, slightly to the south of Kaupapa, using a good supply of totara timber suitable for large carvings which had been uncovered by floods at the mouth of the river nearby. The resident Church Missionary Society missionary, William Williams, believed that the grandiose plans for the new church had been stimulated by a desire to outdo the large Maori church recently erected at Otaki. To achieve this, the Poverty Bay people determined to decorate their church fully with traditional carving, for which they were famous throughout the country. The son of the missionary described the proposed church as follows:

Before Archdeacon Williams left for England, great preparations had been made for the erection of a church in the Maori style of architecture, which was to be 90 feet long

Original carvings from the first Manutuke church which was opened in 1863. The church was dismantled in 1881 and its carvings incorporated in the building erected in 1888-89. Only a few of the original carvings survived the fire of 1910 which destroyed the second church.

Manutuke Church, Gisborne.

Holy Trinity, Manutuke, today.

under the direction of Paratene Turangi. Then, several carvers worked on these slabs, among them Raharuhi Rukupo, Te Waaka Kurei and Te Waaka Perahuka. After the mission moved to a new site, progress on the church lapsed for another decade until about 1860 when a general movement to replace the earlier East Coast churches with more substantial structures stimulated Rongowhakaata to complete their Manutuke church. The carpentry was supervised by Aperahama Matawhaiti from Wairoa, an old Maori mission teacher who had learnt carpentry in the Bay of Islands. Finally, the church was opened on 19 April 1863, still unfinished, before a large gathering of people from the Poverty Bay tribes, Ngati Porou from the East Coast, Ngati Kahungunu from Wairoa, and a party from Waikato. William Williams wrote just a few days later:

> The building is very plain in its exterior and will look heavy until a tower is erected, which is contemplated. Within it is elaborately carved and presents a specimen of native art which is nowhere else to be seen.

When the first carvings were begun for the Manutuke church in July 1849, a disagreement arose between William Williams and his Maori parishioners over the form of the carvings. The editor of the magazine of the Church Missionary Society, the *Church Missionary Intelligencer*, summarised the disagreement:

> The carving was commenced, during Archdeacon Williams' absence from the Station, in the old native style, in which grotesque and hideous figures are conspicuous, as in much of the church architecture of our own country, executed during the usurpation of the Papal power. To this the Archdeacon strongly objected, as being improper for a Christian place of worship. Some of the Chiefs took offence, the carving of their tribe being famous throughout the island; but Archdeacon Williams remaining firm, and suggesting that they should adopt some other mode of carving, these disciples of the old

and 45 feet in width. A large quantity of totara timber had been got together and dressed for the framework of the walls and for the support of the weighty ridgepole. The uprights for the walls were so prepared that they should stand over 15 feet above the ground. They averaged 2 feet in width and the inner surface which would be seen inside the building was elaborately

carved, the grotesque caricatures of the human form so common in the carving of Maori whares being avoided. The two posts which were to support the ends of the ridgepole, and to stand about twenty-eight feet above the ground were also elaborately carved from top to bottom.

About 60 slabs and three ridgepole supports were adzed into shape school gave way. On going to the workshop, the Archdeacon found a man chalking out a new pattern upon a plain piece of timber, in which the character of the native carving remained, without the devices to which he had objected.

After he believed the dispute settled, Williams wrote to his son to report good progress on the carvings:

To the carving there can be no objection but the New Zealander finds it difficult to go out of the old track, and nothing would do but such posts or rather such whakairo as that in Lazarus [Raharuhi Rukupo] house. But there was a sort of feeling that this might be objected to so they hit upon the expedient of working with redoubled energy while my back was turned so that the advance might be too great before I could interfere to allow of an alternative. Nine beautiful posts were in a state of great forwardness when I came back. There was something so horrible in their appearance that I made at once a decided stand against them, but it was many days before I could make any impression. At last your old friend Wakakurei gave way and recommended a new pattern which is quite non descript exhibiting neither man beast or creeping thing but giving a very good specimen of native carving. They have nearly completed the posts for one side of the building which is to be ninety feet long.

However, despite Williams' optimism, the church was still not finished when he left for England in December 1850 and the work was never resumed with the early enthusiasm, even during the 1860-63 period before the opening. Obviously, Williams' interference and criticisms had had a deeper and more permanent effect than he realised.

The actual carvings produced under these circumstances were purely decorative, without any obvious human figures that would have represented ancestors. Instead, each panel was completely covered with a profusion of manaia figure designs that avoided any obvious

Part of the interior of Holy Trinity, Manutuke, showing some of the carvings with which the interior is decorated.

representational reference. The compromise choice of manaia figures produced a unique set of carvings, quite different to any previously seen in the area, yet purposely calculated to display the virtuosity of the famed Rongowhakaata artists. Contrary to Williams' assertions about their conservatism making it 'difficult to go out of the old track', the carvers had demonstrated great innovative ability, once Williams' interference had forced them to question their traditional assumptions about artistic form. Although Williams had taken an interest in the carving of Te Hau Ki Turanga by Raharuhi Rukupo only 7 years before, he had made no attempt to interfere with Rukupo's use of traditional 'heathen' images. But once Williams' criticisms broke the spell of the old assumptions and created a climate of artistic experimentation, subsequent carvings produced at Manutuke were among the most innovative in the country, especially those in the house Te Mana o Turanga, built to replace Te Hau Ki Turanga.

The church that was opened at Manutuke in 1863 was never completely finished and after collapsing it was carefully dismantled in 1881. After much discussion in the district, a new church was built on the same site in 1888-89, using the old carvings from the previous church. Unfortunately, this church was destroyed by fire in February 1910. A few of the old carvings were saved and these are still treasured in the Manutuke area. Once again a new church was erected, being dedicated by Archdeacon Herbert Williams in 1913. This is the present Holy Trinity Church still standing at Manutuke. All the carvings in this building were new ones, produced by the carvers Te Ngaru of Te Arawa and Te Tuhi of Tuhoe.

Further Reading

Fowler, L. *Te Mana o Turanga* (Auckland 1974)

Phillips, W. J. 'Carved Maori Houses of the Eastern Districts of the North Island' *Records of the Dominion Museum* 1(2), 69-119

Porter, F. (Ed) *The Turanga Journals 1840-1850. Letters and Journals of William and Jane Williams, Missionaries to Poverty Bay* (Wellington 1974)

Williams, W. L. *East Coast (N.Z.) Historical Records* (Gisborne 1932)

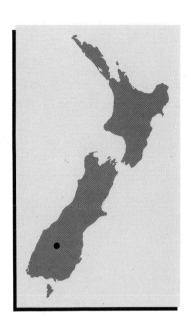

'Claims Taken Up In Every Direction': Gold at Bannockburn

Mark Hanger

THE finds of the pioneers of the Dunstan gold diggings, Messrs Hartley and Reilly, engendered a magnetic attraction to the Dunstan (Cromwell) Gorge among many thousands of gold seekers. The preoccupation of diggers with the gold-bearing gravels by Otago rivers was heightened when, in the spring of 1862, these two men deposited 39.5 kg of gold on a bank counter in Dunedin.

By late spring there were thousands on the new Dunstan goldfield. The adjacent Dunstan and Carrick ranges were foremost in explorations in late 1862 through 1863. A combination of high spring river levels, too high a concentration of miners for the mineable area and a belief that the neighbouring range land must contain gold, led to miners prospecting the major gullies of the Upper Clutha basin and the lower Kawarau Gorge.

The vast extent of 'rude and elevated country' (so described by Vincent Pyke) received a good deal of prospecting, and at its feet a number of payable gullies by the south bank of the Kawarau River, notably Bannockburn, Smiths, Adams, Shepherds and Pipeclay were located. As the eventful year of gold discoveries neared its close, these gullies became the scenes of small gold rushes. Unfortunately for the region, the spectacular

discoveries on the Arrow and then the Shotover drew most miners. For this reason, together with a serious lack of water, growth of the field was only steady. Mining operations consisted principally of sluicing, for which purpose the streams in each of these gullies and their

tributaries were diverted, giving employment to a large number of miners.

By mid 1863 up to 1000 were estimated to be mining at the foot of the Carrick. That year the most readily accessible gold was soon exhausted and this rapid exploita-

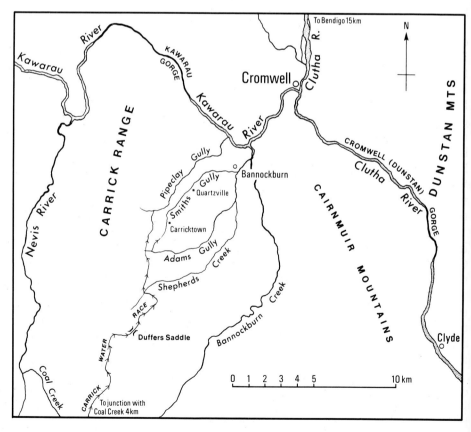

Bannockburn's location in the middle Clutha Valley.

Water was crucial to the successful working of the Bannockburn and Carrick Range claims — for sluicing the alluvial terraces and for powering the machinery that crushed the quartz ore. The Carrick water race crosses the Carrick Range to bring water to Bannockburn from the Nevis Valley. The race is seen here near the summit of the range.

MARK HANGER

tion acted as a natural sifting mechanism, shaking out those miners who could not or were not content to work the inaccessible gold-bearing leads and reefs. As a result the mining population had declined considerably by 1865. Only about 200 miners kept the three hotels and twenty-odd stores busy. But they were a much more stable group than those who had taken part in the initial rushes, prepared to unlearn experience gained on the world's other goldfields and begin to understand the peculiar character of the Otago country. Equally importantly, they were becoming aware of a permanent and prosperous future in goldmining.

Meanwhile a settlement was developing on the banks of the Bannockburn Creek about 1 km from its junction with the Kawarau River. The small flat in the valley had several attractive attributes — good soil, matagouri and manuka to supply timber for firewood and building, clear water and reasonable shelter. As the Bannockburn, Shepherds and adjacent gullies were mined, a settlement of shanties and shops grew.

For the residents, links were initially with Clyde rather than Cromwell for no means of crossing the Kawarau existed and Cromwell was not by then of sufficient size to be a service centre. The track over the Cairnmuir Range to Clyde was a good one for it also served as the route to the Nevis diggings.

By 1866 a number of stores existed. John Richards, one of the leaders of the district at the time, had a wood and calico store in the main settlement. Bakeries and

COLLECTION OF RON MURRAY

Bannockburn last century was a straggle of timber and corrugated iron buildings set in a wide, barren landscape.

The Bannockburn Hotel last century

▲ *Workers at the Rip and Bust It claim at Bannockburn, a venture which recovered gold by alluvial tunnelling.*

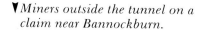
▼ *Miners outside the tunnel on a claim near Bannockburn.*

smithies also existed. But stores were not confined to the Bannockburn Creek itself. In Smiths Gully the Moore brothers operated a store, while Halliday's store was situated in Shepherd's Gully. This indicates the widespread nature of the diggings at this time. Both Richards and Halliday soon opened hotels in conjunction with their stores. Another publican, James Stewart, opened a ferry service across the Kawarau in 1867 at the mouth of Bannockburn Creek. Cromwell was by this stage a town of some size, and with the upgrading of the Dunstan Gorge Road, Bannockburn settlers began to associate with Cromwell rather than Clyde. A good dray road was rapidly built from the ferry to the settlement and then further on up and over the Carrick to the Nevis.

Most mining was now occurring on the Bannockburn terraces. Thus, although close to the ferry, the town was becoming ill-placed to service the mining people. In 1867 John Richards initiated the township's relocation when he shifted his hotel and store to Doctors Flat (its present location). Other businesses followed, and within a year stores and habitations became spread out along the Bannockburn-Nevis Road.

Also in 1866 the quartz fields around Cromwell were first opened. At Bendigo on the Dunstan Range and on the Carrick immediately behind the Bannockburn terraces, gold-bearing quartz reefs had been located. All that were needed for the fields to be developed were an infusion of capital, a more liberal mining lease system and a sufficiently disillusioned alluvial mining workforce prepared to work underground. All were lacking in the Bannockburn area in the mid sixties and the reefs were not then developed.

For the time being, the Bannockburn region remained an alluvial mining area. Mining operations were no longer restricted to the gully beds, but were principally directed to excavating the terraces, where the miners found a series of ancient riverbeds of strategically arranged gravels. Whereas finance hindered the development of the quartz reefs, lack of water was the bugbear for the Bannockburn sluicers and tunnellers. With such a scarcity, and because the concentrated gold-bearing gravels lay deep beneath the surface, tunnelling was the favoured method of mining. This involved driving a tunnel from the terrace bank in the direction of the dip of the gold-bearing layer. Rails laid in the tunnels enabled the rich gravel to be transported in trolleys to the surface. In smaller operations wheelbarrows were used. Once on the surface the gravels were washed with what little water was available down into and along a paved tail race. The flat stones served as riffles for catching gold. Periodically these stones were lifted and the material between washed to separate the gold.

The dramatic physical landscape of the Bannockburn sluicings as seen today is, however, the result of much more efficient methods of goldmining — hydraulic and ground sluicing. These methods became more commonplace in the seventies as water became more readily available with the completion of two major water races. The Bannockburn race was finished in 1873 and the monumental Carrick race in 1876. The Carrick race still stands as testimony to its constructors and continues to supply the Bannockburn settlement and farms with water transported via race, tunnel and aqueduct from Coal Creek in the Nevis Valley. The Carrick is a group of races. One brings water over a low saddle on the Carrick Range (Duffers), whereupon it divides, spilling water into Shepherds Gully, then Adams, Pipeclay and Smiths. Lower down each gully, smaller races again collect the water and redistribute it. Without these races, the region, one of the driest in New Zealand, goes thirsty.

With ample water for mining there arose another problem — disposal from mining claims of water now laden with tailings and

COLLECTION OF RON MURRAY

▲ *Terraces and flats near Bannockburn being sluiced away in pursuit of gold contained in the alluvial deposits. At the bottom left of the picture, a dredge has left regular heaps of tailings in its wake.*

▼ *Buttes and sluiced pinnacles are all that remain of the terraces that once existed between Baileys and Pipeclay gullies at Bannockburn.*

MARK HANGER

silt. The Kawarau, just 1 km distant, was the perfect sewer. All that was needed was to construct links between it and the sluicing claims. The building of sludge channels, the main canals into which the numerous tail races draining the claims fed, occupied the alluvial miners for many years in the seventies and eighties.

Behind, high on the Carrick Range, others were now busy mining the quartz. The discovery, development and rapid demise of the Bendigo quartz field in 1869-71 led to an equally rapid rise and

▲*The Day Dawn quartz mine in the hills above Bannockburn.*

▼*A quartz stamping battery in the Carrick Range, high above Bannockburn.*

nearly finished; another in the course of erection, one store, several respectable private houses, and a goodly number of residences of less ambitious character. We have claims taken up in every direction, and several new lines of our reefs.

Yet, less than 4 years later Quartzville was described as being in a state of deadly liveliness. In the interim new reefs had been found all over the ranges and mining activity had centered on the Young Australian, Star, Border Chief and John Bull areas. Quartzville and Carricktown had blossomed and withered almost overnight. Only one quartz reef, the Heart of Oak (Star of the East) was in any way successful. Once again the promise of a goldfield had not been fulfilled, although it had led several companies to erect expensive crushing equipment. One group had carted machinery to an altitude of nearly 1300 metres, where it still lies. The Young Australian water wheel is a gigantic reminder of the miners' hopes and aspirations.

Despite the ups and downs on the Carrick, the seventies saw growth in the district as a whole. Water was available for all mining, and enterprise was widespread in the area. A bridge was constructed across the Kawarau by a private company in 1874. The area was becoming permanently settled by families and so a school was established, again by private enterprise. In both cases the Government soon took over. As companies formed the Carrick and Bannockburn water races, dug the Pipeclay sludge channel and mined high on the Carrick Range everything had an air of permanence. As the *Cromwell Argus* stated in 1875:

> Once abandoned by the 'moles' (tunnellers) [the land] will become the prey of the 'amphibian' (Anglice — sluicers) and furnish a livelihood to many hundreds of those and succeeding generations of those who also make their living between land and water.

It is, of course, referring to the men who mined by hydraulic sluicing.

During the 1870s an influx of Chinese arrived in the district.

decline of the Carrick field. Disconsolate miners left the Bendigo mines when (except in the case of the famed Cromwell Company mine) yields failed to live up to expectations. They began to test the already known Carrick reefs. Following them came itinerant merchants and retailers. As the Bendigo settlements of Logantown, Wakefield and Bendigo Diggings declined, Carricktown, Quartzville and Bannockburn mushroomed.

In 1871 all looked rosy. One correspondent to the Clyde newspaper, the *Dunstan Times*, stated of Quartzville:

> We are all indulged in great 'expectation'... building a township as fast as we can, prospecting for fresh reefs; and at the close of every day asking as Micawber would do whether anything fresh has turned up. We have one embryonic hotel

The remains of a battery in which the mined ore was crushed on the site of the Young Australian Mine, near the summit of the Carrick Range.

The huge water wheel near the summit of the Carrick Range which is silent testimony to the endeavour of the miners of the Young Australian claim.

While persecuted in many areas, the Chinese fraternity kept to themselves at Bannockburn and became established some distance from the main settlement. Most lived at Shepherds Creek, concentrated about the two or three Chinese stores.

Stability brought with it a wider variety of settlement. Farming and orcharding began to increase in importance. Only the keen and industrious stayed mining. Gold-mining became a way of life for many rather than a get-rich-quick scheme, although striking it rich was always a possibility and the thought driving every miner on.

The make-up of Bannockburn typified many of the inland Otago towns in the late nineteenth century. It was a town of storekeepers, farmers and miners. The usual clubs and societies were supported, along with lodges. There was briefly a digression from the standard when in the 1880s a co-operative general store was formed by the socialistic miners. It followed years of strain between the

mine owners and the working miners. Strikes had occurred which further soured relations. The co-operative was an attempt by working miners to help each other and perhaps to increase solidarity. Unfortunately, by 1883 it was no longer viable.

Those involved in mining fell broadly into three groups — the working miners; those involved in water races; and those involved in sludge channels. Often as not these overlapped considerably, as many water races and channels were owned publicly, the shareholders being a cross-section of the local community plus investors from Dunedin and Cromwell.

As was the case on many a goldfield, it was not the working miners who made the money, rather those who controlled the water, that is the owners of the water races and sludge channels. A reticulated water system was critical to successful mining and water sold by the 'head' earned an income

for the race proprietor, whether gold was found or not. Similarly for the sludge channel proprietor. He charged miners to deposit tailings and waste water into his channel at the rate of sixpence a 'head'. Again this payment was demanded regardless of how little gold was won. The channel proprietor then had a second bite at the golden apple when he paved his channel and caught any free gold contained in the sludge.

The onus was always on the active miner. Water was bought on an 8-hour-day basis, but of course ran for a 24-hour day. Consequently the race company sold three 'days' of water each day. Some unfortunate miners had to rise at midnight to collect their share of water, although this night water

The Lady Ranfurly *(Electric No. 3) dredge, one of the most famous dredges in New Zealand mining history, working the Kawarau River near Bannockburn in 1910.*

A dredge, with those working it posing for the photographer, on Shepherds Creek, Bannockburn.

was somewhat cheaper. Miners now rarely made spectacular money, but worked for little more than average wages. Consequently there was little about the life to attract new blood to the goldfield and as the early miners aged or moved on the total mining population declined. This trend continued through the closing decade of the century. By 1900 only the diehards remained. On the range only the Day Dawn Star and Golden Gate mines were spasmodically worked. On the terraces about 40 men were employed, while 30 Chinese mined old ground by the creeks. A year later the Queenstown goldfields warden reported:

> The gradual decline of alluvial mining referred to in previous reports still continues — the returns have been gradually diminishing, and the industry is surely though slowly dying.

Meanwhile, on the major rivers nearby, gold dredging was assuming greater importance. Twenty-three dredges plied the rivers at and about Cromwell in 1900, compared with 12 the year before. At Bannockburn, dredges were placed on the Bannockburn, Shepherds and Smiths creeks. A much greater number worked the Kawarau below the mouth of the gorge.

Successful dredging had its beginnings when the three McGeorge brothers met Charles Coote on Boxing Day 1894 and began talking goldmining. The McGeorges had a great deal of dredging expertise and Coote along with James Horn of Bannockburn held the mining rights to two stretches of the Kawarau River. They formed a partnership of 12 shares of £200 each to place a prospecting dredge on the two mining claims. After some difficulty in attracting finance, the Electric Gold Dredging Company was registered, so named because Coote, a commercial traveller, had once purveyed a skin stimulant called 'Electric Essence'.

Despite being too small and light, the dredge fulfilled its purpose of prospecting the Kawarau. A second dredge was constructed after frustrating delays at a cost of £5100. This money, although a large sum, was well spent, as within 10 weeks it had produced 1695 ounces (64 kg) of gold with a value of £6780. Two further large sister dredges were later built from the one set of plans — the Electric No. 3 or Lady Ranfurly just below Scotland Point and the Magnetic just above it. The Lady Ranfurly did exceptionally well, beating all previous records for gold production. The highest return obtained was 1273 ounces (48 kg) for four and a half days' dredging. Good returns continued for several years, until a fire destroyed the famed dredge in 1924.

The success of the Electric Company resulted in the second and largest dredging boom in New Zealand. Several hundred dredges were placed on and by rivers in Otago around the turn of the century. Unlike the Electric, few of the dredging companies ever paid dividends. The gold fever was located more in Dunedin's stock exchanges than on the rivers.

For Bannockburn, dredging provided merely a stay of execution. The population of the district stabilised in the 1890s, but with the end of the boom after 1903, decline continued apace. Miners had to compete with agricultural settlers for the available water. The attitudes of the twentieth century were quite different from those of the century before. Bannockburn was no longer solely a gold town. Returns from gold were now low and those obtained from other sources were increasing. Whereas miners almost invariably had first right to use water and destroy land in mining for the 50 years following the Dunstan rush, settlers' opinions began to be listened to following World War I. A new wave of young farmers demanded some security for their land against the ravages of mining, and required use of water for irrigation. Their dominance in the district has increased as the century has progressed. Latterly the residents of Bannockburn itself and local farmers, orchardists and horticulturists have enjoyed sole access to the water brought in by the still-active Carrick water race and other smaller races.

Only the spectacular, man-sculptured landscapes of the Bannockburn sluicings remain as a legacy of the impact of the nineteenth-century gold seekers on the alluvial terraces by the Kawarau River. Higher on the range behind, the evidence of the quartz miners is widespread although the towns of Quartzville and Carricktown are all but gone. The climb up the range is a steep one but the historic reminders do justice to the effort.

Further Reading

Cromwell Historical Society *Guide to the Carricktown/Quartzville Area* (Cromwell n.d.)

Duff, G. D. *Sheep May Safely Graze* (Dunedin 1978)

Parcell, J. C. *Heart of the Desert* (Dunedin 1951, reprinted 1976)

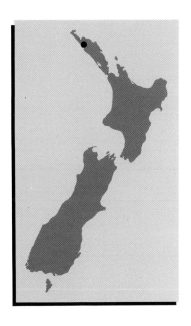

A Hokianga Survivor: Kohukohu

Jack Lee

A TRAVELLER passing through Kohukohu to or from the ferry which connects that side of the Hokianga Harbour with Rawene, the Hokianga county town, might well wonder idly what this peaceful village is doing there. Some 25 km from the heads, and with its age plainly showing, Kohukohu is now little more than a place where live a few hundred people who like a quiet environment. It rose a century and a half ago out of the kauri timber trade which flourished for about 80 years, but is now no more. And until lately, what was left of Kohukohu after many disastrous fires was being taken away piecemeal.

The closure of the town's sawmill early in this century coincided with the opening of a dairy factory at Motukaraka, a few kilometres downstream, and the flickering ember of Kohukohu's departing life was rekindled by an expanding dairy industry. In 1958, however, dairy factory amalgamation left only stark and empty walls at Motukaraka. This closure and calamitous fires seemed to have initiated a descent towards oblivion for Kohukohu. But a decade or so ago another revival occurred. Hokianga became a haven for 'alternative lifestyle' people and others seeking the tranquillity of country

life, and here at Kohukohu was a town ready made for them — the fossilised remnant of a mill town. So deterioration ceased and Kohukohu lives again, no longer the noisy, bustling township of early this century, but a gentle, kindly place for quiet people, which the Historic Places Trust hopes will be preserved in its present state to commemorate its role in New Zealand's first major export industry.

We first learn of Kohukohu in Maori tradition. Here, in the dimly remembered past, Kupe is said to have come with the people of his expedition and it seems that he may have lingered awhile. Many traditional accounts recall the deeds of Kupe and, although some of them are conflicting, many have survived over the centuries, and objects and placenames at Kohukohu and elsewhere testify to his presence. The petrified bailer of his canoe *Matawhaorua* is said to be at Kohukohu and similarly its anchor is downstream a little, at Rangiora. And some say that the name Kohukohu derives from a curse that Kupe laid on some of his people when they opened a hangi there before the food was cooked, a sinister omen in Maori terms. 'Kohu' means a curse, among other things. But between Kupe's presence and the early 1830s little about Kohukohu

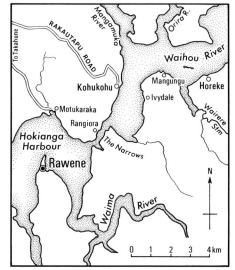

Middle reaches of the Hokianga.

is known. By that time it was within the domains of its chiefs Wharepapa, or Tohu Kakahi, and Tarewarewa, Ihutai chiefs of Nga Puhi.

European occupation at Kohukohu began in 1831. In the previous year Lieut. Thomas McDonnell, a speculator of New South Wales, had purchased at auction in Sydney the dockyard that had been established by Messrs Raine, Ramsay and Browne at Horeke, about 5 km upstream from Kohukohu, on the opposite shore. There, until his own arrival, McDonnell established George Frederick Russell as his factotum and later, it seems, his

Charles Heaphy painted this 'View of the Kahu Kahu, Hokianga River' in December 1839. The locality was already, as the logs under tow in the right foreground indicate, an important source of timber.

partner. This displaced Capt. David Clark, the original dockyard superintendent, who had married in succession two of Wharepapa's daughters. Clark therefore moved his Horeke house over to Kohukohu, intending to purchase land there from his father-in-law. Although he died by drowning in 1831, shortly after his move, Clark and his partner, Fishwick, were the first European occupiers at Kohukohu. Clark, it appears, had not purchased the land before his death, but when this occurred, Fishwick, apparently a none too scrupulous speculator and adventurer, sold Clark's house to Fred-

erick Edward Maning. Maning, with one Kelly, later acquired from its many owners the 20 or so hectares on which the town now stands.

In his journal, Edward Markham, an Englishman of means, but apparently of no useful occupation, describes the tensions and acrimony surrounding this transaction. He lived at Kohukohu in the autumn and winter of 1834. Kelly's role was an ambivalent one. Ostensibly he was there to watch over the interests of a Henry Oakes who in 1833 had arranged an option to purchase Kohukohu and had gone back to Hobart for finance. Unsuccessful, he returned to Hokianga with Markham, where, to his chagrin, he found his man Kelly, and Maning, negotiating on their own account for the land, which they succeeded in acquiring.

The Clark family's claim that

their father had in fact purchased Kohukohu before he died was rejected by the Old Land Claim Commissioners who were appointed after 1840 to investigate early European land acquisitions. Messrs Russell and Webster were then in occupation and, no doubt much to his relief, Russell was confirmed in his title by the evidence of Maori witnesses. The Clarks were finally settled by the Government on the present Maori block Tauteihiihi, which extends from a little south of the town to Rangiora, at The Narrows. This was Wharepapa's territory, while Tarewarewa had been the owner of the pa overlooking Kohukohu.

Maning, the 'Pakeha Maori', later author of the book *Old New Zealand*, employed sawyers and used Kohukohu as a base for preparing baulk timber from kauri logs for export to Australia on the vessels that came up the river and

A view along the waterfront at Kohukohu in the later nineteenth century. The long building with the veranda is the town's first hotel, which was opened in 1882 and burned down in 1900.

Another nineteenth-century view of the waterfront at Kohukohu which underscores the importance of timber to the town. Squared baulks, confined by booms, have been floated down to Kohukohu to be milled in or shipped from the town.

By 1912, when the Northwood Bros took this picture of the Kohukohu waterfront, the town had a more established, permanent air. Many of these buildings survived for many years, as Kohukohu stagnated, until they were destroyed in the major fire of 1954.

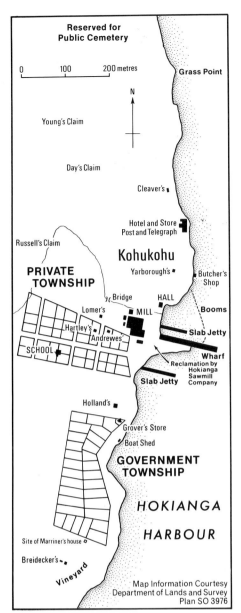

Kohukohu in the 1880s; redrawn from a plan prepared in 1885.

LAURENCE ABERHART

The tide still floods and ebbs on the waterfront of a changed and quieter Kohokohu, no longer the busy timber town of the nineteenth and early twentieth centuries.

anchored close-to in deep water. The trees were felled in the Mangamuka River, some kilometres upstream, and the logs floated down to Kohukohu on the tide. Maning's occupation there in 1833 thus saw the beginning of Kohukohu as a timber town and the main outlet in the harbour for the countless squared timber baulks, piles and spars brought down from the forests at the head of the river.

The land at Kohukohu changed hands many times before, in 1874, it came to Alfred Cooke Yarborough and Alfred Spry Andrewes, who made a township out of a small settlement. Maning had sold to Dr Ross of the Bay of Islands,

whose widow, upon his death, disposed of it to the Rev. Nathaniel Turner, a missionary, who purchased it despite the Wesleyan embargo on land acquisitions. He in turn sold to G. F. Russell and Matthew Marriner and Russell established himself there in the late 1830s with his Maori wife — reputedly a niece of Tamati Waaka Nene — in opposition to McDonnell, his former employer at Horeke. John Webster was in residence at Rangiora in the 1840s and 1850s as agent for John Logan Campbell in the timber business and in 1855, the year of Russell's death, he married one of his daughters. Russell left Kohukohu to Webster and Campbell as executors, in trust for his 'illegitimate children', and Webster acquired the estate with his brother who, until 1869, had a small water-driven sawmill at the Wairere Stream, near Horeke.

The early development of Kohukohu as a European settlement occurred in Russell's and Webster's time, but it was Russell who built its famous stone bridge some time before 1851, since it appears on a sketch of that date with the Journal of John Jolliffe, of the survey ship *Pandora.* And on Old Land Claim Plan No. 65 (Auckland), probably prepared in the mid 1850s, the

bridge and eight buildings are shown. Jolliffe wrote of Russell's '... sweetly pretty garden which is the (sic) by far the prettiest I have ever seen out of England it is a perfect garden of Eden in the Wilderness...'

In 1874, Yarborough and Andrewes appear, taking over Webster's timber business which then seems to have been concentrated in the bay, now reclaimed by the sawdust of subsequent milling operations. Yarborough also bought Webster's house and land. The Websters had acquired large areas of land along the harbour and owned several ships. The new owners continued with the baulk timber trade and the export of totara piles, but by this time the trade had declined somewhat. A log squaring station on the Whangape Harbour was also rafting logs into Hokianga to be picked up by vessels that could not negotiate the shallow Whangape. Hokianga did not attract many Europeans in the mid nineteenth century, and the bush was worked mainly by Maori, of whom Webster employed about

▲ *The kauri timber industry continued to sustain Kohukohu until the early years of this century. This picture is of a winder at work on a bush tramway in the hills behind Kohukohu.*

▼ *The Kauri Timber Company mill at Kohukohu. Logs awaiting milling float behind booms in the bay and sawn timber is stacked on the shore and wharf awaiting shipment to destinations all over New Zealand. The mill was later shifted to Koutu and then to Auckland.*

700. In 1870 the European population was estimated to be about 200, but this increased to about 400 when, in 1879, Greenfield and Stewart, a Sydney firm, set up a sawmill in the bay at Kohukohu. On 1 May 1877 a Post Office was opened there, with Yarborough as postmaster. He was described as a storekeeper, and was shortly followed in the same year by one W. Harrison. This, however, was not the first postal service in the locality, since the chart of Hokianga prepared from the surveys by the *Pandora* in 1851 shows a post office and custom-house at Rangiora.

With the advent of the mill, Kohukohu forged ahead. In 1881 Yarborough and Andrewes acquired the mill and operated it under the name of the Hokianga Sawmill Company. From that point onwards, until the closure of the mill in 1909 and beyond, these two men dominated business in the river, both in timber and in trade generally. However, they retained the mill only until 1885, when it closed for want of capital. It did not reopen until 1889, when a Sydney firm, the Kauri Timber Company, took it over. Then, at about the turn of the century, a local enterprise, the Rangiora Timber Company, opened a mill about 2 km downstream. Its capacity was 5,000,000 board feet a year, compared with Kohukohu's 6,000,000, but none of the Hokianga mills ever achieved their maximum output. All had relied on waterborne timber, easily accessible from the rivers. Inevitably the supply of this diminished and the timber became more difficult and less economic to get out as time went on.

The end came for the Kohukohu mill when in 1909 its licence was revoked and it was closed, due to the excessive discharge of sawdust into the harbour. By 1916 only three mills out of the earlier total of five in Hokianga remained. The Rangiora mill, on its original scale, was finished before 1919, although it operated from time to time until the 1930s.

For over 50 years industry in Kohukohu, and indeed throughout Hokianga, had relied entirely on water transport. This was eminently satisfactory in the early years, when the shores of the harbour were thick with kauri and only manpower was necessary to get it out. But toward the end of the century, when the millers were forced progressively further inland and the flax, kauri gum and farming industries were emerging, the benefits of water transport diminished sharply. The need for roads, steam power and road transport then became imperative.

With the decline of the timber industry had come government action to promote settlement in Hokianga, where three blocks of Crown Land, Punakitere, Waiotemarama and Motukaraka were opened up. Motukaraka is some 5 km downstream from Kohukohu. Thomas McDonnell claimed to have purchased this land from Maori owners in the 1830s, but on a visit to London in 1839 he sold it to the New Zealand Company. However, he later failed to substantiate his claim, so that neither he nor the company got possession of the land. As Crown Land in 1884 it was surveyed and subdivided into blocks on which 51 settlers were located.

By this time the European population of the county had risen to 767, but the settlers at Motukaraka were much better placed than the others, due to their proximity to Kohukohu, then a well established township. They were able to sell the timber off their land to the mill there, supplies were available to them and some casual work could be found. The earlier settlers' blocks were only about 20 ha, but later these were increased to about 40 ha and dairying, rather than subsistence farming, became possible. This, with the opening of other land away from the harbour, led eventually to the formation of the Hokianga Co-operative Dairy Company. In 1908 this company took over a factory at Motukaraka built shortly before by Dalgety and Company.

Behind the old Motukaraka dairy factory is a concrete dam, one of the few relics of the industry which helped sustain Kohukohu after the decline of the timber trade. The site of the factory is now a council yard.

Providentially this came at a time when the economy of Kohukohu had been struck a mortal blow by the sudden dissolution of its only industry, sawmilling. Dairying undoubtedly saved the town from immediate extinction. Road-building too brought government funds into the district and to Kohukohu.

The first important road that affected Kohukohu was constructed in the 1880s as a 2-m-wide bridle track between a point on the shore at Motukaraka, opposite to Rawene, and Takahue, near Broadwood. This joined up with one built from Kaitaia and both were shortly widened to 4.5 m. Before 1890 a bridle track from Kohukohu — the Rakautapu Road — was constructed to meet this about 6.5 km from Motukaraka and the town thus had road access of a sort through Broadwood to Kaitaia.

So Kohukohu survived on the dairy industry and to some extent on public funds spent on works. In the town itself an incursion into horticulture had occurred in 1884 when a German, Heinrich Breidecker, produced wine from his own vines and from grapes brought down to him by Maori from the Mangamuka. He broke in land at the south end of Kohukohu and grew grapes on a trellis of manuka

poles. His press was made from local timber and was operated by a bottle jack. Breidecker produced wine at 10 shillings per gallon, taking up to £400 per annum from his Isabella grapes. His hock won prizes at the Dunedin Exhibition. The vineyard was on an area of about 1 ha in the 'Government Township' laid out in 1886 and is shown as Lot 27 on Survey Office Plan 3976 (Auckland). It was immediately south of Marriner Street, being part of Marriner's Claim, which, on resumption by the Crown, was reserved as Maori land under the name Tauteihiihi. Another Kohukohu resident, Lester, was encouraged by Breidecker's success and terraced a very steep hill rising from the foreshore behind the township for vines and an orchard. But the impetus initiated by Breidecker lapsed and this sort of activity subsequently migrated across the harbour to Ivydale.

The dairy industry that rescued Kohukohu from extinction grew slowly but steadily as government

Looking inland up the upper reaches of the Hokianga Harbour from the look-out point above Kohukohu's old cemetery, the once busy waters of the 'River' now tranquil and almost deserted.

The Catholic church, centre, and the Masonic temple in the background, are among the survivors of Kohukohu's buildings, many of which have been lost over the years to fire.

The facade of Kohukohu's Masonic temple.

land in the interior on both sides of the harbour was opened for settlers. Kohukohu was the commercial centre for those on the northwest side of the harbour and on the south-east side upstream from the Waima River. Photographs of the 1880s and 1890s — perhaps the town's heyday — show substantial buildings, some two-storeyed. There were stores, offices, a large mill establishment in the bay, a town wharf, a mill wharf, a hotel, a school, a church and other public buildings. Large ocean-going vessels anchored or moored off the town. Cottages and substantial houses sheltered a European population of over 500 by the time the mill closed in 1909 and these had their town hall, brass band, Masonic hall, banks and newspaper. A weekly steamer service plied between Kohukohu and Onehunga, on the Manukau Harbour.

Apart from a mill fire in 1882 and the burning of the Wallace Supplies store and the 18-year-old hotel on 28 August 1900, Kohukohu remained much the same until 1920. With its hotch-potch of wooden buildings cheek by jowl, it had always been a fire risk, but this lesson was not learned until most of the buildings at risk had actually been destroyed. A fire in the early 1920s razed the library, courthouse and two buildings across the road at the south end of the town. Then at 2.30 a.m. on 1 April 1937, Kohukohu's last mill, the Kiln Dried Veneer Box Company's complex, located on the old Kauri Company's site, together with all plant and the general store, went up in flames. Known as King's Mill, it had been built in the early 1920s by Bay of Islands interests and cut all useful timbers, but specialised in the manufacture of kahikatea-veneered butter boxes for dairy companies in the north and elsewhere. It was the largest roofed-over space in Hokianga.

But worse was to come. On 19 August 1954, almost exactly 54 years after the original hotel and Wallace Supplies store had been burned, the same two establishments, on the same sites, suffered the same fate, along with two other buildings. Then on 27 January 1967 came the ultimate disaster. Fire broke out in Andrewes's store at 2 a.m. and spread to Andrewes's furniture storeroom, the Andrewes and Cook building, formerly the dental clinic, the police station, the solicitor's office, the Bank of New Zealand and the bank residence. There was insufficient water for firefighting and the tide was out. Although both the Kaitaia and Rawene fire brigades turned out there was little they could do to control the blaze.

Significantly, of the buildings destroyed by the later fires, few were ever replaced. Their work was done and the depressed economy of Kohukohu had no use for replacements. Inevitably the former metropolis of Hokianga reverted to a village of store, post office, hotel and garage — a mere remnant of its early pre-eminence. But as a tranquil place for people to live, in old, mellow houses, it is surviving. The old commercial centre of Kohukohu is no more, apart from a few minor buildings at the north and south ends of the town. There was never an adequate water supply, even for domestic purposes, and this is still the case. There was therefore little chance of the town's survival. Apart from houses, significant buildings that remain are away from the old commercial centre on the waterfront. They include the town hall, the Masonic hall, the old school and St Mary's Church.

The final chapter in Kohukohu's colourful history and the decline of its commercial eminence on the Hokianga was written in 1958 when, in the interests of the amalgamation of dairy factories, made possible by improved roads, the Motukaraka factory was closed. And in 1960 the Bank of New Zealand moved out.

In the author's lifetime, fern and scrub have replaced much of the county's grassland of the 1930s. Many smaller farms have become uneconomic due to rising costs and excessive distances to markets and have been incorporated into larger ones. This, too, has been a significant factor in Kohukohu's decline, together with road improvements which have minimised the discomfort and time lost in travelling to the larger centres.

A few years ago the last building to be removed from the town, the Union Church, was taken across the river to Mangungu to the site of the old Wesleyan mission station, where it is now part of the Historic Places Trust's complex there. But another, Fell's old boatbuilding shed on the waterfront, from which so many boats were launched in earlier times, has been preserved for the town by the present owner, who has donated it to the local Boy Scout troop.

In a letter to the *New Zealander* in 1864 F. E. Maning, then a judge of the Native Land Court, wrote of Hokianga:

The state of this district, and the positions which the native and European inhabitants hold towards each other, are peculiar . . . *every* settler, every householder, in this district except one have been here from twenty-eight to forty years except such as has been born here . . . *there is not one European female in the whole district* but one, who is not a settler's wife, *all* the settlers being married to native women or women of Maori descent . . .

Maning was saying that the Hokianga community was essentially a bicultural one. And so it remains to this day.

Further Reading

Earle, A. *Narrative of a Residence in New Zealand* (London 1966)

Harrison, E. *Kohukohu* (Kohukohu 1983)

Markham, E. *New Zealand or Recollections of It* (Wellington 1963)

Ramsden, G. E. *Busby of Waitangi* (Wellington 1942)

Ross, R. M. *Clendon House* (Wellington 1978)

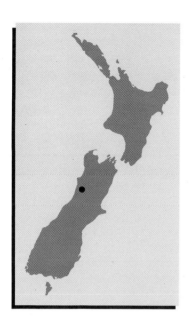

'A Distinctive Pocket of West Coast Settlement': Blackball's Militant Past

Brian Wood

Can new industry be set up in the town? Can it be made prettier or more attractive? Can Blackball be publicised as something other than a coal mining town?

THESE questions, asked in 1966 by the editor of the *Centennial of Blackball*, had been given urgency by the closure of the Blackball mine in 1964. Like many small West Coast townships, Blackball owed its existence to coal mining, but the beginnings of European settlement there were due to gold. In the winter of 1866, following reports of rich washes, the creeks of the lower Grey Valley including Black Ball Creek were rushed. Sizeable nuggets were found. In October 1867 an Irishman exclaimed to his mates, 'Arrah boys, these are the praties I like to be digging.' After the frenetic creek rushes, sluicing claims provided more permanent work for parties of diggers. In 1916 a veteran digger, Peter Passeni, struck it lucky in Moonlight Creek when he found the 87.5 oz 'Victory' nugget.

The goldminers' independence and capitalistic enterprise were in contrast with the collectivist, unionist attitudes of the coal miners. However, some Blackball coal miners also had gold claims which supplemented their incomes in

times of unemployment; following the disastrous strike in 1931 and the deepening of the Depression, large numbers of loyal Blackball unionists enrolled on subsidised goldmining relief schemes as their only means of livelihood. Quartz-crushing operations, begun in the 1890s, were also revived at this time. On the flats below Blackball, the tailings left by the dredges operating between the 1930s and the early 1950s can still be seen. Goldmining was significant but not pervasive; Blackball was first and foremost a coal mining town. As such it

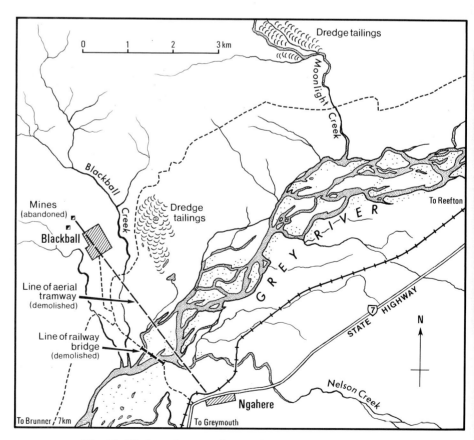

Blackball's location on the north bank of the Grey River.

ALEXANDER TURNBULL LIBRARY / AUCKLAND WEEKLY NEWS

► *The Blackball Coal Mining Company's engine house and workshops in 1902. The mine entrance is behind the workshops. The coal industry gave Blackball its economic base and its place in the history of radicalism in New Zealand.*

became a centre of radical working class protest in New Zealand.

Sited on the 'Plateau' fringing the eastern slopes of the southern Paparoas, Blackball was physically isolated. The Midland Railway Company extended the Greymouth-Brunner government line to Ngahere in the late 1880s and an aerial tramway for carrying the coal across the Grey River was completed in 1893. However neither the ferry services, nor the goldfields track from Brunner provided easy access. Its location and isolation helped Blackball develop a distinctive identity. When the Ngahere-Blackball branch line was completed in 1909, the rail bridge became the linchpin of the transport system. Increased coal output, population growth and more regular contacts with other townships in the Grey Valley contributed to

Blackball's growing self awareness.

Immigrant coal miners and their families made up the bulk of the population. The dozen or so from Newcastle, New South Wales, who put up their tents near the mine entrance in November 1894, were the first from Australia. Most Blackball miners came to New Zealand directly from the United

Kingdom, many from coal mining districts in the north of England but a growing proportion from Scottish pits. Some had worked in North America. Relatives and

▼ *All that remains near the entrance to the Blackball Mine are a few concrete structures and scraps of rusting metal, ruins of the fan housing near the mine's return airway.*

Among the more interesting industrial remains on the site of the old Blackball Mine is a huge fan which, part of the mine's ventilation system, extracted stale air from the mine's workings.

FRANK SIMPSON

FRANK SIMPSON

▲ *Early Blackball was physically iso-lated. Between 1893 and 1909 coal mined at Blackball was conveyed across the Grey River to the Mid-land Line at Ngahere by an aerial tramway. People crossed the river by boat.*

▼ *A branch railway line was laid in to Blackball in 1909, making the aerial tramway redundant. Black-ball's links across Grey River remained precarious, however, and spans of the bridge were often washed away by floods. In floods in 1950, two spans of the combined road and rail bridge collapsed into the Grey River, severing the town's link to Ngahere. The bridge has now been demolished.*

▲ *Some of the old standards which carried the wires and buckets of the aerial tramway on which Blackball coal was transported across the Grey River from 1893 to 1909 still rise out of the bush near the town.*

workmates often migrated together or followed an initial immigration. The extremes of miner militancy that developed at Blackball owed much to the previous experience and perceptions of these immigrant miners. Circumstances and events at Blackball tended to reinforce rather than lessen their sense of struggle.

In 1911 Edward Hunter, a social-ist militant from Lanarkshire, was forthright in his praise when he wrote:

Truth needs must out!
  It speaks from every tree;
It calls from every track, and every
  shack —
'The Blackball men fought ever to
  be free
And never turned a fighting com-
  rade back.
    Oh, Blackball men!'

The Blackball Coal Company Lim-ited, its headquarters in London, was held in low regard by the miners. The interests of overseas owners were seen as the main concern of the Christchurch-based board of directors. Few amenities

▲ *Miners about to go to work in the Blackmall Mine, c.1913–14, gathered for one of their number to take their photo.*

➤

At the coal face in the Blackball Mine, probably in the 1950s. By the time this photograph, and the photograph below, were taken conditions in the mine had improved from those of the earlier times when Blackball was a centre of radical labour action.

➤ *A trucker at work in the Blackball Mine, a photograph taken at the same time as the one above, probably the 1950s.*

Housing provided by the mining company at Blackball for miners and their families was often primitive and came under criticism. This miner's hut, one of a long row built by the company, was pictured in a report of a Board of Trade enquiry into the coal industry as an example of the less than satisfactory standard of housing prevailing.

were provided for the town. Monopoly capitalism made it in the eyes of some 'a pup' of the New Zealand Shipping Company, an association which became closer after 1899 when the ill-fated Midland Railway Company sold the freehold on the Blackball leases to Sir Edwyn Dawes, chairman of directors of the shipping company. Miners alleged that the connection with the shipping company permitted the production of false information on the profitability of the mine.

Conditions underground and the periodic lack of work frequently caused dissatisfaction. The mine was free from potentially explosive firedamp, but 'black damp', caused by spontaneous combustion, was a major danger. The flooding and sealing off of large sections of the mine due to underground fires was one cause of irregular work and unemployment. Downturns in trade reduced demand, particularly for shipping. Blackball coal was steam coal and conversion of ship-

ping from coal to oil, which began in the late 1920s, coincided with the onset of the Depression in the 1930s.

The poverty and insecurity of Blackball miners and also their transience contributed to the low standard of housing in the township. Many of the sparsely furnished, two-bedroomed cottages still to be seen lacked porches or verandas and had no drying facilities for miners' clothes. Water ran off tar roofs into tanks and was contaminated with soot. The water to the mine manager's and company officials' houses ran fresh and clean from a tributary of Blackball Creek. No agreement could be reached to have it reticulated to the township. The general environment also left much to be desired. With the bush cleared, the town assumed a sparse, unkempt appearance. Poor drainage and poor soils discouraged the planting of gardens. The West Coast's wet weather compounded the ill effects of overcrowding. Rainwater gathered in pans which in some cases became cesspits. Only later were drainage ditches dug.

According to an official report on miners' housing and social conditions in 1919, the sordid conditions helped explain much of the industrial unrest in Blackball. In some cases they were said to be

The mine manager lived in a substantial house which was in marked contrast to the small, often inadequate cottages or huts in which the miners and their families lived. The mine manager's house is being restored for use as a community centre.

'similar to that found in the Old World only as a result of extreme poverty'. A row of huts, totally lacking in ventilation, built by the company for single men, came in for special criticism.

Many miners had large families. In 1931, 80 families were dependent on company housing, much of it inconvenient and unhealthy.

Blackball was a working class township, a pit village. There was a strong sense of community. A common poverty, traditional loyalty, union solidarity and hostility to their employer helped heighten class consciousness there.

A case for the provision of bathhouses was argued before the Royal Commission on Mines in 1911. Miners had to walk to their homes not only dirty but also sweaty and frequently wet. Few of their homes had bathrooms and at the boardinghouses they had to queue to use the wash tubs. A bathhouse was eventually provided near the mine entrance. At the end of each shift the miners could exit directly to it. However, during the strike of 1931 a condition of return to work required that the miners climb 300 steep steps to another exit and walk through the bush to the bathhouse. The requirement so inflamed relationships that miners' wives offered to work for the company if the condition was removed.

Miner militancy made its first successful appearance at Blackball with the crib time strike in 1908. This strike established a tradition which put Blackball miners in the vanguard of radical labour protest in New Zealand for almost a generation. The Blackball Miners Union, formed in 1899, was registered under the 1894 Industrial Conciliation and Arbitration Act. Under their award agreement, the miners were allowed only 15 minutes for their crib or lunch. Attempts to negotiate an increase to the 30 minutes enjoyed by other West Coast miners had not succeeded, although improved conditions and increased wages had been obtained.

The Industrial Conciliation and Arbitration Act was central to industrial relations in New Zealand for 80 years after its passage in 1894. It gave the power of final decision on awards to the Arbitration Court Judge. During the decade after the Act's passage, New Zealand became known as a 'country without strikes'. However, by 1908 the measure was becoming less popular with some unionists, among them the Denniston coal miners. A nil award there in 1905 had caused dissatisfaction and during 1906 and 1907 the Denniston miners pursued the objective of reducing their working day to 8 hours 'bank to bank' with increasing vigour. Indeed Seddon's Liberal Government had conceded it in the 1905 Coal-mines Act, but the Arbitration Court Judge, W.A. Sim, held that the award agreement requiring 8 hours work at the coal face took precedence over the legislation. Seddon's successor, Ward, intervened in December 1907 and a compromise solution prevented a strike.

Four of the seven militants who were to lead the Blackball miners in their crib time strike had been prominent in the agitation at Denniston. Others had worked at the nearby Point Elizabeth state mine where 'Fighting Bob' Semple was union president. The most prominent of the new arrivals at Blackball were Patrick Hickey, who had returned to Denniston in 1906 bearing his card from the United States Western Federation of Miners, noted for its militancy, and Paddy Webb, whose socialist convictions had contributed to his blacklisting in the Victorian miners strike of 1903. 'A splendid capitalistic measure for keeping the workers in subjection', was how Hickey described the Industrial Conciliation and Arbitration Act in his first speech at Blackball in January 1908. Socialist perceptions of the class war and syndicalist ideas of industrial labour organised into One Big Union could have no truck with the Arbitration Court system.

In early February Hickey decided to test the management. He refused

Blackball's image in the rest of New Zealand during the 1908 crib-time strike is illustrated by this cartoon from the New Zealand Observer, *14 March 1908, titled 'His Imperial Highness Labour'. The Premier, Sir Joseph Ward, backed by his ministers, makes his obeisance. The chorus of ministers is pleading: 'May it please Your Highness, we implore you not to strike. Bear patiently with the Arbitration Act a little longer, and, if it does not please Your Mightiness we will amend it still further so that it will please you.'*

to resume work after 15 minutes' crib. Following his court appearance for refusal to obey the manager's lawful instruction, agitation intensified. A Socialist Party branch was formed by Hickey and Webb, assisted by party organiser H.M. Fitzgerald. Their youthful enthusiasm and audacity began to win over the more conservative and cautious miners. Supportive labour meetings in Greymouth attracted audiences of up to 1500.

The crib time strike began on 27 February when Hickey, Webb and five other Socialist Party miners repeated Hickey's offence and were discharged. The strike's illegality and the strikers' defiant attitude towards the Arbitration Court gave national prominence to the strike

◄

In the bar of the newly opened Dominion Hotel, Blackball, 1912. An unidentified, cloth-capped miner watches the proprietor, Jim Irvine.

and its leaders. Company attempts at a compromise settlement were rejected. The union was fined £75 but refused to pay. The miners refused to return to work. The leaders blatantly used the courts to publicise their anti-arbitration position. An attempt by the company to divide the union failed in the face of union and community solidarity.

The victory after 11 weeks was due in part to a more conciliatory attitude by the company but it was a victory nonetheless. On 10 October, with elections impending, an Act to amend the Coalmines Act of 1908 provided for 30 minutes' crib time in an 8 hour working day, bank to bank, 'not withstanding the provisions of any award or industrial agreement in existence'. The Denniston issues of 1906-7 were won at Blackball in 1908.

In the wake of the strike a Federation of Miners was formed at Greymouth, which in 1909 became the 'Red' Federation of Labour. New Zealand's larger unions deregistered from the Industrial Conciliation and Arbitration Act and adopted militant unionist and socialist policies. Hickey and

Webb were increasingly prominent in what became a period of growing conflict in New Zealand industry and ferment within the New Zealand labour movement. To some, the socialist millenium was at hand. However, the Red Feds met defeat at Waihi in 1912 and in the 1913 waterfront strike Massey was more than a match for them. Their call for a general strike was not heeded. The appearance of a 'scab' arbitrationist union at Blackball in December 1913 marked the end of the struggle there.

Politics were not entirely ignored. As a Social Democratic Party candidate, Paddy Webb was elected M.P. for Grey in July 1913. Indeed, the future of the Red Feds was to be in politics. After the 1913 defeat, their leaders faced the realities of power in New Zealand and were prominent in the formation of the Labour Party in 1916. Their socialist opposition to war and conscription helped them maintain a high profile, but their compromise acceptance of arbitration led to their rejection by many Blackball unionists.

Opposition to World War I was at first confined to the Socialist Union leadership. The Marxist

study classes established at Blackball in 1914 led to increased socialist awareness but opposition to the 'capitalist war' gained momentum only after conscription was introduced in 1916. There is no war memorial at Blackball. The V.C. won by Scottish-born miner Samuel Frickleton at Messines is commemorated in Greymouth but not in his home town. Miners could be exempted from military service but as the war progressed the unequal sacrifice of capital and labour and the evidence of 'war profiteering' became increasingly apparent. Socialist Bill Bromilow, a veteran of the 1908 strike, led the Blackball Union in a strike against conscription in November 1916. However, they were not supported by the Miners Federation executive. Solidarity for the go slow of 1917 and the intermittent strikes of 1918 only followed the arrests of union and labour leaders for anti-conscription activities. The demand for improved wages as the cost of living increased helped win support for the union leadership from rank and file miners. The 'Red Fed' Miners Federation, re-established after the 1913 defeat, was able to assert itself as the miners' negotiating body and obtain wage increases considerably larger than those obtained by unions under the Arbitration Court. The 1919 Report of the Board of Trade Investigation on the Coal Industry commented adversely on housing and social conditions, but to little effect.

Blackball militancy, continuing in its vanguard role, took new forms in the 1920s. Economic insecurity reinforced a growing class consciousness. The New Zealand Communist Party, formed in 1921, was probably at its strongest between 1925 and 1928 when its headquarters were at Blackball.

Blackball's Marxist study classes provided most of the party's foundation members. Yorkshire-born William Balderstone, whose communism was influenced mainly by his time in British Columbia, in 1921, as secretary of the Blackball Union, led the miners out of a docile Miners Federation which in 1919 had joined the Alliance of Labour. In 1922 with the aid of J.A. McDonald, a Canadian socialist propagandist, he set up the West Coast Communist Federation. Their belief in strong local organisation appealed to the miners in the West Coast 'colliery villages'. During the 1923 lockout, which lasted 4 months, Balderstone claimed in his *Appeal to the Wage Workers of the Dominion* that 'We are fighting your fight. If we win you win!' The Arbitration Court was labelled 'an instrument of the Exploiters and Profiteers'. They were defeated, but out of the defeat a revitalised Miners Federation, the United Mine Workers, was formed. Its organisation and methods were along the lines proposed by Balderstone, giving the employers greater cause for concern.

The General Secretary of the Communist Party was another Blackball miner, Scottish-born Angus McLagan who had come to Blackball in 1911. In 1926 he became secretary of the United Mine Workers; by 1927, this organisation was largely controlled by Communists. A Blackball Communist initiative, not unlike that of the Red Feds after 1908, seemed possible.

The stage of the newly built Union Hall and the streets of Blackball provided the platforms from which Balderstone, McLagan and other prominent Communists such as Alex Galbraith and Jack Doyle, expounded their message.

Propagandists, idealists and other radicals gravitated to the township intent on being part of the new dawn which the Russian Revolution had shown to be possible. The union provided for most of the educational, social, welfare and medical needs of the Blackball community. From April 1926 to

▲*Cordials manufactured in Brunnerton being delivered to Campbell's Hotel, Blackball, by horse-drawn cart in 1905. Hotels and boarding houses played an important part in Blackball's social and political life and one of the last sputters of protest by Blackball miners concerned the price of beer.*

▼*This old building is one of Blackball's survivors. The old miners' hall stood nearby until its unfortunate demolition in the early 1980s.*

1929 the *Workers' Vanguard* was produced monthly from the press of the *Grey River Argus*, the pioneer labour daily established in 1919. Through it Blackball miners and New Zealand workers were kept informed on Marxist-Leninist interpretations of international and class issues. Class consciousness and solidarity were promoted at Sunday morning union meetings. 'Blackball reeks with an

Blackball miners and their wives outside the courthouse at Greymouth, there to face charges of stone throwing and the use of insulting language. The year is 1931 and these people of Blackball were maintaining a tradition of radical action that had begun in 1908.

atheistic Socialism which bids fair to ruin our Church work,' the Anglicans complained. Annie Balderstone took lessons at the socialist Sunday school. The inspiration of Blackball was *The Peoples Flag*.

However, between 1926 and 1928 attempts by McLagan, assisted by F.P. Walsh and the Seamens Union, to exert a Communist influence over the Alliance of Labour failed, due to the opposition from 'Big Jim' Roberts and Labour Party/arbitration-minded unions. Economically the times were inauspicious. At Blackball also the Communist red dawn began to fade. In 1928 Balderstone attacked the party and was expelled; the Communist Party headquarters were moved back to Wellington. In 1929 the refusal of McLagan to follow Communist Party executive instructions and call a strike in support of Australian miners led to his expulsion and the resignation of most other New Zealand coal miners.

Under pressure of power struggles and personality conflicts, the unity of Blackball unionists and their community was shown to be more fragile than many had imagined. In January 1931, the Blackball Coal Company issued dismissal notices, indicating that miners wanting work should re-apply. When fewer men were required, union policy was to share available

work. The company's refusal to accept this was seen as an attempt to break the union. The unionists stood firm. However, after 10 weeks the pumps were withdrawn from the dip section of the mine allowing it to be flooded. The possibility of other parts of the mine being worked by tribute parties (who contracted to work a section of the mine for the owner, who in turn bought the coal produced at an agreed price) was mooted. In June, after 5 months on strike, it was announced that a tribute mine was indeed to be worked by a party of Blackball miners, led by none other than its former Communist union secretary, William Balderstone. As tributers they would not belong to, or be controlled by, the union. Balderstone took pleasure in describing the union leadership of McLagan and Clark as 'pitiful short-sighted and useless'. It was said that Balderstone had been drawing strike pay while negotiating with the company.

At the demonstration on 1 June the anger was immense. Other Grey district coal miners joined those at Blackball with their wives and children in Union Hall. McLagan warned that 'if the tribute system were got away with... they would be down to a coolie level'. The meeting resolved 'to fight the tribute system to the last ditch'. Led by the Highland Pipe Band, the

procession of demonstrators circled the township, stopping at the house of each tributer. Roofs were pelted with stones and windows broken. One estimate put the number present at 1250. *The Peoples Flag* was sung at the barbed wire protecting the tributers' workplace, where extra police were stationed. In the afternoon the tributers, returning to their houses under police protection, were abused by between 250 and 300 unionists and their wives. Phrases such as 'You scabby yellow mongrel' were typical. Prosecutions for using insulting language, stone throwing and assault resulted in fines. The use of the courts to promote the union case did not repeat the success of 1908 when Blackball had been 'practically one family'. The division in the township brought a long, lasting bitterness. Its social cohesion was shattered.

McLagan continued to lead the United Mine Workers during the Depression and in 1934 formed Councils of Action on the West Coast advocating a nationwide strike to restore wage cuts. The solution that emerged, however, was a political one, with the election of a Labour Government in November 1935. Under Labour, New Zealand was to reap some of the benefits of the Blackball experience, although not in the 'heady' form that had existed there. Paddy

The most impressive relic of the old Blackball Mine is the high chimney, built of bricks fired in nearby Brunner, which served the boilerhouse. The boiler generated steam for the winches and winding gear of the mine.

In the bush on the opposite side of the hill from the old mine entrance are two chimneys which were part of the mine's ventilation system.

The square chimney, the larger of the two old ventilation chimneys in the bush some distance from the mine mouth, is 20 m high.

Webb became Minister of Mines in a Government led by his friend Michael Joseph Savage, whom he had encouraged to come to New Zealand in 1907. Angus McLagan, who in April 1937 became President of the New Zealand Federation of Labour (so named after the 'Red' Federation of Labour), entered Cabinet in 1942 as Minister of Industrial Manpower.

The Labour Party brought to the New Zealand working class an economic and social security absent in previous generations. Its leaders had had to forsake most of their radical ideology in the process and acknowledge that political action could achieve what industrial action could not. For the next generation at least, a greater degree of security and equality of opportunity could exist.

Blackball's recovery was slow. In 1940 there were still over 40 miners enrolled on unemployment schemes, but nationalisation of the mine, justified by the war situation as well as Labour Party policy, helped improve employment opportunities. In 1947 rising prices, in particular an increase in the price of beer from 6d to 7d, provoked protest by West Coast miners

in the form of the Beer Boycott. Bill Pearson's fictional synthesis of Blackball in *Coal Flat* is set in this year. The Beer Boycott is used in the novel to delineate some of the attitudes and tensions present in the community. It was for Jack Doyle, President of the West Coast Trades and Labour Council, to advise the Licensed Victuallers Association, 'sell sevenpenny beer and your pub will be declared "black" '. On 1 October the boycott, which was to continue for over 4 months, began. Union discipline required action against boycott breakers but the result was a victory. The move to establish licensed working men's clubs had begun before Christmas 1947. Blackball's is chartered as the 'Blackball Working Mens Club and Mutual School of Arts'.

Blackball's population has declined markedly. Its coal mining and union past is no more, but relics of coal and goldmining activities and surviving township buildings are reminders of a bustling township where hardship was the norm and radicalism once flourished.

Like echoes from the past, protest and conflict still occur. A new

community leadership is emerging, hostile to large-scale goldmining proposals. Over protest, Union Hall has been demolished. Ironically the former mine manager's home has become the town's community centre. A high proportion of Blackball's present residents receive benefits introduced by the first Labour Government. The questions asked in 1966 have not yet been answered. Perhaps the key to Blackball's future will lie in its past. In the meantime the centres of New Zealand radicalism have moved to other places and other industries.

Further Reading

Bennett, F. *A Canterbury Tale* (Wellington 1980)

Howitt, G. ed. *Centennial of Blackball* (Greymouth 1966)

May, P.R. ed. *Miners and Militants: Politics in Westland 1865-1918* (Christchurch 1975)

Pearson, W. *Coal Flat* (Auckland 1963)

Roth, H. *Trade Unions in New Zealand: Past and Present* (Wellington 1973)

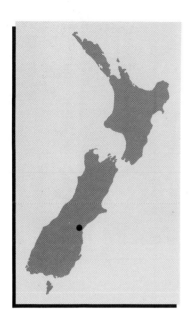

In a Land of Wheat: Timaru's Flourmills

Noel Crawford

FACING the railway in Timaru, south of the station, are a large stone store built to accommodate landing boats, and four flourmills. No other centre in New Zealand has a comparable group of early flourmills, or a landing service building. They have, together, been classified as an industrial precinct by the Historic Places Trust.

The name Timaru is possibly derived from Te Maru — 'the shelter' — referring to a shallow indentation in the coastline, where Patiti Point offered limited protection from the open sea. George Rhodes chose Timaru as the site for his first house on The Levels Station in 1851, for although it was not a natural harbour, there was sufficient shelter for him to load and off-load ships. His initial landing service was taken over by H. J. Le Cren and Capt. Henry Cain in 1857. The Provincial Government took over the service in 1866, but was unable to operate it satisfactorily, charging high rates for a poor service.

In August 1867, the dissatisfaction of runholders and merchants led to the formation of the Timaru Landing and Shipping Company, which had as promoters many of South Canterbury's leading businessmen. The company tried unsuccessfully to lease the Government

service, then leased a section on the beach at the foot of George Street, where it erected two or three modest sheds and began operating in January 1868. The adjoining section was bought in the name of Richard Turnbull, a director of the Landing Company, in June 1869, but a year later was taken over by a bank, as mortgagee. This was almost certainly a reflection on the company's rather than Turnbull's financial position, for its objective of providing as cheap a service as possible ensured that its operations were not lucrative. In September 1870 the company sold by auction its entire plant, gear and lease to Capt. Cain.

Peter McRae, owner of the nearby Club Hotel, bought the section from the bank and by early 1871 had built the original part of the present landing service building. This was a two-storeyed, hip-roofed, stone building with a 25 m facade of cut stone facing the sea and a width of 11 m. It had three portals for drawing landing boats into it. It seems likely that the Landing Company was not financially able to erect this essential large store and that it persuaded McRae, with more funds or credit available, to buy the section, build the store and lease it to the service. McRae sold the landing service building in February 1875 to the

New Zealand Loan and Mercantile Company.

Before 1876 the building was doubled in size with the erection of an addition at the rear. The New Zealand Loan and Mercantile Company erected a third, similar, though single-storeyed, addition behind the others in July 1876 to bring the building up to its present size.

In 1875 the railway was built along the shore, separating the landing service from the sea. This caused the service the inconvenience of having to operate across the line. Then in 1879, soon after construction of a breakwater began, shingle began to accumulate against the breakwater, burying both of the company's launching ways. Another had to be built. Shingle has continued to accumulate relentlessly behind the extending port works, until today the sea has moved out 400 m and numerous industrial buildings stand between the landing service building and the sea.

Landing services in Timaru ceased in 1881 after the first wharf was built. Until 1984 the landing service building was used continuously by the New Zealand Loan and Mercantile Company, then Dalgety Ltd, which took it over, for its original purpose of storing inward merchandise and wool for

▲ *The George Street Landing Service in the early 1870s. The service began on the site in 1868. The stone building, which still stands though it is now hemmed in by other buildings and several hundred metres from the sea, was built probably in the early 1870s.*

➤ *The George Street Landing Service building has survived for more than 100 years on a site now some distance from the shore. Its future is uncertain but part at least of the country's only surviving early landing service building will probably survive.*

export. Now owned by the Timaru City Council, it stands as a reminder of an important early service which, in the absence of a natural harbour, bridged the gap between ship and shore and set Timaru on the way to becoming a thriving centre.

There were earlier flourmills in South Canterbury than the four remaining in Timaru, but after railways and improved roads began to open up the countryside in the mid 1870s it became practical to build larger, centralised mills.

The freeholding of land, mostly in the 1870s, triggered a large increase in wheatgrowing and led to the erection of these mills. Once they had the security of freehold tenure, new farmers and station owners began to plough their land for the first time, growing wheat to improve returns and to improve the land itself before sowing English grasses. South Canterbury had large areas of land that were easily worked and an equable climate.

Between 1871 and 1881 the area sown in wheat in South Canterbury rose from 5300 to 24,500 ha. This was a time of good prices for wheat and almost total lack of demand for mutton. South Canterbury's wheat crop peaked at over 40,000 ha a year about 1910 and dropped to 28,500 ha in 1922. Canterbury was then producing seven-tenths of the wheat grown in New Zealand and more than half of this was grown in South Canterbury.

The Belford, the earliest of the remaining Timaru mills, was built early in 1878 by Arthur Ormsby, a local solicitor. The four-storeyed

▲ *The history of flourmilling in Timaru opened, as it did in many other New Zealand towns and cities, with a substantial windmill, shown here in a Burton Bros photograph, probably taken in the 1880s. No windmills of this age and size have survived in New Zealand.*

◄

Henry Winkelmann photographed Timaru from Chalmers Church in 1904, showing the southern side of the town dominated by large brick mill buildings and their smoking chimneys.

brick mill has a 13 m frontage onto the railway and is 7.5 m wide. Most of it is built into an excavation in the cliff side which allowed grain to be loaded into stores at third-storey level.

Originally there were three pairs of French millstones, each weighing 15 hundredweight, on the second floor and room for three more pairs. Millstones were normally about 1.5 m in diameter with the lower one fixed and the top stone turning against it crushing the wheat which was poured in

through a hole in the middle. As the wheat was ground between the two stones, carefully cut grooves in the rock guided the grain along progressively smaller channels to the outside rim.

Richard Allen, later owner of the Riccarton Roller Flourmills in Christchurch, bought the Belford Mill in 1881 and sold it in 1890 to a partnership of D.H. Brown, John Jackson, a Timaru timber merchant, and C.W. Turner, who was a merchant in Christchurch. In 1892 D.H. Brown left the part-

nership and began the flourmilling company in Christchurch which still bears his name. Turner sold his interest in 1895, leaving Jackson as the sole owner. He had the mill completely remodelled and installed a modern roller plant. Between 15 and 20 hands were employed at that time, and the Belford's 'Golden Gem' brand of flour sold well throughout New Zealand.

Jackson transferred the mill in 1904 to a private company, Belford Mills Company Ltd, in which he

The Belford Flour Mills, photographed at the turn of the century. This, the earliest of Timaru's remaining mill buildings, was built in 1878.

ALEXANDER TURNBULL LIBRARY

The Belford mill is the oldest of Timaru's surviving mill buildings. It now houses a plating business and, in an old grain store attached to the mill, a night club.

BRUCE FOSTER

retained an interest. By 1947 the mill had ceased production and was sold to New Zealand Breweries, which used it for storing barley. In 1974 it was bought by Chrome Platers Ltd which operates a plating business in the mill. The Old Mill Nightclub leases a grain store which was part of the mill, and other stores are leased for storage. Though old, the mill is still sound and is well used.

James Bruce, founder of the Timaru Milling Company's mill, operated a large sawmill in Waimate before building adjoining timber and flourmills beside the railway in Timaru in 1878. The Waitangi flourmill, four storeys high and designed by Bruce himself, had a capacity of 100 tons a week, which was large for those times. When fire destroyed it in May 1881 it was only partly insured.

Bruce was determined to rebuild his mill and to obtain the very best machinery for it. He made up several samples of New Zealand wheat and sailed to America, where he found it could be ground very efficiently by the roller system. Bruce therefore bought a complete roller mill, the first to be brought to New Zealand. In September 1882, just 16 months after the fire, he threw the mill open for all interested to see it begin operation.

The system was a resounding success and brought about a revolution in the New Zealand flour-milling industry.

The six-storeyed brick mill, built on the site of the one destroyed, is an impressive and sturdy building, which still operates without apparent modification after a century of milling. It has a 22.5 m railway frontage and extends back 36 m including a lower oatmeal department. There was also a three-storeyed grain store beside the railway. The main architectural feature is the row of circular headed windows, which give good interior lighting.

The second floor housed 17 rol-

BRUCE FOSTER

▲ *The Royal Flouring Mills build-*
ing remains in use today by the
Timaru Milling Co., founded in
1886. The building itself has
changed little. The large grain
silos behind it were built in 1956.

▶

In the early 1930s, when this pic-
ture in a booklet Come to Sunny
Timaru *was taken, the Royal*
Flouring Mills were owned by the
Timaru Milling Co. The building,
somewhat altered and added to
from when it was first built,
appears much as it still does today.

DUNEDIN PUBLIC LIBRARY

ler mills, each with two pairs of rollers. Only one of the mills was fed whole grain; the others each reduced it a little further in what was called the gradual reduction process until a very fine flour was produced. There was an excellent demand for the new 'Bruce's Silver Dust' flour. Although the mill ran day and night grinding about 250 tons of flour a week, it could not

keep up with demand. The capacity of roller mills was two or three times that of the old stone mills and most were converted to the new system as soon as possible. The Timaru mill was, and still is, one of the largest in New Zealand.

Bruce's Royal Flouring Mill began work in September 1882, but stopped again early in 1883 following the death of Julius Mendel-

sohn, Bruce's main financier. With encouragement from Bruce, a company was formed to take over the mill. The Royal Flouring and Oatmeal Mills (Bruce and Company Ltd) bought the mill in October 1883 and work resumed. Bruce continued as manager, but left in March 1885 after a dispute with the managing director. The company planned to borrow

£10,000, which Bruce felt could endanger the interest of those he had persuaded to take up shares. Bruce was dismissed, but he retained the support of share-holders. This led to the directors withdrawing their guarantee to the bank, and to the company's liquidation. The Timaru Milling Company was then formed in 1886 and took over operation of the mill.

At the turn of the century A.S. Paterson and his partner George Shirtcliffe bought a large interest in the company, which is now a subsidiary of Goodman Group Ltd. The main changes at the mill this century have been the replacement of the entire plant of the flour and oatmeal mills in 1924 and 1925, the erection in 1956 of 36.5-m-high grain silos beside the mill and diversification of the company's range of products, particularly into pasta.

After leaving the Royal Flouring and Oatmeal Company, James Bruce formed Bruce's Oatmeal Company which in 1887 built a large, five-storeyed wooden mill and its associated tall brick chimney alongside the railway, just south of his previous mill. In the first 3 months of production the drying kiln caught fire twice, but was repaired by December 1887 when the company's second annual meeting was held. Here it was stated that a further call for capital would be needed to provide necessary equipment, but when that was done the company should be profitable.

This expectation was not realised. The machinery was not entirely suited to the purpose and the market was not big enough to keep the big mill going. There were already two oatmeal mills in Otago and it was at about this time that the Timaru Milling Company opened its oatmeal plant. After running for about 6 months the mill was closed.

In October 1888, soon after the closure, a severe nor'west gale almost blew the mill over. Ropes tied around it were anchored to the base of the chimney and gradually tightened to pull the mill back to

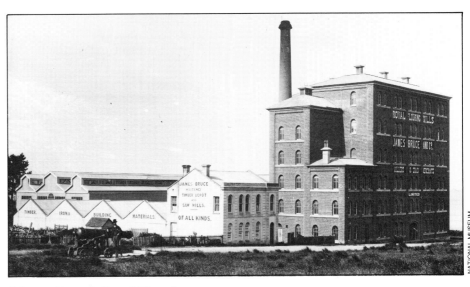

James Bruce's Royal Flouring Mills, opened in 1882, housed the first roller mill to be brought to New Zealand. This photograph was taken before the three-storeyed store was built facing the railway attached to the mill.

In the left foreground of this photograph is the tall wooden oatmeal mill which was built by James Bruce in 1887. It never operated successfully and was eventually burned down in 1904. Its chimney survived the fire and was taken over by the Timaru Borough Council for its lighting plant early this century. The chimney has only recently been demolished.

vertical. It was then strengthened by adding bracing timbers. A month later, by order of the Supreme Court, the mill was put up for auction. There were only two bidders, Bruce and the mortgagees. It went to the latter, for less than they were owed, and was never reopened.

The machinery was sold, and the mill was used occasionally for storage before being burned down in a spectacular early-morning blaze in 1904. Many spectators commented that smoke was issuing from the chimney for the first time since 1888.

Early in 1907 the chimney

The Atlas mill before the brick grain store was built alongside it, when grain brought in sacks was stacked in an open shed beside the railway line.

suddenly became important for Timaru. Because it was in sound condition, the Timaru Borough Council chose the site for an electric power generating plant. A new, single-storeyed building was erected and two steam engines and three generators were installed and operated by Scott Brothers of Christchurch. By 1915, when the Timaru Borough Council bought the plant, 128 km of streets were being lit.

Lake Coleridge, the first hydro power station in New Zealand, began operating that year, but Coleridge power did not reach Timaru until 1923. The steam-generating plant was scrapped then, but the building and old chimney remained and were used for pottery production for several years from 1935.

William Evans, founder of the Evans Atlas Mill, was an Irishman who went to the Australian gold diggings, then to Gabriels Gully where he became a storekeeper. He was then a general merchant in Hokitika, before moving to Timaru in 1875. There he bought the unoccupied Atlas foundry and set up business as a coal, grain and timber merchant.

When Evans formed the Evans Atlas Roller Mill Company in 1888 he told shareholders why he had decided to start another flourmill in Timaru. As a grain merchant he had found grain trading to be depressed. Home shipments in almost every case had shown losses. Timaru was a cheap place to manufacture flour, for besides

An early view of the Atlas Roller Flour Mills, erected by William Evans when he decided to enter the flourmilling business in Timaru in 1888. The five-storeyed mill was designed by James Hislop of Dunedin.

▲ *The Atlas Roller Flour Mills after a large brick grain and wool store had been built to one side of it in 1897. In front is a 'D' class locomotive, shunting trucks.*

▼ *The Evans Atlas Flour Mills building as it appears today from the railway line.*

▲ *J.R. Bruce's Dominion Roller Flour Mills, built in the early 1920s, is newer than Timaru's other old mills. This photograph, taken c. 1930, appeared in a booklet* Come to Sunny Timaru.

➤

J.R. Bruce's Dominion Roller Mills today. The 1920s building was burned out in 1941 but rebuilt, although the main building is not now in use.

ample wheat there was plentiful labour, a good port and railway close at hand, and coal and water were as reasonably priced as elsewhere in the colony. With prudent management, milling should pay in Timaru if anywhere.

The Evans Atlas Mill, designed by James Hislop of Dunedin, is a five-storeyed brick building. It is built against the cliff and, like the Belford, has its third-floor level with grain stores on the cliff top. Incoming wheat was therefore closer to the start of its gravity-assisted passage through the tall mills. The roller plant was supplied by Henry Simon Ltd of Manchester, an important English mill machinery firm. In 1897 a large, four-storeyed grain store, similar in style to the mill, with an imposing brick front and paired windows, was built on the south side of the mill.

The 'Atlas' brand of flour enjoyed a good demand throughout New Zealand and for a long time 30 to 40 mill hands worked in two 12-hour shifts 6 days a week. Almost 10,000 tons of flour was produced in 1914. Evans was the principal shareholder in the company, and was managing director from 1888 until he retired 42 years later in 1930 at the remarkable age of 92.

James R. Bruce, a nephew of James Bruce, worked for some years in a Temuka flourmill before becoming a grain merchant in Timaru. In 1915 he helped establish J.R. Bruce Ltd, which built a small mill, the Dominion Roller Flourmill. Although Bruce supplied the management and name, most of the capital was raised by others. John Hutchison, a Timaru baker, was chairman of directors until 1927. He was succeeded by Miss Margaret Wilson, whose name is perpetuated in a Timaru old people's home. Her father, James Wilson, and James Macauley were the other original directors.

A larger mill was built beside the original one in 1921, but production was barely under way when the new mill was destroyed by fire. It was immediately replaced with the present five-storeyed mill. Fire struck again in 1941, burning out the mill, but again it was rebuilt.

Like his uncle, J.R. Bruce was the first to introduce new equipment which was to gain acceptance throughout New Zealand. In 1922 he installed into this mill the plansifter system, which gave a purer and whiter flour than the earlier real sifters. There was keen demand for this flour.

In 1925 the company erected a biscuit factory, which employed 30 people in producing 2.5 tons of Gingernuts, Arrowroot and water biscuits a day. They were cooked while passing by conveyor belts through a long gas oven. Production was doubled with the installation of a second oven in 1927 and during World War II more than 4000 tons of biscuits were sent overseas on armed services contracts. The company went out of biscuit production in 1955, but was to continue producing flour for another 10 years.

In recent times, there have been interrelated changes involving all the mill sites except the Belford. In 1960 the Timaru Milling Company bought the oatmeal factory site and chimney for use as a stock food plant. Evans Atlas and Company merged with J.R. Bruce Ltd to form Bruce Evans Ltd in 1964, in a move intended to form a strong, locally owned company which could counter the strength of the Timaru Milling Company. However, after only 10 months Bruce Evans was taken over by A.S. Paterson and Company and in 1966 its operations were merged with those of the Timaru Milling Company.

Bruce Evans had already stopped producing flour at the J.R. Bruce Mill, concentrating on stock food production there instead. Because of this, the Timaru Milling Company transferred its stock food plant to the J.R. Bruce site in 1968 and sold the old oatmeal mill site to Hurricane Wire Products. The chimney was pulled down in 1985.

Milling ceased at the Atlas Mill in 1970 and its milling equipment was removed and sent to Wellington to fit out a new mill. Very large storage bins, which were built beside the Atlas mill in the 1950s, are now important as the company's main grain storage area. The larger J.R. Bruce flourmill is now not used, but the original mill of 1915 houses the stock food plant. Other buildings are used for storing other company products, or have been leased out.

Although wheatgrowing and flourmilling have declined in South Canterbury, the Timaru flourmills provide to this day impressive reminders of that era.

Further Reading

Andersen, J.C. *Jubilee History of South Canterbury* (Auckland 1916)

Gillespie, O.A. *South Canterbury. A Record of Settlement* (Timaru 1971, first published 1958)

Hassall, C.E. *The Port of Timaru* (Timaru 1955)

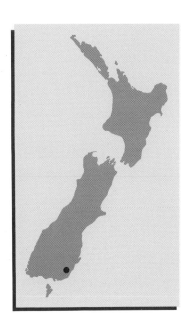

The Lifeblood of a Town: Benhar and its Pottery

Gail Lambert

TO turn off State Highway 1 just north of Balclutha and drive the 5 km to Benhar township is to step back in time. The road meanders through sheep country, often divided into fields by precise stone walls, which sets the scene for what is to come. The road drops away to the main street, lined by small, wooden, workers' cottages which form a mute guard of honour, so closely do they hug the road's verge. The town is devoid of embellishments that signify lifestyles of the 1980s. There is no theatre, no hotel, no corner dairy. The windows of the general store and post office stare blankly out onto the street. Hoardings advertising popular tea brands and cough cures were long ago souvenired and local residents no longer gather on the veranda to await eagerly the midday mail train. The building's countenance, like that of the town, has a dream-like quality.

An aerial view of Benhar taken about 1950 by Owen Hurst. The South Island Main Trunk Line enters the picture at bottom left, passes the main cluster of pottery buildings and begins to curve as it passes the pipeworks. The town lines the street which rises from the pottery works to leave the picture at top right.

The striking anomaly within this apparently sleepy township is hidden from the casual visitor. Nestled in the valley floor, at the bottom of the main street, is the Benhar Pottery, a factory which produces high quality ceramic sanitary ware for world markets. The modern technology of this successful industry has developed within the walls of buildings erected over 60 years ago.

It is a picturesque and unique village, unique in that it grew and developed around this one industry. That the factory and its associated community have survived the adversities of depression, war, geographical isolation and competition from alternative materials such as plastics, emphasises its uniqueness. Perhaps even more significant is that the adversities were overcome and the successes

▲ *Benhar and its pottery works in the late 1920s. The factory buildings are at the foot of the hill, on each side of the railway line. The 'main street' of the town itself climbs the hill, lined mostly with the simple wooden dwellings of workers in the pottery.*

▶

A general view of Benhar today, little changed since the 1920s except for the modern technology of the pottery which has seen the almost total demise of brick kiln chimney stacks. One of the clay pits on which the town's industry is based can be seen to one side of the works. The South Island Main Trunk Line still runs through Benhar, passing close to the old kiln and office and other factory buildings, but the pottery's production now leaves Benhar by road.

achieved by the efforts of one family, the McSkimmings.

Long before clay seams in the Benhar area were utilised, however, coal reserves in the valley were being mined. The Benhar Coal Company, the earliest in Otago, was established by John Nelson in 1864. Although only lignite coal, it found a ready market at 4/6 a ton with the operators of steam-powered threshing mills, used on surrounding farms, and of steamers plying the Clutha River. The

steady supply of local coal and suitable clays for pottery making, together with the completion of the rail link between Stirling and Benhar, were factors which influenced Nelson's decision to establish a pipe-making factory in 1876. During these early years of operation, staff lived in the nearby town of Stirling and walked the 4 km to work each shift.

The factory grew steadily and in 1888 Nelson expanded into brick making and flax dressing; fire-bricks, vases and pots were added to his output and staff numbers increased to 50.

Two employees at this time were to have a personal and lasting influence on the development of Benhar and its pottery industry.

Peter McSkimming, a Scotsman possessed of much drive, determination and ambition, had emigrated along with his wife and family from Glasgow in 1878, lured by the promise of riches on the Otago goldfields of Lawrence and Waitahuna. After 4 years of panning for the elusive metal, the McSkimming family moved to Stirling where Peter McSkimming and his eldest son, Peter McNish McSkimming, became contract workers for John Nelson. Within a few years they were able to lease the business and by 1894 father and son owned both mine and factory.

Impatient to improve and increase production, McSkimming wasted no time in advertising 'back home' in Scotland for experienced

▲ *Dressed in their Sunday best, workers and management alike enjoy the company picnic. The picnic was an annual event on which no expense was spared. Everyone was transported to destinations like Mount Stuart and Taieri Mouth on company trucks. This group was photographed some time before 1923, the year of Peter McSkimming senior's death. He is the elderly gentleman with a white beard in the centre rear of the photograph.*

▼ *Although domestic pottery was produced at Benhar, the main production was sanitary ware. This photograph was taken in the slip casting area of the factory in the late 1920s. In the left foreground are slip cast moulds for lavatory pans.*

clay workers. He also wrote to relatives working in Scottish potteries, offering them work in his Otago factory. Realising the need to diversify, in 1907 he sent his son-in-law, Parker McKinlay, a man who had a formative influence on McSkimming Industries, to England to investigate the feasibility of moving into the manufacture of sanitary ware. At that time British potteries jealously guarded their processes and recipes and Parker recorded in his diary that a cold shoulder was the usual response to the enquirer. However, he somehow managed to obtain the necessary assistance and brought back to Benhar glaze and body recipes which enabled the sanitary ware section of the factory to commence production in 1908 using a muffle kiln to fire the wares. By 1912 staff in this section of the factory had increased to 30. The decision to specialise in sanitary ware proved an astute one and is a major reason that the factory still continues successfully in the 1980s.

The amalgamation in 1917 between McSkimmings and two ceramic enterprises owned by James H. Lambert (Water of Leith Brick and Tile Works, Dunedin) and Thomas Todd (Woodlands and Waikiwi, Southland) ensured the continuing development of the company. Two years later Abbotsford Tileries joined up and shortly afterwards the Wingatui Brick Company came into the fold. A successful new line introduced in 1922 was acid bricks. For quite some years, the firm was the only supplier of this product in New Zealand.

Serious attempts to produce domestic pottery at the factory were first made in 1890 when two potters named Phillips were employed to make such items as jam jars, basins, jugs, crocks and teapots. Production lasted only a short time, as the factory was unable to compete with imported wares in price or quality. Despite this and several other abortive attempts to produce domestic lines, McSkimming remained convinced that manufacturing domestic ware could be viable. In

Marjorie Marshall painted the Benhar potteries probably in the 1930s.

1921 Parker McKinlay was once again sent to Britain, this time to spend a year attending the pottery school at Stoke-on-Trent. Here he was able to confer with architects, engineers, potters and glazers, to gain knowledge which would enable the company to set up a domestic pottery section at Benhar. Before returning to New Zealand he engaged as pottery division manager Thomas Norman Lovatt, an experienced craftsman from the Lovatt and Lovatt factory in England. Lovatt arrived at Benhar in 1922 and immediately set about preparing plaster moulds and

training staff in slip casting techniques. Additional bottle kilns and buildings had been erected in readiness and by 1922 a variety of pottery was being made. However, following the resignation of Lovatt in 1925, domestic pottery production declined to become eventually a small sideline.

An article in the *Clutha Leader* in 1923 indicates the extent of the firm's holdings at that stage — 200 ha for clay resources, a family farm running 70 to 80 cows, the coal mine employing eight miners and producing 10,000 tons annually and eight downdraught kilns

operating at the factory. At the time of the article the pottery was constructing a new sanitary ware building with the name 'Benhar Pottery' built into the end gable in white glazed bricks so as to be visible to passing rail passengers. This building is still part of the factory today. It was on moving into this complex that new technology for making sanitary ware was introduced. With the change from press moulding to slip casting, production increased dramatically. Two years later another major step into the twentieth century was made at Benhar when

The railway siding at Benhar was situated beside the pipeworks. The salt-glazed conduit pipes used to support the loading dock are visible in the picture. Workers are loading sanitary pans into railway trucks using straw as packing. The building behind the trucks was part of the pipeworks which ceased production in the mid 1960s and was demolished, along with several remaining bottle kilns, in 1982.

electricity was installed.

Although work seemed to be going well and the firm received a prize at the Dunedin South Seas Exhibition in 1925–26, production was not without its problems. A rather terse telegram from the Hutt Valley Horticultural Society in April 1926 referred to an order of specimen vases: 'Spills (vases) very unsatisfactory, breakages heavy, workmanship disgraceful, writing'.

Following the outbreak of World War II the factory was declared an essential industry. During these difficult years many jobs in the factory were mastered by women manpowered to the industry. Domestic pottery was once again made, as import restrictions on non-essential goods created a demand for items such as electric jugs and mixing bowls.

The men unable to board the troop ships for the battlefields of North Africa and the Pacific formed the Benhar Home Guard to protect the town in the event of an invasion. For the men, the Home Guard was a serious responsibility. For the women of the town it provided welcome light relief. They could scarcely conceal their mirth at the sight of their menfolk's clumsy attempts to drill in the long grass of the back paddock, sporting broom handles for rifles, many having great difficulty distinguishing their left from their right foot.

Since World War II the fortunes of the company have fluctuated. In the main, the problems have been the same as those faced by others in the clay industry in New Zealand — of keeping pace with overseas technology and of attempting to retain tariff protection, so as to be able to compete with imported wares. Transport costs were a particular problem facing McSkimmings as a South Island firm. Today all wares are transported out of Benhar by road although the rail line runs through the town's centre.

The town of Benhar seems to have begun to develop in the early years of this century, coinciding with the growth of the factory. As the numbers of workers increased, the demand for housing probably exceeded the supply in the nearby town of Stirling. Many of the workers found the trek home to Stirling by foot or cycle exhausting after the long hours of shift work. The increasing success of the factory meant that the McSkimmings had sufficient means gradually to build houses for their employees.

The first house occupied by Peter McSkimming senior still survives on the far side of Snake Gully, a road which loops around to the side of the township. (The name Snake Gully was bestowed by locals after the fictional community of the long running Australian radio show 'Dad and Dave'.) Peter McSkimming's first house is a simple, four-roomed wooden dwelling with no central passage, the front door opening directly into the living room. The bathroom and wash house were located in an out house.

Gradually similar houses dotted the valley, most of them rented to employees although several workers purchased their homes, including Jim Parker, who added a room and veranda to the front of his house and opened a general store and post office. Now unoccupied, this house stands opposite the brick church on the main street of Benhar. In the 1920s a group of portable homes, made by Loves of Dunedin, were brought to Benhar in two halves and erected on the bottom side of Snake Gully. By 1908 there were sufficient local residents to band together and build a multi-purpose wooden hall cum church, with assistance from the company.

In April 1909 the Benhar School opened in the hall with a roll of 27. In the following year a school committee was formed. As the roll rose steadily, the committee requested a schoolroom from the Education Board. This was opened in September 1921. The following year a schoolhouse was added. All those living in Benhar had a common bond, with their livelihood dependent on the fortunes of

Benhar's finest house, Lesma-hagow, was built in 1914 by Peter McSkimming senior and his wife. They named the house after their home town in Scotland and laid out around it gardens of legendary beauty. While the gardens have lost most of their former glory, the house and brick pergola remain impressive.

ROSS COOMBES

ROSS COOMBES

▲ *A detail of the brickwork and terracotta decoration, with Scottish motif, on the side of Lesmahagow.*

the factory. Self-sufficiency seems to have been a byword for the school committee and pupils. Extensive landscaping and planting won them several awards for having the most attractive school grounds. Pupils held concerts, raised chickens and sold eggs, built a glasshouse and grew tomatoes for sale, activities which enabled the school to establish its own library and tennis court, astounding achievements for such a small community.

The roll at Benhar School rose and fell with the fortunes of the factory. It survived several attempts to have it closed and the pupils transferred to Balclutha School. Long-time residents of the town watched with mixed emotions as the old wooden school was demolished after being replaced in 1982–83.

By 1914, with the business on sound footing, Peter McSkimming senior and his wife had a new home built. Called 'Lesmahagow' after

his home town in Scotland, it stands on the top of the hill overlooking Benhar. A brick home with an almost 'Spanish villa' appearance, the house in its heyday is best remembered for its fine gardens. Two gardeners were employed to build an extensive brick pergola, a sunken rose garden, a croquet lawn and a tennis court and to plant out borders. At the rear of the house, three glasshouses were heated by steam pipes fuelled by an insatiable boiler. The perfection of the flowers and succulence of the tomatoes is legendary. Today the pergola still supports wisteria planted over 60 years ago and the outlines of the flower beds are still evident, gradually being returned to their former splendour by the present owners.

The other home of substance in Benhar was built by Parker McKinlay. Known as 'Bainsford' it can still be glimpsed to the left of the road which winds its way across the valley floor towards Stirling. It too

is remembered for its resplendent gardens. In stark contrast a group of brick houses built just below 'Lesmahagow' on the right side of the road as you enter the town were nicknamed 'Rotten Row' by the locals, so poorly were they constructed in the lean years of the 1930s.

During the 1950s a group of houses were transported from the sawmilling town of Glenomaru and relocated on the top side of Snake Gully. The most impressive building erected by the McSkimmings was a hostel built about 1939. Located in Snake Gully, it was a two-storeyed brick building, constructed to meet an accommodation shortage during World War II when the factory was declared an essential industry. It was accidentally burnt out and subsequently demolished in the late 1970s.

A long-time dream of the McSkimming family and many other residents of Benhar to build

ROSS COOMBES

The continuous kiln is one of the finest of Benhar's older industrial buildings, but it is now gutted and used as a workshop.

a new church was finally realised in 1952. A family of strong religious convictions, the McSkimmings had never felt comfortable with using the original church for other activities. But plans to build a church were delayed, first by the outbreak of World War I, then by the Depression, which was followed by World War II. Finally, a builder from Balclutha erected the church using mosaic bricks from the Abbotsford factory. A Sunday school room was built into the basement. It was a moving occasion in the village when the Rev. F. Barton blessed and opened the church. Those who listened outside, sheltering under umbrellas, were unaffected by the rain,

proud to know that they had contributed much of the finance to build the church.

It is somewhat ironic that the building of the kirk came at a time when the social patterns of the town were changing. The community had worked together and, despite long and arduous shift hours, created its own leisure activities. These included debating, a black and white minstrel group and various sports teams. The residents welcomed new families with a morning tea and quickly made them feel a part of the community, regardless of their position in the factory or mines. The intimate social structure of the little town began to crumble in the 1950s as itinerant workers came in to work at the pottery. Unsettled in spirit, these displaced persons from many different countries wrought lasting changes on the

town, which was never to revert to what many of the old-timers recall as halcyon days.

Benhar has often been described as a 'feudal' township, with its founder as its laird. It is, in fact, probably the only town surviving in New Zealand that was established using concepts translocated half way across the world, those of the social system associated with nineteenth-century English industrialism. Undoubtedly McSkimming's fiercely independent nature and uncompromisingly strict moral standards had a strong effect on the town. But his reasons for establishing the township around his business seem to have been practical, born of economic necessity, rather than feudal or paternalistic. The isolated location of the factory must have made it difficult to attract and retain staff and to entice skilled workers from Britain, vital if the business was to progress. To know that they were coming to a job and a roof over their heads must have encouraged many.

McSkimming imposed stern standards on the town, insisting that staff attend kirk each Sunday and discouraging smoking by docking a shilling from the wages of 'culprits'. Such practices perhaps stemmed from a wish to establish a core of permanent skilled workers who would provide strong moral foundations for a community. If some felt rebellious about strictures imposed on their personal lives, many others accepted these, knowing that there would always be fuel to warm their hearth in winter or a pot of paint for their house when it was needed. Although a strict disciplinarian, McSkimming inspired loyalty in many. He never failed to visit a family with a newborn child and to leave a £5 note in the cradle. Everyone was encouraged to keep a house cow and to graze it on the McSkimmings' farm. A community byre was provided for milking.

In later years, the company established the first reticulated water supply in the area. The reservoir, situated at the top of the hill coming into the town, was built late in 1945. It supplied water to both Benhar and Stirling. This ready supply of water enabled the company to establish its own fire brigade. A staff member was sent to Auckland for firefighting training and the engine was housed in an old garage opposite the pipe factory.

The relationship between this family and its employees has endured many hardships and seen many changes. Coal-fired bottle kilns have given place to modern tunnel kilns fired by LPG. Quality control has become a scientific exercise instead of rule-of-thumb guessing. The township itself has come a full circle. At the turn of the century staff lived in Stirling from necessity as the township of Benhar did not exist. Today workers once again prefer to commute, now from nearby Balclutha. Modern roads and vehicles make the distance insignificant and the larger town offers trappings of modern society not available in Benhar.

The future of Benhar the town is in question but the pottery continues to thrive. The inability of the town to change is the reason why it is now a ghost of its former self; McSkimming Industries, the firm, has adapted and the future of the factory seems secure. Since its takeover by Ceramco in 1980, the pottery has been linked to a West German ceramics conglomerate, Villeroy and Boch, and now produces that firm's prestige range of sanitary ware, mainly for the Australian market. This gives the firm international support at a time when the Industries Development Commission has recommended withdrawing protection against imported pottery wares, a decision many believe could toll the death knell for the pottery industry in New Zealand. Whatever lies ahead for this company, its future seems more secure than that of the town to which it gave birth. Benhar township, its purpose for life apparently gone, is, sadly, unlikely to survive.

Further Reading

Lambert, G. 'A Family of Potters', *The Summer Book 2* (Wellington 1983)

Lambert, G. *Pottery in New Zealand: Commercial and Collectable* (Auckland 1985)

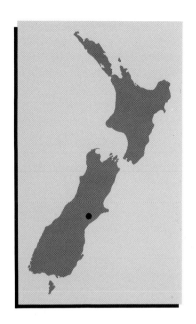

'The Mushroom of the Plains': Ashburton Builds in Brick

Michael Hanrahan

KNOWN in its earliest years as 'The Mushroom of the Plains' because of the speed at which it grew from just a single building, Ashburton had by 1882 reached the stage where a Christchurch journalist could say that 'the era of rickety new buildings had passed'. Substantial brick and stone buildings were replacing many of the original jerry-built buildings and were giving the town the beginning of the air of solidity it has today.

While the view of the commercial area from the main street no longer provides much evidence of the use of brick, thanks to modernisation and the liberal use of plaster and paint, the rear of these same buildings in places presents an imposing brickscape and illustrates that Ashburton at one time had the highest per capita use of bricks in New Zealand.

The use of brick in Ashburton has declined in recent years with the advent of the ubiquitous concrete block and Summerhill stone, together with the closing of the last local brickworks in 1978, but bricks made in other centres are still used and quite an industry has developed reclaiming bricks from demolished buildings for reuse in new ones.

Before European settlement, the area that is now the Ashburton County was virtually a wasteland. In 1844 one of the first Europeans to travel through the area, Bishop Selwyn, described the country between the Rakaia and Ashburton rivers as 'a dry and gravelly plain'. People travelling across the plain, especially those travelling north, would rest overnight at the Ashburton River before beginning the long trek to the next water source.

Why Ashburton turned to brick, at least in the early days, is not hard to explain. The earliest houses, or huts, built by squatters and the first runholders during the 1850s, were rude affairs of wattle and daub, thatched with tussock, with the chimney often just a hole in the roof.

The nearest source of building timber was Alford Forest, some 40 km from the site of Ashburton, situated in the foothills between the two branches of the Ashburton River. Without roads, timber wasn't easily obtained from this source. In 1855 one squatter reported that he and a companion had been lost in a snowstorm for 2 days while on their way to Alford Forest for timber and that they had to navigate by the feel of the wind on their faces.

The site of Ashburton was chosen by William Turton and a Government agent as the most suitable place for a river crossing. It was downstream from the confluence of the two branches of the river, but inland from the swamp which stretched to the coast on its south side. However, it was a very long way from the source of building timber at Alford Forest.

Turton had other problems besides distance in obtaining timber for the accommodation house he and his brothers built at the river crossing. After bringing one load of sawn timber back from Alford Forest, they found, on their return for a second load, that the remainder had been burnt in the bush while they were away. After that experience, they carted squared logs back and sawed them on the site of the accommodation house.

This accommodation house saw brick enter onto the Ashburton building scene. Suitable clay was found on the North Branch of the Ashburton River and bricks for the accommodation house chimneys were burnt at that spot in 1858; these were the first bricks made in the area.

Timber, despite its local scarcity, remained a relatively common building material in the area. Timbers such as kauri were brought in from other areas to be used along with the local timbers. A railway line was laid to the mineral-rich Mount Somers area in

BRUCE FOSTER

The 12-chamber circular kiln at Crum's brickworks had been producing bricks for almost 100 years when the brickworks closed down in 1978. Although it is an important industrial monument in Ashburton its condition is poor and its future uncertain. It will probably be demolished.

1886, allowing timber to be transported more easily from the foothills and also giving access to the stone quarries at Mount Somers. By 1887 large quantities of stone were being sent from Mount Somers to other places, especially Melbourne and Napier. The stone was described as 'the finest stone produceable to work in New Zealand'. It was likened to white marble, capable of receiving a highly polished surface. Production in the late 1880s ran at between 150 and 200 tons per week with the bulk of the output being shipped to Australia.

In spite of the source being close at hand, little of this building stone was used in Ashburton, probably because of the expense. The only significant building of Mount Somers stone in the town was St Stephen's Anglican Church, built in 1876 and demolished in 1963, the stone for which was donated by C. P. Cox. Concrete was also used to a limited extent. One of the more notable concrete buildings was the Holy Name Catholic Church, built in 1882 and demolished in 1931.

Brick remained the most common permanent building material because clay was readily available. The first brickmakers were itinerant, moving to a suitable source of clay near the new building and making the bricks on the site. One of the more notable of these was Ben Ede. He made some of the first bricks for the Lyttelton rail tunnel and then moved south under contract to J. B. Acland and C. B. Tripp to make the bricks for the Mount Peel homestead. He bought a section in Ashburton County in 1864 and settled his wife and family

there while he continued brickmaking.

The next stage of brickmaking saw the establishment of permanent brickworks with large kilns. About 1880 one of the earliest of these was built in Creek Road with a 12 chamber circular Hoffman kiln. Hugo, Max and Rudolph Friedlander bought this brickworks in February 1882 from Montgomery and Company. Montgomery had owned the land for less than one year, although he must have built the kiln before this as the hospital was built beginning in late 1879 from Montgomery bricks.

In 1895, Albert Crum bought this business, known as the Kolmar Brickworks, from Friedlander Brothers. Albert's father, John Crum, had in 1878 set up in trade in Ashburton as a bricklayer. He is recorded as having made his own bricks, apparently on a site near Beach Road, in competition with the existing brickmakers. Albert Crum modernised the works, installing a steam engine in 1902 to replace the existing hand and horse power. Clay was obtained from the surrounding land and, initially,

barrowed to the machine. Later a horse tramway was used.

The kiln had a capacity of 60,000 bricks with an output of 25–30,000 per week, enough to build five houses. During the building boom after World War II, when many brick houses were being built, the fire burnt continuously for 13 years. Many other items were produced, including chimney pots, field pipes for drainage, plain pipes and specially moulded bricks for architectural features. Many bricks went to Christchurch from this works for factories and houses. They were also used to line the Otira Tunnel and later in the building of the Princess Margaret Hospital, Christchurch.

By 1966 the 8 ha of clay pits surrounding the works had been worked out to a depth of 2.5 m. Attempts to obtain more land nearby for clay were blocked by the local authorities. By 1973 it looked as though there would be no option but to close down. A further year's production was made possible by using clay from excavations for a community swimming pool near the works, and then for three years clay was brought some distance by

▲ *The grandest of Ashburton's old brick public buildings was certainly the post office, built in 1901 and demolished in 1963. This 1904 photograph views the 3-year-old building across the main south railway line and road which bisect the town. The round roof to the left of the Post Office is the Radiant Hall, serving, in 1904, as a livery stable.*

◄

One of the more charming of the several public buildings built of brick in Ashburton at the turn of the century was the borough's public library. For most of its life the building served as the Borough Council Chambers. This photograph of the now demolished building was taken in 1904.

truck from Mount Somers. This costly operation was made possible by the demand from as far away as Auckland for clinker bricks, which were not made elsewhere. Clinker bricks, originally made unintentionally by overburning bricks in the kiln, became prized for their decorative effect and were later made deliberately.

In 1978 Crum's brickworks closed, bringing to an end the production of bricks in Ashburton. Some of the bricks produced in the final year were used to pave Baring Square, the town's centennial project, a fitting tribute to an industry which helped to build much of the town. The kiln still stands, its future uncertain. The

chimney has a distinct lean and the walls are cracked. While it appears likely that this last reminder of brickmaking in the town will soon go, hundreds of brick buildings still standing provide tangible evidence of the size of the industry.

Three other major brickworks were built in the area, but none outlived Crum's works. In 1875 Alfred Saunders decided to build a flourmill in the town and obtained the services of a brickmaker named Thomas Andrews to make the channels for the mill. Andrews had been a stone carver on the Christchurch Cathedral, a trade he had learnt from his father at the age of 9. He brought his two eldest sons, George and Albert, to Ashburton

with him. He established a brickworks on the west side of Eton Street between Wellington and Nelson streets. The date of this is uncertain, but would have been in the late 1870s or early 1880s. This works was in production until the turn of the century when the clay surrounding the works gave out.

About 1900 a new brickworks was built in Nixon Street (at that time called Brickfield Street) in Tinwald by Thomas Andrews's son Albert. The Tinwald kiln was a circular kiln of the Hoffman type. This works was purchased by Crums in the late 1920s but it does not appear to have been working at that time. It is believed that the clay in the area was unsuitable for

▲►
Two early twentieth-century brick school buildings erected in Ashburton were the High School (above) and Technical School (right). The buildings of the High School have been demolished, the rectory (to the left of the main building) in the late 1950s and the main building in the 1960s, but the Technical School has been retained and now serves Ashburton as the town museum.

brickmaking. The kiln was demolished and the bricks from it used to pave the Atlantic Oil Company yard in West Street.

John Grigg of Longbeach built a kiln on Surveyors Road in 1887, primarily to produce pipes for the draining of the swampy land to the south of Ashburton. The bricks for the second Longbeach homestead and other buildings were made there as were those for some other homes in the district. The Eiffel Tower was built in Paris about the same time as this brickworks and the height of the kiln's chimney above the otherwise flat landscape led to the district being called Eiffelton. The brickmaker at this works was James Hillyer. A statue of John Grigg in Baring Square in Ashburton shows him with his foot resting on a drainage pipe, a reminder of the work he did in draining the swamp land using pipes made in the Eiffelton

brickworks.

Several other brickmakers were working in Ashburton from the 1880s to the early twentieth century. While most were probably employed at one of the main works, some may have operated on a smaller scale as itinerant brickmakers. They included Stephen Potter, Henry and William Shears, and Benjamin Haines.

While Ashburton still boasts many fine brick buildings, several brick public buildings have been demolished in recent years. These include the post office (1901–63), the borough school, the borough council offices (1884–1971), the old high school buildings and the fire station built in the 1870s. In spite of these losses, many interesting buildings remain. In particular, two groups of buildings, the hospital and the Catholic church, each with a variety of brick buildings, provide interesting examples of

changes in style over the years.

The oldest part of the hospital dates from 1880. It was the first brick building of public character to be erected in Ashburton. Rather more prosaically, it later became one of the first buildings in New Zealand to be equipped with septic tanks. In recent years some ornamentation has been removed from this building, but enough remains to recall its original Elizabethan-style architecture. Adjacent to this building, a two-storeyed superintendent's house was built in the late 1940s. Chalmers Ward, donated by Miss Jane Chalmers, was opened in 1924. In the early 1970s a new brick maternity ward was opened. Its clean modern lines contrast with the older hospital buildings. Other hospital buildings are also interesting. One, the mortuary, with its distinctive windows, has the appearance of a small chapel. During redevelopment over the next few

▲*Several old brick buildings, some dating back more than 100 years, are still standing at the Ashburton Hospital, but most are slated for demolition. This is an early twentieth-century view of some of the oldest buildings of the hospital group.*

▼*Tuarangi Home, built in 1902, was only 2 years old when this picture was taken of it. It was built as an old men's home and is still standing, though some embellishments, such as the battlements on the tower, have not survived.*

years most of the present hospital buildings will be demolished.

Elsewhere in the town, but associated with the hospital, Tuarangi Home was built in 1902 as an old men's home. It has a three-storeyed tower which was once graced with battlements. The former Malvern Hospital, now converted to other uses, was a private nursing home until it was taken over by the hospital board in 1922.

The other large group of brick buildings in Ashburton, is the Catholic church. Its six main buildings all replaced earlier structures. The ornate, two-storeyed presbytery opened in 1907 is the oldest. Opened in 1931, the Lombardy style Church of the Holy Name is one of the town's most distinctive buildings, besides being one of the highest. Designed by H.St.A. Murray, it has a massive

square tower and the walls are in places five bricks thick. The exterior of its rounded sanctuary wall has been described as one of the finest examples of rounded brickwork in the country.

St Joseph's School was built in 1950. It presents a plain and businesslike appearance, with no excess of decoration. The two-storeyed convent opened in 1959 has a little more embellishment.

BRUCE FOSTER

▲*Probably the finest of Ashburton's brick buildings is the Catholic Church of the Holy Name, designed by H.St.A. Murray and opened in 1931. Its companion is the presbytery, built in 1907.*

BRUCE FOSTER

◄ *The superb brickwork on the Church of the Holy Name is especially evident at the building's rear. The rounded sanctuary wall has been particularly admired by architectural historians.*

▲ *The presbytery, which stands beside the Church of the Holy Name is itself one of the finest of Ashburton's several large brick houses. Built in 1907, it is almost 25 years older than the church.*

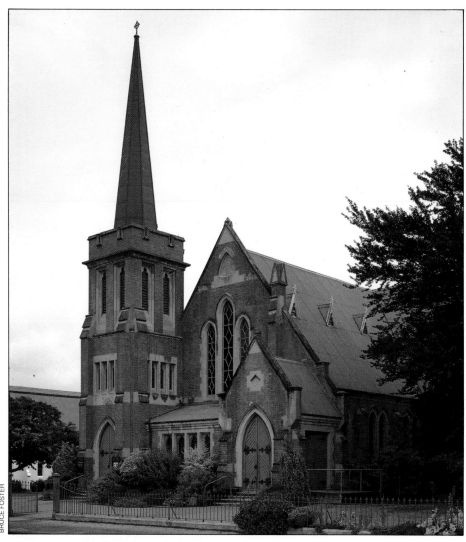

▲ *Ashburton's oldest brick church, St Andrew's Presbyterian, was built in 1907. It is a conventional Gothic building, like the great majority of New Zealand's churches of all ages, sizes and materials, but appealing despite its conventionality.*

▼ *Of the many commercial premises built of brick in 'downtown' Ashburton, the Westpac Bank, built in 1898 in a restrained classical style, is one of the better maintained. Many have been altered with scant regard for their architecture, some in very recent years.*

Another school building and the parish community centre, formerly a classroom block, both date from the 1960s and can only be described as utilitarian in appearance.

Most of the town's major churches are, like the Church of the Holy Name, built in brick. Adjacent to the Catholic Church, St Andrew's Presbyterian Church, built in 1907, is the oldest brick church in Ashburton. The building's steeply pitched roof and many changes of roofline make it one of the more interesting churches in the town. Other examples of brick churches that stand out are the Baring Square Methodist Church, designed by E.H. Gabites and built in 1926, and the Baptist Church, built in 1930. Brick churches in more modern styles in outlying areas are St David's, Allenton, and St Paul's, Hampstead.

Commercial buildings of brick are numerous, although many have been shorn of ornamentation and many more are now hidden behind modernised frontages. One of the oldest, Bullocks Arcade, was built in stages between 1882 and 1891 as a venue for horse and wool sales as well as offices and shops. Its curved roof is supported by laminated wooden beams, an advanced technique for its time. It has recently been modernised to the point where it is almost impossible to realise that it is in fact a brick building. The former Radiant Hall — another curved-roof building of a type once common in the town — was built in 1882 by Edward Cookson as a livery stable. It was considered one of the finest livery stables in the country. It later became the Scottish Society Hall, but is now used for commercial purposes.

Two major two-storeyed commercial buildings have been more sympathetically altered and better maintained. The Westpac Bank in Burnett Street, built in 1898 with bricks from the Eton Street brickworks, presents pleasing views from all angles, although the pleasant enclosed garden it used to have has now given way to a car park. In West Street the former

Bank of Australasia building, built about the turn of the century, is now occupied by Federated Farmers. Additions to it, although much more modern, blend in well.

A little brick building in Havelock Street has probably suffered more changes of use than most buildings. It started life as an office, later became women's rest rooms, still later the town's museum, then again an office, and is now a drop-in centre for Birthright. The Ashburton Club and M.S.A. (Mutual School of Arts) in Burnett Street is one of the few buildings in the town built of other than standard red brick. It is a handsome, two-storeyed building with large, rounded bay windows at one end. It is built of yellow, salt-glazed bricks from Glentunnel. The Plunket Rooms are of an unusual design, with one side circular, and are also unusual for Ashburton in having walls half brick and half roughcast.

Ashburton has never been a major industrial centre, but has supported a number of industries over the years and many of these have operated from brick buildings. Many of these buildings remain, although few date from later than World War II. The largest industrial complex is the Fairton freezing works, a short distance north of the town. The first buildings were erected there in 1889, although it is, of course, much extended now, with almost all buildings being brick. The former Alford Forest woollen mill is a similar complex featuring a variety of functional brick buildings. Established in 1885, it was enlarged in 1900, and also has many later additions.

Crum's brick kiln itself is the town's oldest brick industrial building still standing. Adjacent to it is a two-storeyed building which housed the brickworks's steam engine and blacksmith's shop. For a purely functional building, it has some interesting brickwork above the doors and windows.

In the late 1920s an attempt was made to establish a glassmaking industry in Ashburton using silica

One of Ashburton's finest brick industrial buildings was erected in the late 1920s as a glassworks. But the industry failed after functioning for only a few weeks and the building has since been used for storage purposes.

One of the houses in Ashburton associated with the Crum family, which owned the town's longest lasting brickworks, is the brick bay villa at 19 Wakanui Road. Plans for the house were drawn by the Ashburton architect Harry E. Vincent. The house has been re-roofed and had its bargeboards replaced, but appears otherwise much as it does in the architect's original drawings.

BRUCE FOSTER

Another house associated with members of the Crum family is the rather larger brick bay villa at 50 Bridge Street. Like 19 Wakanui Road it dates probably from the early years of this century.

BRUCE FOSTER

Brigadoon, in Tinwald, is one of the Ashburton area's grandest brick houses. The house is now a restaurant and reception centre and has been unobtrusively added to.

sand from Mount Somers. A large brick building was built just north of the town to be used as a glassworks. The industry failed after the works had functioned for only a few weeks. The buildings lay idle for many years until they were converted for use as a grain store, with very little change to their appearance. The main building has a high clerestory roof and is dominated by a large concrete chimney.

Few industrial buildings have been built in brick in recent years. Tilt slabs and steel have proved to be more versatile and economic, although often lacking in character.

By far the greater number of brick buildings in the town are houses. Most have been built since 1950. In 1902 the town had only 471 houses, an increase of 242 from 1881 when the first census of the town was taken. Most were small — the number with six or more rooms increased from 46 in 1881 to 127 in 1902. Few of these were built of brick, but some early brick houses remain. A large brick bungalow in Short Street has a very decorative veranda. In the Wakanui Road area are two small, two-storeyed brick houses and an elegant brick bay villa of a style common throughout the country in wood, but only rarely seen in brick. These three houses all had connections with the Crum family.

Some of the houses belonging to churches and professional people were built of brick and were often two storeyed. The Catholic presbytery and hospital superintendent's house have already been mentioned. The former vicarage in Burnett Street and a former doctor's house almost immediately opposite are others of this type. So is Brigadoon, now a restaurant, in Tinwald.

There are some examples in Ashburton of brick houses built between the two wars but these are not numerous. Today, reclaimed bricks from demolished buildings are being used for new residences and other buildings. While the work involved in cleaning these bricks can be arduous, the effect is pleasing.

In the rural areas there are practically no examples of pre-World War II brick houses except in the area near the Eiffelton brickworks. This reflects the state of the farming industry prior to the 1950s, brick being a more expensive material than wood. However, in the last 30 years most new rural houses have been built with brick.

The use of brick in structures other than buildings in Ashburton must not be overlooked. Most brick chimneys belonging to factories have long been demolished, the sole remaining examples being at the brickworks, at Tuckers joinery factory and an isolated chimney on Wills Street. The long brick wall along the West Street frontage of the Domain, built by unemployed labour in the late 1920s, is a landmark and an excellent example of this type of work. Its demolition was recently proposed, but it has received a stay of execution and had storm damage dating from 1975 repaired.

With its variety of types of brick buildings, built over a long period of time, Ashburton should appeal to those interested in the different ways brick has been used for construction and adornment over the years. Much can be seen in a relatively small area, in spite of the losses by way of demolition. The town is not noted for preserving its old buildings, so with brick construction now having slowed down, its distinctive appearance as a red brick town will in all probability one day largely disappear.

Further Reading

Ashburton Borough Council *Our Heritage* (Ashburton 1978)

Bayliss, E.R. *Tinwald. A Canterbury Plains Settlement* (Tinwald 1970)

Hewson, A. *Early Days in Ashburton County* (Ashburton 1918)

Scotter, W.H. *Ashburton* (Ashburton 1972)

'This Really Noble Thoroughfare': Princes Street and Albert Park

Wynne Colgan

THE area of present-day Princes Street and Albert Park is the site of a volcano that erupted possibly more than 60,000 years ago. The Maori knew it as Rangipuke (Hill of the Sky). Of Maori occupation, however, there appears to be little evidence, although a pa is known to have existed on the headland above the Waitemata Harbour.

As David Rough, the first harbourmaster, remembered: 'It was here on Flagstaff Point on September 18th 1840, in the presence of all the Europeans and Natives assembled round, that I had the pleasure of running up the British colours for the first time in Auckland.' Several weeks after that auspicious spring afternoon, the Surveyor-General, Felton Mathew, produced his plan for the capital, little of which was to come to pass. He did, however, designate the historic clifftop 'Pt Britomart (Flag Staff)' in honour of the surveying brig of that name. The thoroughfare running inland from it he named 'Prince Street'.

Locally, 'Point' Britomart soon came to be called 'Fort' Britomart as Governor William Hobson, fearful of attack on the town by some of the many Maori tribes which had not signed the Treaty of Waitangi of February 1840, ordered a military barracks erected

on the headland. By January 1842 the work was completed. Major Thomas Bunbury, in command of the 80th Regiment of the Imperial troops, described them as forming:

> ... two sides of a square, one side containing two stories, was loop-holed, and was capable of containing two hundred men. The building was of stone, built on a tongue of land separated from the mainland by a broad, deep ditch and parapet. It had evidently at some time or other been a fort of the natives. The entrance was across the ditch, a part of the parapet having been thrown down to fill it up for that purpose.

Clearly this was the site of the pa of earlier days. Second only to Government House, Fort Britomart was to become Auckland's social centre in the 1840s. Balls were held there, its barracks square was a meeting place for the townsfolk and plays were frequently performed in its military theatre.

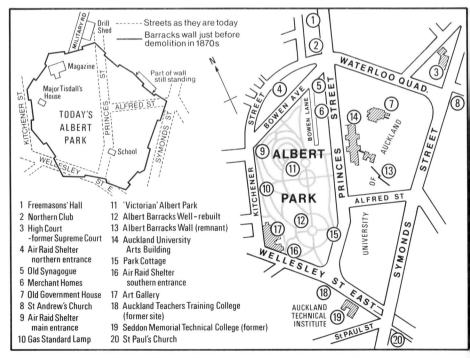

1 Freemasons' Hall
2 Northern Club
3 High Court -former Supreme Court
4 Air Raid Shelter northern entrance
5 Old Synagogue
6 Merchant Homes
7 Old Government House
8 St Andrew's Church
9 Air Raid Shelter main entrance
10 Gas Standard Lamp
11 'Victorian' Albert Park
12 Albert Barracks Well – rebuilt
13 Albert Barracks Wall (remnant)
14 Auckland University Arts Building
15 Park Cottage
16 Air Raid Shelter southern entrance
17 Art Gallery
18 Auckland Teachers Training College (former site)
19 Seddon Memorial Technical College (former)
20 St Paul's Church

From military barracks to park and university.

Within the walls of the Albert Barracks in the 1860s, men in military uniform pose along with others in civilian dress amid the accoutrements of war. Behind them, to the left, is the military store.

From 1842 Auckland began to take shape as a town, fanning out from the barracks on three sides. To the west, 'Fore' Street, the original trading area on the foreshore of Commercial Bay at the foot of today's Queen Street, came to be known as 'Fort' Street because of its link with the barracks on the hill above it. Eastwards, the artisans or 'mechanics' set themselves up in Mechanics Bay to work in Niccol's shipyards, Robertson's rope-walk or Low and Motion's flourmill. By day officialdom largely occupied the high land between the two bays. Off-duty, administrators like the Colonial Secretary, the Surveyor-General

and the Colonial Treasurer, along with those aspiring to their rank, retired to their framed wooden houses in the quiet of little Official Bay just east of the Fort.

Inland from the barracks the Anglican church of St Paul was under construction in 1842. Completed in 1843, it was consecrated a year later by Bishop Selwyn as the Metropolitan Church of Auckland. It was the town's most substantial building to that time. Built of bricks not very satisfactorily made, it had soon to be plastered over to forestall weathering. Within only months of its opening, it was noted by William Bambridge, the writing master at St John's College, 'the congregation have to hoist umbrellas, put on rain coats and shift from one side of the church to the other to endeavour to get out of the wet.' St Paul's too was loopholed and prepared as a refuge for the women and children

of Auckland in case of attack arising from the war in the north against the Maori.

Just to the south of St Paul's were grouped the post office, the premises of the New Zealand Banking Company and Wood's Hotel, diagonally across from the gates to Government House. As early as 1844 Princes Street was the address also of a tailor, a general dealer and two carpenters, in addition to a bank manager, a surveyor, a solicitor, the consul for Belgium and two 'Esquires'. One of them was Daniel Pollen, the physician turned politician, the other James Dilworth, the philanthropist.

The dominant building on the eastern side of the street was Government House. Shipped out from England, it was said to have been modelled on the one to which Napoleon had been exiled on the island of St Helena after his defeat at Waterloo in 1815. One wing of it had been put up by March 1841 when Governor Hobson and his family moved in. In the following August Mrs Hobson was writing to a friend, 'You will be glad to hear that we are now comfortably established in our new house in Auckland.' The prospect was not so attractive to Mary FitzRoy, the wife of the succeeding Governor. 'A barn' she called it in 1843, 'divided into unpainted and unpapered rooms, dirty to a degree. The children have two tiny, little nurseries out of which I am told they will be driven by wind and rain in winter.' And, in 1845, Colonel Godfrey Mundy, while grateful for the hospitality extended him by Governor George Grey, was less than admiring of the house which he thought 'to have been built in half an hour out of a dozen or two old packs of cards.' Eliza Hobson must surely have been of a most accommodating nature. For all that, Government House and its spacious grounds remained the setting, for 7 years, for fashionable weddings, performances by the band of the 58th Regiment and for the dances that ended the weekly meetings of the Philharmonic Society. Fire destroyed the building in 1848 and it was another 8 years before a second house replaced it.

Meanwhile, military activity had moved south along Princes Street to what became known as the Albert Barracks in deference to the consort to Queen Victoria. The barracks and Fort Britomart were together able to hold nearly 1000 men. In December 1846 Governor Grey had ordered the erection of 'A loop-holed wall with flanking defences round the barracks at Auckland.' Five months later, Captain William Marlow of the Royal Engineers was able to report: 'I had a party of Maoris instructed in dressing stone which in a few weeks they accomplished in a very superior manner. The stone used for building is a hard kind of scoria.' The stone itself was quarried by 'friendly' Maori and the work carried out by 25 sappers and miners despatched from England. Within several years the barracks

▲ *Auckland's second Government House and its slowly maturing trees seen in the 1860s from the newly opened Supreme Courthouse in Waterloo Quadrant. To the rear are the buildings of the Albert Barracks inside the northeastern rim of the encircling wall.*

▼ *Backed by the sprawl of buildings of the University of Auckland, old Government House today nestles amid mature trees. To the right rises the 'wedding cake' tower of the university's original arts and library block.*

covered some 10 ha. Their appearance in 1853 was recorded by William Swainson, the Attorney-General, thus: 'The Albert Barracks, the larger of the two, are built upon the same ridge, but about a quarter of a mile inland. The Stores, Hospital, Magazine and Commissariat Offices are built of scoria. The rest of the buildings are of wood, plain in style and of a sombre colour.' Of their siting,

though, he was critical: 'Being commanded by a rising ground within a few hundred yards and being within view from ships in the harbour, and within range of their shot and shell, the site, in a military point of view is not happily chosen.'

In the event the Albert Barracks, like Fort Britomart, were never attacked. Nor could they readily have sheltered the entire popula-

In this view of 1885, 'old' St Paul's in Emily Place is about to be demolished. In front of it the hill-top site of Fort Britomart is being cut down for fill in harbour reclamation. Right foreground are buildings in Custom Street East, behind them Shortland Street rises to meet Princes Street and at right rear is the Northern Club.

tion of Auckland as some had claimed. During the Waikato Wars of the 1860s, the barracks became a training centre for the local militia and a base for the Imperial troops. And with much of the barracks square sown in grass, Aucklanders were quick to take it over, unofficially, for playing cricket and rugby on one of the few flat areas in the town.

With the danger of further fighting largely over by 1871 and the last of the Imperial troops having departed, both sets of barracks were closed. By order of the provincial council, the land on which Fort Britomart stood was handed over to the harbour board as an inducement to improve waterfront facilities. The council instructed that the site occupied by the Albert Barracks be retained as a public endowment and entrusted development to a body of 11 improvement commissioners who were obliged to set aside at least 15 acres (6 ha)

for public recreation, form certain streets and as seen fit 'improve' or lease the remainder. Short of funds, however, the commissioners were forced to subdivide and lease all the area, except for what is today's Albert Park, at low rentals for a period of 99 years. It was a requirement of lease that lessees build nothing less than a two-storeyed house worth at least £700. So were erected in the late 1870s and early 1880s a number of substantial residences of which, on the perimeter of the park, four remain. As John Stacpoole succinctly put it: 'The town houses in Princes Street became the Auckland stuccoed equivalent of Kensington as the man of property replaced the soldier as the colonial beau ideal.'

The entertainer, Charles Thatcher, had poked fun at the *nouveaux riches* of Auckland in 1869 in a parody drawn from an American stage turn of the day:

Oh! The would-be swells of
Auckland
With their trousers cut so tight,
A short, flash coat and curly hair
In which the girls delight;
A paper collar, price one penny,
A black bell-topper tile,
And whiskers clipped so carefully
In the Lord Dundreary style.

The new men of business in Auckland, though, were a far cry from

the indolent, blundering, empty-headed swells of Thatcher's burlesque. With Wellington having become the capital in 1865 and with the Imperial troops gone, the social vacuum in Auckland — now with a population of about 23,000 — was being filled, as Frank Rogers reminded a seminar on the Princes Street area some years ago, by those who, because of wealth, ability, occupation and education, were the emerging natural leaders.

One may smile at the 'fairy tale' written by a clergyman of the church of St Andrew for a small girl in 1883:

... At length the old man came to the street called the Street of Princes which was filled with grand palaces as befitted its name: and he went up to one of the most beautiful of them and rang a bell and a young maiden, all wreathed in smiles, and beautiful to look upon opened the door to him and ushered him into the presence of the charming princess who owned the palace...

Since almost the time of the founding of Auckland, Princes Street had been the private address of families prominent in its history, beginning with Dilworth and Pollen. It was the last quarter of the nineteenth century, though, that saw the rise of the mercantile aristocracy as typified in the houses built side by

In Princes Street in 1902, horse-drawn carriages await departing guests in front of Auckland's leading hotel, the Grand, resplendent after the fire of a year before.

side from the synagogue to the entrance to Albert Park opposite the 'wedding cake' tower (1926) of the university. As it happened, the owner of the 'palace' to which the Rev. McKinney made obeisance was not a princess but a beer baron, one Thomas Whitson. Two other brewers were at one period or another occupants of others of the five 'protected' homes of the street, one of them the public benefactor, Moss Davis. In addition to these, and probably even more-widely influential, were James Sharland, the chemist, Henry Brett, owner of the evening newspaper, the *Auck-*

land Star, William Hellaby, the butcher, Arthur Nathan, a member of the pioneer trading family, and W. Scott Wilson of the *New Zealand Herald*. Largely making their money in the burgeoning city little more than the proverbial stone's throw from their doors, they lived their tight social lives on the ridge above it. As befitted heads of Victorian households, they met their friends and did business along at the Northern Club (established 1867) and gathered with their fellow Lodge members a few steps further on at the Freemasons' Hall (1881). Sundays they went to church with their families, Anglicans to the new St Paul's (1895) opposite the Auckland Grammar School (1880) in Symonds Street to which some of them sent their sons,

Presbyterians to St Andrew's (the first part of which had been erected in 1847 as the 'Scotch church') on the edge of Constitution Hill, those of the Jewish faith to the even closer synagogue (1884). Braving the shortcomings of the Supreme Courthouse (1865) in Waterloo Quadrant (where, a visiting judge commented, there were 'as many fleas hopping about the matted floor as there are lawyers in Auckland') they heard cases argued before Chief Justice Sir George Arney. And they would entertain visitors at the Grand Hotel (1889) and be entertained, as others of their rank had been since 1856, at nearby Government House.

The successor to the first, ill-fated Government House could come none too soon for William Swainson. 'Its non-replacement,' he had written after the fire of 1848, 'materially detracts from the dignity which ought to hedge about the Queen's vice regent.' Designed by the first Superintendent of Public Works, William Mason, the second Government House was Italianate in style and far more generously proportioned than its predecessor, with rooms 30 m long, 7.8 m broad and 4.85 m high. Even so, Vicesimus Lush was, for one, critical of it. 'It is far from a good design,' he wrote in his diary, 'being too much pretence, the elevation showing columns, pilasters, architraves, a pediment etc as though it were a stone building in the Grecian style — instead of being but of wood.' There were those who said that the clergyman must have been talking to his friend Frederick Thatcher who was, like Mason, an architect. All the same there was some truth in what he wrote, although later alterations have to a degree masked the 1856 building's somewhat blank look. Like Swainson, if for other reasons, socially conscious Aucklanders were delighted with the weekly 'at homes' of Governor Thomas Gore Browne and his lady. 'You meet everyone worth knowing and have excellent music in one room while there is dancing in another,' wrote one who attended.

▲*Bustles, boaters and small children in their Sunday best gather around Albert Park's fountain. The turn-of-the-century photograph taken by Henry Moss Keesing shows, at right, the backs of several of the merchant houses fronting Princes Street and, middle distance, the statue of Queen Victoria.*

▼*In the 1980s there are fewer inner-city families to stroll in Albert Park. Trees now all but mask the protected houses of Princes Street, but from her pedestal Queen Victoria continues to gaze on the flower-encircled fountain erected on a section of the old military barracks.*

One of the fine old houses on Princes Street has been taken over to serve as the premises of the University Club.

KRIS PFEIFFER

With the Albert Barracks closed, nothing was more reasonable, as *The Cyclopedia of New Zealand* later commented, than 'that the name "Albert" should be retained for the park that would be developed from much of it, its situation now that Point Britomart has been sacrificed to the greedy grasp of commerce, being the finest in the whole town area.' From the early 1880s, the city council formed and realigned adjacent streets like Wellesley, Coburg (during World War I it would become Kitchener), O'Rorke, Symonds and part of Princes itself, laid out gardens and paths, embellished the area with a flagstaff, a bandstand, a fountain and various pieces of vintage artillery. In 1899, at the exact centre of the old barracks, they mounted a statue of Queen Victoria. At the park's south-western corner land was lopped off in 1883 for the

library, art gallery and municipal offices; and on the Princes Street frontage on the south-east was built the attractive lodge (1882) meant for the park gardener but shortly to be occupied by the librarian and his family.

Today, students stroll past the remaining small remnant (some 85 m of the original 1300 m) of the once-encircling wall within which troops drilled more than a century ago; in Albert Park workers from offices in downtown Auckland relax under the spread of oaks, macrocarpas and Moreton Bay figs and eat their lunches beside gardens ablaze with the flowers of summer, where 125 years ago a cluster of ugly, bluestone buildings indicated the military prison and the barracks magazine; returning, they may peer some 7 m down a partly rebuilt well, one of several that served the barracks, walk beneath

one of Auckland's few remaining gas lamps or, probably unaware of their existence, pass close to three now blocked-up entrances to air raid shelters dug hastily in early 1942 following Japan's entry into World War II; from the direction of 31 Princes Street, to which the name Pembridge was given in 1894 and which is today the university's conservatorium, the sound of music replaces the bark of the sergeant-major; and on the street's eastern side, the skyline from the rear of old Government House to the intersection with Wellesley Street East is dominated by multi-storeyed blocks of the university, broken only by the gracious late-nineteenth-century Alfred Nathan home, now the registry of the university.

Inevitably some of what was pleasing has been lost in the near-150 years since the pioneer Pakeha and few selected Maori drank the health of Her Majesty at the flag raising ceremony of 1840 on Flagstaff Point. Gone that high headland, its approximate site indicated by an Historic Places Trust marker at the point where Quay Street meets Kings Low Landing; effaced, too, with the sea pushed a full 500 m northwards, the indented bays, Commercial, Official and Mechanics; and obliterated as well, in the sprawl of university development, tree-lined O'Rorke Street and all but five of the handsome Victorian homes of Princes Street.

Much, though, that has come in their place is for the better. Like, for example, the pocket handkerchief park with its pohutukawas and palms in Emily Place where St Paul's stood until 1885. And, most notably, the much larger park that sprang up in place of the Albert Barracks.

Elsewhere on the ridge of Rangipuke, the flavour of a part of Auckland of the second half of the nineteenth century lingers on. Half-hidden in mature trees, native and exotic, 'old' Government House serves today as the senior common room of the university. Alongside the once fashionable Grand Hotel, itself made over into offices, the Freemasons' Hall continues to stand solid behind ornate, cast iron railings as a youth hostel. Men of business still foregather in the Virginia creeper-clad Northern Club. Across on the corner of Bowen Avenue, the 100-year-old synagogue awaits conversion into a small hotel. Their wealthy owners long since fled to addresses more distant, the five 'protected' houses (one of which dates from as late as 1934) are hosts to educational and cultural institutions, bank agencies, architects and lawyers. And, overhung with elms and poplars and overlooked by a line of towering Washingtonia palms, Princes Street can still claim the title which the newspaper *The New Zealander* awarded it as far back as 1849: 'This really noble thoroughfare.'

Further Reading

Easdale, N. *Five Gentlemen's Residences in Princes Street Auckland* (Auckland 1980)

Lennard, L.M. 'The Albert Barracks' *Journal of the Auckland Historical Society*, no. 9, 1966

Platts, U. *The Lively Capital: Auckland 1840–1865* (Christchurch 1971)

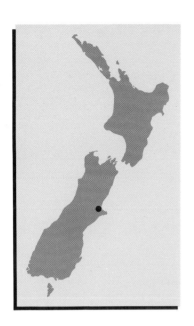

Homes for the People: Workers' Dwellings of Christchurch

Barbara Fill

DESPITE the common belief that state housing began with the Labour Government in 1937 under the direction of the fiery and enigmatic John A. Lee, government involvement in providing housing for the low income worker of New Zealand was first introduced in 1905 under the Liberal Government headed by Richard John Seddon. An outbreak of bubonic plague in 1900 and the increasing number of reports tabled in the House by concerned members documenting the overcrowded and unsanitary living conditions of many of their constituents prompted the Seddon Ministry to draw up the Workers' Dwellings Act in 1905.

Seddon's aim in promoting the Act was to provide low-cost housing to maintain a stable and happy workforce. He had himself seen workers' houses being built by local councils in London and Glasgow in the late 1890s. The Secretary of Labour, Edward Tregear, submitted a memorandum to Seddon in 1904 pointing out that rents had increased and 'acquired an utter disproportion to earnings'. Seddon saw the Workers' Dwellings Act as a means by which the state could take over as landlord in opposition to profit-hungry city landowners, to the benefit of responsible and industrious mem-

bers of the working class.

The Act aimed to provide 5000 houses for landless people who earned less than £156 per year — amended in the following session to £200 per year. The houses could

be leased for 50 years with the right of renewal or purchased outright with the proviso that on the death of the owner the house was to be returned to the state. In return the worker was 'to maintain the dwel-

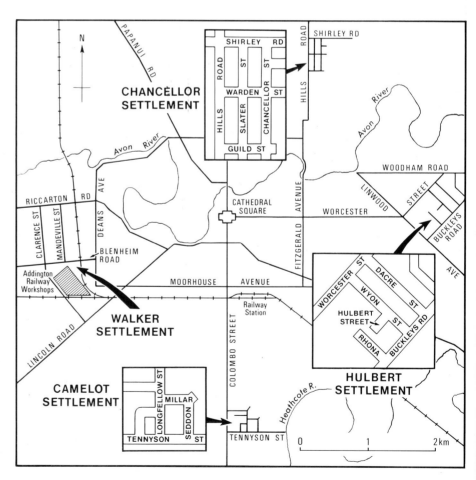

The Workers' Dwellings settlements of Christchurch.

Workers' dwellings on Longfellow Street, Sydenham, soon after they had been erected. At the end of the row is the house first erected at the Christchurch International Exhibition as an example of a workers' dwelling. The rents for the five-roomed, single-storeyed houses in the picture ranged from 9/6 to 10/6 per week.

ling in the manner the Premier would have liked, keep the garden properly tilled and cultivated, and have the chimneys swept once a year'.

However, for many workers, bringing home a pay packet of £3 per week, the rents, which varied between 10 shillings and 15 shillings a week depending on the city, added to general daily living expenses plus local rates and insurances, meant the houses were too expensive.

The workers failed to flock to the offices of the Land Board. The Government was, in turn, not prepared to build lower-quality housing, if building houses to the original high standard was to prove uneconomic at an affordable rent. Thus, although the Government started out with good intentions, the scheme failed to have any significant impact on New Zealand's housing problem. When the scheme finally ground to a halt in 1919, only 648 houses had been built throughout the country — less than a fifth of those originally intended. Meanwhile the newspapers of the day continued to feature articles on the slums which were spreading out over the cities in

every direction, bringing 'dishonour and unhappiness on those that lived in them'.

The Camelot Settlement

In Christchurch the housing situation was like that in the other main centres. Annual outbreaks of typhoid, diphtheria and scarlet fever in many of the poorer areas took their toll on the working man and woman and their families. Sydenham, Christchurch's most decisively working class suburb, was home to many of the low income workers who had found work in the factories which had sprung up in the area in the latter half of the nineteenth century. Appropriately, Sydenham was the suburb chosen for the first group of state houses to be built in Christchurch.

Building of workers' dwellings began in 1906 on a section of Crown land known locally as the 'Police Paddock'. Renamed the Camelot Settlement in 1909, it bore little resemblance to Tennyson's 'long fields of barley and of rye' beyond which lay the 'many towered Camelot'. The land in Sydenham was little more than a shingle former riverbed fringed by the raupo swamps which lined the Heathcote River.

New streets were formed, drains laid and the paddock subdivided into 35 sections, although initially only 13 houses were to be built. These first houses were designed by local architects S. Hurst Seager and Cecil Wood, R.W. England and F. Barlow. Their designs were a

marked departure from the grand Christchurch houses which Hurst Seager and R.W. England in particular had previously designed for members of Christchurch's elite and which Cecil Wood was to design later in his career. Certain restrictions were placed on the type of house that the Government was willing to build for workers. The houses were to consist of five rooms including a bathroom and scullery with the cost of erection of each dwelling not to exceed £350 if in wood, or £400 if constructed of brick, stone or concrete. The aesthetic quality of each house was considered important, however, and to achieve this the Government sponsored a competition which resulted in accomplished and established architects designing houses that varied in style. Where more than two houses of the same design were built in an area, they were placed at random down the street to avoid both monotony and any hint of the stigma which might be associated with those living in a state-built 'hand out'.

Hurst Seager's and Cecil Wood's design, 'Comfort', which was placed first in the South Island section of the competition, was selected to be part of the Labour Department's exhibit at the International Exhibition held in Christchurch from November 1906 to April 1907. The house was prefabricated and erected in the exhibition grounds, to show the world how the Liberal Government was taking care of its workers. The

▲ *The house designed as a workers' dwelling by S. Hurst Seager and Cecil Wood in a free Tudor style which was erected in the grounds of the 1906-7 International Exhibition held in Christchurch as an example of a workers' dwelling.*

▼ *After the exhibition closed the house was moved to the Camelot Settlement in Sydenham, where it still stands on Longfellow Street, housing now the Beckenham Pottery.*

'model' dwelling was fully furnished, fenced and planted with a typical worker's garden.

The house was designed in a free Tudor style which owed much to the English Arts and Crafts Movement. Although on a smaller scale than the usual Hurst Seager houses, it had many of his hallmarks, with its half-timbered upper storey jettied out over the weatherboarded ground floor, a steep-pitched iron roof, tall Arts and Crafts style chimneys and leaded casement windows. The entrance porch featured a built-in seat and opened into a rimu panelled living room with a coal range. Off the living room was a larder with a scullery adjoining and a separate bathroom. Stairs led up from the scullery to three bedrooms. The two larger bedrooms had tiled fireplaces and all three had dress cupboards. When the exhibition closed the house was moved to its present site in Longfellow Street and was first leased by William Lucas, a gardener, who was married with six children.

Of R.W. England's and F. Barlow's designs, three houses were built in brick and the remaining nine in wood. Unfortunately many of these houses have been altered dramatically over the years and several have been demolished to make way for blocks of flats.

The remaining Sydenham sections were built on under the changed terms of the 1910 Workers' Dwellings Act. Under the new Act the over-all value of the land and dwelling was increased to £600 and a worker earning not more than £175 per year was able to purchase his or her home outright by making either weekly payments or monthly instalments at 7 per cent interest on the capital over a period of 25 years and 6 months.

The Labour Department architect, Woburn Temple, took over responsibility for the designs of the houses and on 21 November 1911 the Hon. Mr Miller, Minister of Labour, laid the foundation stone for the first of these dwellings. The weatherboarded house was situated on the corner of Seddon and Millar

Top: one of the workers' dwellings erected in Sydenham's Camelot Settlement. This five-roomed house rented for 10/6 per week.

Middle: a six-roomed house in Sydenham's Camelot Settlement for which the rent was 11/4 per week.

Bottom: a smaller, four-roomed house, also erected in Christchurch's largest and earliest group of workers' dwellings, which rented for 9/4 per week.

streets and still stands today, surrounded by its laurel hedge and fir trees, planted shortly after it was built. However, most of these later houses have suffered the same fate as their earlier counterparts, and of those that remain standing few have retained any discernible features from their original design. Aluminium windows have replaced the original sash or casement windows and stucco has been plastered over brick and weatherboarded exteriors to give a 'Spanish' effect popular in New Zealand in the 1970s.

The Walker Settlement

A second group of workers' dwellings in Christchurch was built in Riccarton in 1909. Six houses were erected in ferroconcrete and a seventh house already on the site was extensively renovated. The ferroconcrete houses were constructed on a trial basis using day labour and were of a similar design to those previously erected in Wellington. The Government architect, Woburn Temple, believed that the use of ferroconcrete should be encouraged as much as possible. The extra cost was a mere £6 per dwelling and it was more than compensated for by the houses' extra durability, with consequent savings in cost of maintenance and insurance, and their being 'warmer, more weatherproof, and less sensitive generally to external influences'. The outward appearance of the houses was not adversely affected by the use of

BRUCE FOSTER

One of the few workers' dwellings of the Walker Settlement in Riccarton which is still lived in and still in good repair is 23 Mandeville Street. The house was purchased by the Hoy family in 1923, after they had rented it for some years. Members of the same family have lived in it ever since.

concrete for construction as ornate wooden verandas and porches were added to alleviate any severity in the design. The trial proved quite successful because the materials were available locally and a further ten houses were built in 1912.

The settlement was named after William Campbell Walker, a former Speaker of the Legislative Council, and Governor of Canterbury College. It was situated on 1.25 ha of land in Mandeville Street within easy walking distance of the Railway Workshops and the stockyards. It was from these local industries that the Government hoped to attract workers to live in its houses. Posters and application forms outlining the conditions of the Act were posted in the workshops, but when applications for the houses closed only two had been received from railway employees. Other railway workers had already found cheaper accommodation in the shanties in nearby Crewe township. This township lay between the railway line and

Lincoln Road to the south and Riccarton Road to the north and was bounded to the west by Pigeon Lane — now Clarence Street — and to the east by Chinaman's Lane — now Mandeville Street. The cottages and workshops were surrounded by Chinese market gardens and paddocks used for grazing dairy cows and polo ponies that belonged to the two large property owners in the area — the Beaths and the Halls.

It was at the original Hall homestead, Oakford, that Joseph Hoy, an early tenant in one of the Government's workers' dwellings, had found employment on his arrival from Scotland before World War I. Mr Hoy worked as a gardener and his wife helped out in the house. On the outbreak of World War I, Mr Hoy left to fight overseas. In return for his services to King and country, his family — along with other soldiers' families — was indemnified by the Government against any inability to keep up payments on their homes. The Government relaxed the conditions of tenancy and/or purchase of the houses by charging only the interest on the balance of principal owing at the date of enlistment. In some instances payments were waived altogether, leaving families only the rates and insurance to pay.

After the war Joseph Hoy worked

as a linesman for the Municipal Electricity Department in Christchurch and eventually purchased the freehold of his dwelling in 1923. The Hoy family have lived in the house ever since, Joseph Hoy's son taking possession of it when he returned from World War II. The other houses that were built as part of the Walker Settlement have succumbed to 'progress' but Mr Hoy intends making sure that his home remains — at least as long as he does. The first houses were demolished when Mandeville Street was realigned and Blenheim Road was put through. Over the years other houses have 'bitten the dust' as the neighbourhood has changed from residential to industrial. Butlers ran a timber mill in Mandeville Street from the turn of the century but it was the advent of Fletchers' asbestos cement factory during World War II that brought about the change. Mr Hoy believes that 'people got sick of the smoke and dust from the factory's chimney and the ladies got fed up with having to wash their curtains every month.'

Although the factory has since closed down, Fletchers have gradually bought up the east side of the street from 'the Creek to Blenheim Road; while on the western side two of the workers' cottages next to Mr Hoy's place have recently been demolished by B.J. Phillips to make way for new offices and showrooms. Ironically the cabbage tree which stood in front of one of the houses was protected by the local council — but not the houses. The same fate has overtaken these houses as houses in other Christchurch working class suburbs. As the areas have been rezoned from residential to industrial, speculators have moved in to profit from new developments, pushing the workers further out. Factors such as accessibility to transport and the proximity of the houses to the workplace which were a major consideration when the Liberal Government was selecting areas for its workmen's homes in 1905 seem no longer relevant in a commuter-computer age.

Seven houses of the Chancellor Settlement, St Albans, erected in 1911 under the amended 1910 Workers' Dwellings Act. The four- and five-roomed houses commanded rents of between 12/7 and 15/3 per week, already somewhat higher than rents charged for similar houses in the earlier Camelot Settlement in Sydenham.

The Hulbert and Chancellor Settlements

Two other workers' dwelling settlements were built in Christchurch, the first in Chancellor Street, St Albans, in 1911 and the second in Hulbert Street, Linwood, in 1915. The houses were similar in style to those built on the Walker and Camelot Settlements. Those on Hulbert Street remain relatively unchanged, but those on Chancellor Street have not been so fortunate. A house which stands on the corner of Chancellor Street and Shirley Road has undergone the most dramatic changes. Over the years it has served as a worker's dwelling, the local dairy, and more recently the offices of the St Albans branch of the Labour Party.

The surviving houses, in Christchurch and other New Zealand cities, built under the Workers' Dwellings Acts of 1905 and 1910 are to some extent memorials to a goal never realised. More successful than the Workers' Dwelling Acts in providing housing of a good standard for New Zealand's working class families at the opening of the twentieth century was the Advances to Workers Act, 1906, which made low-cost loans available to enable working and lower middle class families to build their own homes. Nevertheless, the houses built under the Workers' Dwellings Acts are important as reminders of the first attempt by New Zealand's central government at housing its people — as New Zealand's first state houses. Though some of Christchurch's workers' dwellings have been demolished and many of the survivors unfortunately changed, they are as important in the city's history as many of the grander mansions of the rich in which Christchurch already takes interest and pride.

Further Reading

Appendices to the Journal of the House of Representatives 1906–20 H11B

Fergusson, R. 'The Workers' Dwellings Act and the Auckland Settlements (Research Essay, School of Architecture, Auckland 1978)

Fill, B. *Seddon's State Houses. The Workers' Dwellings Act 1905 and the Heretaunga Settlement* (Wellington 1984)

Many of the houses of the Chancellor Settlement, built in St Albans in 1911, have been modified or allowed to deteriorate, but some, like 66 Chancellor Street, have been well maintained.

The least changed of all the workers' dwellings erected in Christchurch are probably those of the Hulbert Settlement (the picture is of 9 Hulbert Street) built in Linwood in 1915.

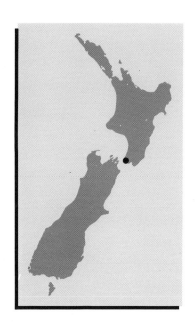

Head Office Country: South Lambton Quay

Jim McKenzie

A SMALL part of Wellington's 'central business district', centred around a triangle of land bounded by Lambton and Customhouse quays and Hunter Street, contains a variety of historic commercial buildings, most owned by banks and insurance companies. Unlike the rest of central Wellington, it has been relatively unaffected by the destruction of historic buildings during the city's latest building boom. In 1984 the Historic Places Trust declared it a conservation area, that is to say an area of land and its associated buildings and objects that have architectural, historic and visual interest meriting conservation. Today, the district contains New Zealand's finest concentration of historic 'head office' buildings of different ages and varying styles. A number of retail/office buildings on the fringe of this financial core are also included in the conservation area. They form part of Wellington's 'retail ribbon' running from Lambton Quay to Courtenay Place.

The land on which these buildings lie has long been a key part of the town and has many historical associations with the early growth and development of Wellington. These associations reach right back to the early years of the Wellington settlement, following its foundation by the New Zealand Company in 1840. At that time the shoreline followed the line of today's Lambton Quay. The Lambton Quay-Willis Street corner (where Stewart Dawsons Jewellers now stands) was

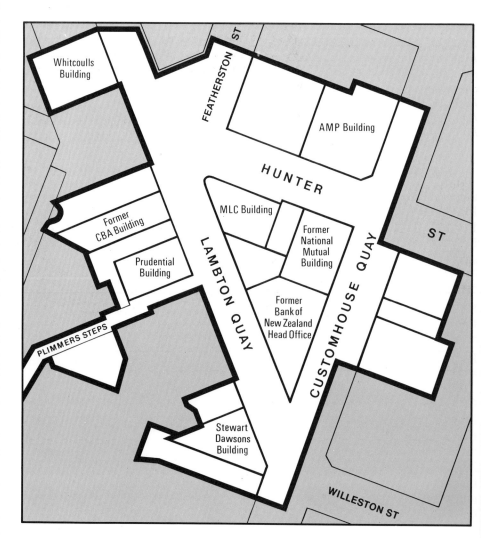

The South Lambton Quay Conservation Area.

When W.H. Holmes sketched the beach at Wellington in 1856, John Plimmer had already beached the hulk of the Inconstant *for use as a wharf and warehouse on the seaward side of Lambton Quay. Land has since been reclaimed and Lambton 'Quay' is now several hundred metres inland.*

at the bottom of a steep promontory known as 'Clay Point' or 'Windy Point'. Wellington was then a beachfront village, with a line of small stores and cottages strung out along the shore at Te Aro and Thorndon. Clay Point formed something of a barrier between these two parts of town. The sea washed right up to the base of the promontory at high tide, often making passage difficult.

Clay Point itself was the site of Charles Heaphy's flagstaff, an early landmark. In 1839 Heaphy came to Wellington on the *Tory* as draughtsman and artist for the New Zealand Company. Later he was to be renowned for his exploits as an explorer and winner of the Victoria Cross in the Land Wars. Heaphy's flagstaff, sitting atop Clay Point, can be seen in his own watercolour

views of early Wellington. The best known work was painted in 1841 from above Clay Point, looking north to Lambton Quay and Thorndon.

In 1843, Clay Point was selected as the site for the Waterloo Redoubt. This fortification was erected by the Wellington settlers in the general panic that followed the Wairau Affray. A number of Englishmen were killed in this conflict between Maori and Pakeha over land in the Wairau Valley of the northern South Island. Despite the panic that inspired its construction, the redoubt was never used. It was dismantled several years later when Clay Point was cut back to allow a proper road to be built around the promontory, connecting Lambton Quay and Willis Street.

The first commercial enterprise to occupy the area was a brickworks located between Clay Point and what are now Plimmer's Steps. It was owned by a Mr Millar and operated from the 1840s until some time after the 1855 earthquake. Millar's business presumably suffered enormously from the huge drop in demand for bricks follow-

ing the earthquake. For 25 years thereafter, wood was almost exclusively used as a building material in Wellington.

A noted early resident and entrepreneur in the area was John Plimmer. He owned a house and workshop on a site up the steep path that ran alongside the waterfall which originally cascaded down Plimmer's Steps. The location of Plimmer's property is remembered today by the historic oak tree that sits beside the steps. This tree is believed to have been planted by John Plimmer in what was then his garden. It dates from the mid-nineteenth century and was possibly grown from an acorn given to Plimmer by Sir George Grey.

One of Plimmer's more remarkable early enterprises was 'Noahs Ark'. This was a combined wharf and warehouse built from the hull of an American barque, *Inconstant*, which ran aground at Wellington Heads in 1850. It was salvaged and bought by Plimmer who propped it up on the beach where the old Bank of New Zealand head office now stands. He removed its upper works and erected a building over

The southern end of Lambton Quay, about 1860. The reclamation of 1857-63 is in progress. Many of the buildings of today's conservation area stand on ground won in this early reclamation.

the hull. The 'Ark' was surrounded and partially buried by reclamations in the 1860s.

The reclamation which enclosed 'Noahs Ark' was the first of any size undertaken in Wellington. Approximately 3.25 ha in area, it was carried out by Charles R. Carter, the founder of Carterton, between 1857 and 1863, on contract to the Wellington Provincial Council. The land created by this reclamation was both flat and centrally located and therefore a prime site for development. Many of the buildings standing in the conservation area sit on this early reclamation. From the 1860s the area began to establish its commercial character. One of the earliest institutions to acquire a site there was the Bank of New Zealand. In 1863 the first permanent Wellington branch of the bank was opened on the corner site still occupied by its former head office building.

The shift of the seat of government from Auckland to Wellington in 1865 eventually resulted in the head offices of most major companies operating in New Zealand converging on the new capital. All banks in the colony had head offices in Wellington before 1900. By that time, banks and insurance

companies were major landowners in the area at the southern end of Lambton Quay. They included some of the most powerful companies operating in New Zealand. Australia-based organisations were well represented. Insurance companies such as the Australian Mutual Provident Society and the National Mutual Life Association had their main New Zealand offices in the area. Australian banks included the Commercial Bank of Australia and the Bank of Australasia (now part of Westpac and the Australia and New Zealand Bank respectively). The most important organisation of all established in the area, however, was the Bank of New Zealand, New Zealand's most influential bank.

These organisations gained several locational advantages by establishing their head offices in part of Wellington's central business area. The financial heart of the capital city and the country was established close to central government decision-making. Another advantage was proximity to major customers and to organisations performing similar functions, facilitating business transactions and inter-house communication.

High land values have resulted from the desirability of central city office space and the wish to maximise the economic potential of restricted sites. This led to considerable pressure to redevelop parts of the central business district at various times during the last cen-

tury and this. The city centre has, accordingly, passed through several phases of reconstruction. Three phases in particular affected the conservation area. The first was at the turn of the century. Many new buildings were erected including the Bank of New Zealand head office, the former Bank of Australasia and several retail buildings. The second, from 1926 to 1930, saw the construction of the Australian Mutual Provident Society's third and present head office and the Commercial Travellers Club building. The third was between 1935 and 1938, as New Zealand began to recover from the Great Depression. Offices for the Commercial Bank of Australia, Prudential Assurance Company and Mutual Life and Citizens Assurance Company were erected.

Since the early 1970s large areas of central Wellington have undergone more prolonged and intense reconstruction than ever before. Despite an economic recession, large amounts of capital have been available for investment and there has been a huge demand for new central office space. The Wellington City Council edict requiring the demolition or strengthening of all earthquake-risk buildings according to a strict timetable has also hastened redevelopment. A very large number of older buildings in central Wellington have now been demolished, but the conservation area at the south end of Lambton Quay has so far largely escaped the destruction of this latest period of redevelopment.

The marks left by earlier phases of rebuilding are still apparent in the area and give it its historic character. The variety of ages and architectural styles evident in the conservation area is an important aspect of its value. The ages of existing historic buildings range from the early 1880s to the late 1930s. Four main architectural styles are exhibited in the area. Many of the area's buildings follow the forms of the Classical Revival. Others are transitional in design, incorporating both classical elements and twentieth-century fea-

▲ *More than 40 years separate the building of the National Mutual Life Assurance Company of Australasia, constructed 1883-84 (left), and the building of the Australian Mutual Provident Society, opened 1928 (right). The N.M.L.A. building is an early Classical Revival building, the A.M.P. building an example of the transition from the Italian palazzo forms of the Classical Revival to simpler, modern styles. The A.M.P. building has recently been strengthened and refurbished. The future of the N.M.L.A. building, now part of the old Bank of New Zealand group, is unclear.*

► *A pair of triangular pedimented windows on the Hunter Street facade of the National Mutual Life Assurance Company of Australasia building.*

tures. The art deco style is expressed in the Prudential Assurance Company building, while the Mutual Life and Citizens Assurance Company's head office can be described as an early modern building. In many ways the buildings are representative of the history of 'financial' architecture in Wellington before World War II. The oldest buildings in the area belong to the classical architectural tradition. Classical Revival styles were used extensively by mid and late Victorian architects for commercial buildings. Believing all possible architectural styles had already been invented, Victorian architects took features of past styles and adapted them into designs of their own. Classical Revival architects borrowed ideas from earlier phases of the classical tradition, particularly the Italian Renaissance.

The former National Mutual building, built in 1883–84 on the corner of Customhouse Quay and Hunter Street, is probably the finest example of Classical Revival architecture in the area. Now part of the former Bank of New Zealand group, it was designed by Thomas Turnbull who was responsible for other major Wellington buildings such as the General Assembly Library and the old Central Post Office (now demolished). Its three-storeyed facade is well proportioned and richly decorated, although the overall effect was somewhat diminished when the parapet was removed because it was an earthquake hazard. On the ground floor, rustication has been reduced to narrow piers that still give an impression of classical solidity. This creates larger spaces for windows and admits more light. Above, each storey has a different design. The narrow, paired, round-headed windows of the upper storey contrast with the square windows surmounted by triangular and segmental pediments below. The exterior plasterwork features a series of sculptured heads on the keystones of the ground floor windows, each with a different expression. These faces and other plaster embellishments

NATIONAL MUSEUM

The Bank of New Zealand's Wellington branch building late last century. The first permanent Wellington branch of the bank opened on the site in 1863.

such as festoons of fruit and gorgons' heads give the building considerable visual interest.

By the 1920s architects no longer adhered strictly to Classical Revivalism and styles were more innovative. Classical elements were still incorporated into the facades of many buildings, however, often mixed in with more contemporary features. Such buildings can be described as 'transitional' in style. The Australian Mutual Provident Society and former Commercial Bank of Australia head offices in the conservation area both follow this pattern. The Commercial Bank of Australia building, for example, retains a roofline cornice and other classical forms but in a very simplified form.

In contrast, the style of the Prudential Assurance Company building, opened in 1935, is firmly rooted in the twentieth century. Designed by Australian architects Hennessy and Hennessy, its facade shows the art deco forms of applied decoration popular in the 1920s and 1930s. Structurally, art deco buildings were plain and therefore well suited to the economic stringency of the depressed 1930s. The geometric patterns and decorative motifs displayed around entrances and windows, however, served to give them visual interest.

The Mutual Life and Citizens Assurance Company building, opened in 1940, was one of the first modern buildings to be erected in

Wellington. It was designed by local architects Mitchell and Mitchell. With the exception of a panel showing a motif of the Mutual Life and Citizens Assurance Company symbol repeated around the corner tower and above the original main entrance, it is virtually undecorated. Its facing of faience tiles gives it an attractive golden brown colour. Prominent piers rising from the second storey and recessed spandrels create vertical lines.

As well as being visually attractive, bank and insurance company buildings were designed as symbols of the companies' power and prestige. Appropriate images of solidity and dependability were created in the design to impress clients. Visual prominence was also sought to attain a high public profile and attract custom. To this end, corner sites were often chosen. These requirements are expressed in all of the area's historic banking and insurance buildings. Although they were erected over a span of 60 years and show a diversity of architectural styles, the demand for buildings of imposing design and high visibility remained constant.

The Classical Revival architecture of the area's early buildings was particularly suited to these

The Bank of New Zealand's former head office building, opened in 1901 on the site of the Wellington branch which was demolished to make way for the new head office.

The banking chamber of the Bank of New Zealand's head office, opened in 1901.

requirements. These buildings with their solidly rusticated bases, columns and pediments admirably symbolised the security and prestige of the institutions within. The former Bank of New Zealand head office at the intersection of Lambton and Customhouse quays is the best example of this imposing classical symbolism. When its new head office opened in 1901, the Bank of New Zealand was by far the most influential bank in New Zealand. Almost half of all banking business transacted in the colony passed over its counters. It had, however, suffered a severe financial crisis in 1889. Brought about largely by the depression of the late 1880s, the crisis was compounded by the unwise and speculative business practices of the Bank of New Zealand's Auckland board, leaving the bank in a precarious position. In 1890 the headquarters was removed from Auckland to London in an effort to clean up its management. London was too remote to make effective decisions, however, and the bank's financial situation worsened. By 1894 the bank's total collapse was imminent. Disaster was averted only by the last minute intervention of the New Zealand Government. Under the Bank of New Zealand Guarantee Share Act, government stock was issued to rescue the bank's finances. In return, the Government became a major shareholder in the bank and the bank's headquarters was shifted to Wellington where it could be kept under close scrutiny.

A new head office was needed to accommodate the increased staff required in Wellington. The bank desired a suitably prestigious building that would restore its somewhat tarnished image in the public mind. Thomas Turnbull was selected as the architect and designed a building neo-Renaissance in style. Originally the structure was to have been an impressive four storeys high with a dome at each corner. The Prime Minister, Richard Seddon, who was able to take a direct interest in the bank's affairs following the crisis, felt this

TONY ATHFIELD

in 1877, progressively larger buildings being required as business expanded. The architects for the present building, Clere and Clere, chose to reinterpret the Renaissance palazzo style of the Classical Revival. The facades are characterised by a rusticated base, pedimented windows on the floors above and a cornice. The grand main portal on Customhouse Quay rises to almost one-third of the height of the building and is decorated by a plaster frieze embellished with motifs showing mythical griffins. This leads to what was, in its heyday, a magnificent main chamber supported by columns of Italian marble. These features all combined to give the building a suitably imposing air, well befitting the largest insurance company in Australasia. Sitting on top of the splayed corner is the 'Amicus' sculpture, the symbol of the Australian Mutual Provident Society. The sculpture was prominently placed on all society offices and served to advertise the company's presence to potential customers and pedestrians. The company made a happy decision in the early 1980s to strengthen and refurbish this important building rather than replace it.

The Mutual Life and Citizens Assurance Company building also commands attention from passers-by. It is situated on a superb corner site, highly visible from Lambton Quay. The company followed a deliberate policy of selecting corner sites to show its buildings off to best advantage. This can also be seen in the company's Auckland building. The clock in the tower above the corner makes the building an important landmark. The

design to be too lavish. A budget limit of £20,000 was specified, causing the domes and upper storey to be removed from the plan. Even so, the final cost exceeded the limit by £5000.

Turnbull's design drew its inspiration from Italian palazzo forms of the Renaissance. Its distinguishing characteristics included a heavily rusticated ground floor; colonnettes framing pedimented windows on the third storey and a heavy cornice and crowning parapet (since removed). The large main banking chamber is very impressive. It is supported by Corinthian columns and has a superb plastered ceiling. The building is sited at a focal point in the city, on the intersection of two of Wellington's major thoroughfares. The snub-nosed facade fills the acute angled corner to best advantage and stands out prominently from Willis Street. In this way it acts as a landmark to attract the maximum number of potential customers.

The area's insurance company buildings also expressed the corporate prestige of their owners. The Australian Mutual Provident Society building, opened in 1928, is a good example. It is the third Australian Mutual Provident Society building to sit on the site since the first offices were erected

The fine art deco lines of the Prudential Building are evident in this photograph taken soon after it was opened in 1935.

The Prudential building is today more tightly hemmed in by other buildings but remains a fine example of how the use of art deco forms of decoration can give visual interest to even a simple building.

clock originally sat in the old Central Post Office tower but was removed after the 1942 earthquake damaged the tower. It was installed in the Mutual Life and Citizens Assurance Company building in 1955.

Although dominated by financial institutions, the conservation area also contains four retail/office buildings. All were designed in variations of the Classical Revival style. The group of three on the Willis Street-Lambton Quay corner is most interesting. The centrepiece is the recently refur-

bished building erected for Stewart Dawsons Jewellers in 1900 and occupied by them ever since. Its two neighbours were erected around the same time. All three buildings are notable for having their original parapets in place, a rarity in Wellington where most masonry embellishments have been removed because of the earthquake threat. As a group they provide an interesting reminder of how Wellington's main shopping street looked before the latest phase of reconstruction devastated the city.

While the conservation area still

retains its historic integrity, it is under pressure to be redeveloped in the same manner as the rest of Wellington's commercial area. Central city sites offer highly attractive investment opportunities for financial organisations. Insurance companies in particular, with their large funds available to invest, are major developers. The ongoing process of demolition and high-rise reconstruction will make it increasingly difficult to keep the character of the area intact.

The value of the area has already been diminished. A serious loss in

The building of the Mutual Life and Citizens Assurance Company, photographed by Gordon Burt soon after it was opened in 1940. The building, virtually without decoration, is a precursor of the age of modernism in Wellington.

The Mutual Life and Citizens Assurance Company building, today. The building is plain, but the faience tiles with which it is faced give it an appealing golden-brown hue. Behind, the new Bank of New Zealand tower shows what modernism came to in Wellington.

1981 was the Colonial Mutual Life building on the corner of Willeston Street and Customhouse Quay. Built in 1934, the building was notable for the magnificent series of Romanesque style arches on the ground floor and colourful use of stone of varying hues in its construction. Decorations in the form of lions' heads, gargoyles and zigzag patterns further enlivened the facade. This building has been replaced by a smaller, modern building. The former Bank of

Australasia building on Customhouse Quay was demolished in 1985, shortly after the conservation area was declared by the Historic Places Trust. Despite vigorous protests, the building was destroyed by Norwich Union and replaced by a modern tower block. A fine, classical building erected in 1905, the Bank of Australasia was especially noted for a fine main banking chamber which had an ornate plaster ceiling. Other buildings are also under threat, includ-

ing some of the important Bank of New Zealand group buildings despite earlier hopes that all the buildings of the group would be retained.

It is imperative that no further destruction occur if the historic character of the area is to be maintained for the future. Although the Historic Places Trust can designate historic areas, it can only encourage, not enforce, their conservation. There are no legal means of providing the buildings

The finest example of Edwardian Baroque in the South Lambton Quay Conservation Area is the Whitcoulls building, which faces onto Lambton Quay itself. The building, which opened in 1907, was designed by William Turnbull of Thomas Turnbull and Sons for Whitcombe and Tombs. It is one of the few remaining examples in Wellington of ornate Edwardian commercial architecture.

TONY ATHFIELD

in such an area with adequate protection. Until the laws regarding preservation are strengthened, the existence of this important reminder of central Wellington's former glory hangs in the balance.

Further Reading

Cyclopedia Company Ltd   *Cyclopedia of New Zealand, Wellington Provincial District* Vol. I, 1897

Main, W.   *Wellington Through a Victorian Lens* (Wellington 1972)

Ward, L.E.   *Early Wellington* (Wellington 1928)

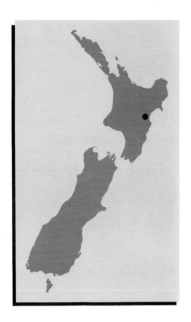

'A New Place in the Sun': Napier Rebuilt

John Cattell

THE art deco character of central Napier was established between 1931 and 1933 at a time of severe economic depression. This remarkable achievement was made possible by one of the worst natural disasters New Zealand has endured, the earthquake of 3 February 1931. The earthquake all but levelled the old town centre, making necessary urgent reconstruction and offering an unparalleled opportunity for civic improvement. This disaster and the subsequent determination of the local population to build a safer, more attractive city has shaped the appearance of present day Napier.

The ferocity and suddenness of the earthquake and the fires that followed stunned the nation. Emergency workers saw to the immediate needs of the victims, helping to provide temporary shelter and distributing food. As the dust settled, labourers and tradespeople arrived from around New Zealand to help with the cleaning up and rebuilding. A rehabilitation committee was set up to oversee the reconstruction work. The local architects, quickly entering into the spirit of community co-operation, formed themselves into the Associated Architects of Napier under the chairmanship of René Natusch. The Associated Architects

were represented on the Rehabilitation Committee by local architects J.A. Louis Hay and René and Stanley Natusch. These architects acted as advisors to the committee and had considerable influence on the rebuilding of the city centre.

This pooling of ideas and labour on the part of the whole community was seen by the politicians as the best means of healing the dreadful wounds inflicted by the disaster. By getting together, the local people could forget for a moment the traumas of the immediate past and concentrate on building a bright modern city; in short create a phoenix out of the ashes of the old town. E.H. Wright of the Rehabilitation Committee put it this way: 'Nothing will restore confidence in Napier quicker than to have a town to be greatly proud of.'

There was much discussion in the newspapers about what the new Napier should look like. Pre-quake Napier had been an attractive city of ornate commercial buildings and narrow streets — almost a Nice of the South Pacific. It was quickly realised that streets could be widened, utilities improved and, most importantly, a planned city constructed. This feeling of optimism was summed up by the editor of the *Hawke's Bay Herald* on 4 February 1932 when he wrote: 'In

our case why should we not endeavour to establish at Napier a City of the Pacific which might easily become the Mecca of holiday-makers from all over these islands?' This sense of opportunity was also uppermost in the mind of the editor of the *Daily Telegraph*:

...we are informed by leading architects that the town is on the eve of a big building boom. Dozens of plans are in the course of preparation and others have reached finality. The next few weeks should therefore witness the commencement of a comprehensive town development and rebuilding scheme which will produce a city both beautiful and bright, safe and attractive of which every citizen will feel justly proud. (11 November 1931)

The style the new buildings should take was debated in the newspapers as well. The editor of the *Hawkes Bay Herald* stated: 'There appears to be a strong feeling that the aim should be a white city in Moorish Spanish style which is considered appropriate for the climate' (9 June 1931). The Spanish Mission townscape of Santa Barbara in California was seen as a possible model. The connection with this city was reinforced in October 1931 when J.W. Mawson, Director of Town Planning in New Zealand, wrote from Santa Barbara to the Chief

▲ *The devastated city. Part of central Napier after the earthquake and fire of 3 February 1931.*

▼ *Rebuilding of the city began very soon after the initial clearing up following the disaster. The view is looking down Emerson Street in 1932, with the Criterion Hotel under construction on the corner of Hastings Street.*

HAWKE'S BAY ART GALLERY AND MUSEUM

▲ *A new city takes shape. This view of Hastings Street in the 1930s shows the reconstruction of the city well advanced and Napier taking the shape which it still largely retains today.*

▼*On the right in this picture of the newly reconstructed city is the Market Reserve building, designed by Natusch and Sons before the earthquake and the first substantial building to be erected in Napier after the disaster. The building stands on the corner of Hastings and Tennyson Streets. To the left is part of the Masonic Hotel which was rebuilt in 1932.*

HAWKE'S BAY ART GALLERY AND MUSEUM

Commissioner for the Rehabilitation of Napier, J.S. Barton. Mawson praised the Spanish Mission buildings he saw there and also sent Barton a booklet containing illustrations of that city's public and commercial buildings.

These grandiose ideas of a wholly Spanish Mission style city did not eventuate. The depressed international financial situation and what many locals regarded as delaying tactics by the Government in deciding what sort of assistance to give those who had lost everything, spelled doom for any thoughts of a planned approach to the reconstruction of the city centre. Local business people, mostly shop-owners, could not afford any delays in rebuilding their premises, 'to make haste slowly' as they had been asked to do by a member of the Rehabilitation Committee. The Government offered loans to those wishing to rebuild, advancing in many cases up to 100 percent of costs on first mortgage. With these heavy financial commitments, most of Napier's inhabitants simply could not afford to build on anything approaching a lavish scale. The new buildings had to be cheap and capable of being erected quickly so that earnings could be generated and the loans paid back. Certainly, local businesspeople were aided immeasurably by the availability of cheap labour which, as René Natusch later wrote, meant that in many cases construction costs were 50 percent of normal.

Despite the fact that a planned, stylistically uniform city was not possible, the townscape that eventually emerged was remarkably homogeneous in terms of the scale and appearance of its buildings. It is a townscape of two-storeyed buildings of various related styles. Much of the credit for the uniformity there is must go to the Associated Architects. Although this group's members favoured different styles, versions of which could all be built for approximately the same cost, each architect was aware of the need to relate his buildings visually to others going up alongside. The architects were also painfully conscious of the need to ensure that their buildings met certain minimum safety requirements. Their own offices had all been wiped out by the earthquake and ensuing fires, but they were quickly back in business with several years of frenetic activity before them. Natusch and Sons were operating from a new office in the Hawke's Bay Motor Company building within a fortnight. This firm was responsible for the first substantial building erected after the earthquake, the Market Reserve building on the corner of Hastings and Tennyson streets. This was a plain, two-storeyed building of no particular style with large, round-arched windows allowing for the maximum entry of light into the interior. It had been designed before the earthquake and its steel frame construction allowed for two additional floors to be added if necessary. The building stands out prominently in early photographs of the reconstruction as an example to all of what could be achieved. Although the plans were prepared by Natusch and Sons they were signed 'Associated Architects'. However, most of the designs prepared by members of the Associated Architects were signed by the architect in whose office they had been drawn up. Accordingly, there is little evidence of firms co-operating on the joint design of individual buildings.

There is at least one case, though, where co-operation did occur. In February 1932 four property owners in Hastings Street combined to produce one building with four slightly different facades, one for each owner. It was hailed in the *Daily Telegraph* as the first example of community construction and described as follows:

Plans for the work for the community building have been drawn by Mr E.A. Williams, Mr J.A. Louis Hay, and Messrs C. Tilleard Natusch and Sons. The drawings provide for the structural work to be carried out as one job, although the facades of the three buildings will be such that any one of them will be readily distinguishable from the other two. (18 February 1932)

The style most favoured by the Napier architects was what we now call 'art deco'; in the 1930s it was described as being 'of the most modern design'. The influences behind the creation of the art deco style are many and various, making it a difficult one to define. The style is recognised as the last 'total style', by which is meant that its central themes and characteristic motifs

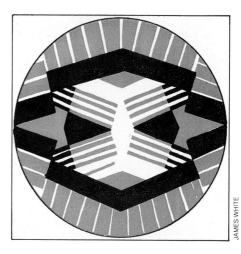

▶
Knowledge of the art deco style reached New Zealand from overseas in a variety of ways. Stanley Natusch, of Natusch and Sons, a firm very active in the rebuilding of Napier, had three catalogues of the 1925 Paris Exhibition in his office. The exhibition saw the beginnings of the art deco style. This is the motif from one of the catalogues, which is still in a Napier architect's office.

JAMES WHITE

JAMES WHITE

▲ *An art deco interior — a room for a young girl — illustrated in the 1925 catalogue. In this interior can be seen elements of art deco design which are visible in many of Napier's buildings.*

embraced everything from the tallest buildings, such as the Empire State Building in New York, right down to the smallest household items.

The development of the style can be traced back to the early 1900s in the decorative art works of European designer artists. It takes its name from the *Exposition Internationale des Arts Decoratifs et Industriels Modernes* held in Paris in 1925. With this exhibition art deco became an international phenomenon. The style became popular in America where in the late 1920s architects applied its distinctive ornamentation to new buildings in cities like Los Angeles and New York. It was these American interpretations of the style which provided Napier architects with their inspiration.

Art deco was an attempt to blur the traditional distinction between art and industry in a style that subordinated ornament to form and function and accepted new materials and mass production as suitable vehicles for artistic expression. Although 'modern' in this sense, art deco did allow for individual interpretation as witnessed by the successful assimilation of traditional Maori patterns into such Napier buildings as the Bank of New Zealand in Hastings Street and the Ministry of Transport building in Church Lane. The

JAMES WHITE

▲ *Part of the facade of the Bank of New Zealand, Napier, designed in 1932 by a Wellington firm, Crichton, McKay and Haughton. The building is one of the most distinctive in Napier in its use of Maori motifs in its decoration.*

▼ *The Ministry of Transport building is a severely plain, single-storeyed building with a frieze in which Maori motifs have been incorporated. The building illustrates the ability of art deco to assimilate traditional patterns into buildings of 'modern' design.*

JAMES WHITE

emphasis of the style was on geometrical patterns which could be easily and cheaply turned out by machine. The characteristic trademarks of the style — the sunrise, the ziggurat (an upward progressing stepped pattern) and the zigzag — are all symbols of the sense of optimism and gaiety that we associate with the 1920s.

Although blunted by the rigours of the Depression, something of this spirit lingers on in many of Napier's art deco buildings. Many of the patterns universally connected with the style are clearly discernible in Napier.

The connections of some local architects with the style are worth noting. H.A. Westerholm, in part-

nership with W.P. Finch for 3 years after the earthquake, was an American and it can be assumed that he was aware of the latest developments in architecture in that country. C. Tilleard Natusch, born in England in 1859, set up practice in Napier in 1890. He specialised in large country houses and many of these show a marked American influence. One of his three sons who continued the practice, Stanley Natusch, worked in London and later with Alfred C. Bossom in New York before returning to New Zealand in 1923. We know that Stanley Natusch owned three catalogues of the 1925 Paris exhibition from which the style took its name. These catalogues contain a series of illustrations of art deco interiors and show that Natusch was familiar with the early phase of the style. Many other New Zealand architects who did not travel abroad would have received their indoctrination in art deco through architectural magazines. E. Arthur Williams, who can be credited with designing the best art deco buildings in Napier such as Masson House, the Daily Telegraph and Scinde buildings and the Hotel Central, was one architect who did not travel overseas at the time the art deco style was evolving.

Three members of the Associated Architects, Aleck and Stanley Natusch and E.A. Williams, were also qualified engineers. This enabled them to identify accurately the structural defects that led to the collapse of so many buildings. Inevitably there was much soul searching on this topic following the earthquake. The architects blamed the disaster on unsound structural designs and the use of lime mortar instead of cement mortar between bricks. The general view was that buildings had not been properly tied together and strengthened. Many parapets and other ornamental features were also not properly tied back. Most of the 258 people who died in the earthquake were killed by falling masonry and parapet embellishments. The immediate result of these findings was that all plans for new buildings had initially to be sent to Wellington to be passed by a committee working on formulating a national building code. It was the Napier earthquake that brought home to the Government the need for a national code and, of course, the dangers associated with building in an earthquake-prone land. It was clear that soundly constructed buildings were capable of surviving severe earthquakes. The buildings that survived the Napier earthquake, such as the Public Trust building, a neo-classical structure built in 1920 on the corner of Tennyson and Dalton Streets, and the Returned Servicemen's Association building in Dickens Street, provide ample evidence of this.

It was felt that 'a building should be complete and "all of a piece" in itself, well "tied" and with no overhanging excrescences or elements' (*Daily Telegraph*, 4 February 1932). The art deco style was perfectly tailored to these requirements. The geometrical lines of these buildings meant that they were suited to construction in reinforced concrete. They could be built quickly and economically, and they were safe. Ornament was inset into panels within the structure and in openings around doors and windows. These decorative elements were firmly applied to the structure and were made of concrete or plaster. They gave added spice and a modern look to what were essentially plain, earthquake-resistant buildings.

Reinforced concrete was the predominant construction material although some buildings were of brick strengthened by a structural steel framing. Many tons of cement were used in the rebuilding of Napier. In February 1932, perhaps anticipating the demand for their product the building boom would create, three New Zealand cement companies together donated 39 tons of cement to the Reconstruction Committee. It was used to pave an area around the old skating rink on Marine Parade as part of a beautification scheme for the parade. The use of timber

The Hotel Central was designed in 1931 by E. A. Williams, one of the most accomplished practitioners of the art deco style to be involved in the rebuilding of Napier. Its facade (above) and balcony (below) illustrate Williams's carefully controlled use of art deco motifs and stylistic features.

for new buildings was avoided. Many of the city's old timber buildings had burned in the fires which followed the earthquake and the locals were not about to endure a repeat performance. Also art deco, with its reliance on smooth surfaces and applied decoration, was not a style that could be readily translated into timber.

Another advantageous feature of the art deco style was that it had been used successfully in earthquake zones, especially California, in the 1920s. It was logical for Napier architects to model their buildings on those developed and tested in seismic regions overseas. This also helps explain their interest in the Spanish Mission style architecture of Santa Barbara.

Probably the finest example of

The interior of the Hotel Central continues the art deco design and decoration of the hotel's street facades. A comparison of Williams's drawing, on his plans, of the upstairs lounge of the hotel (above) with how the lounge appears today (below) illustrates the remarkable state of preservation of the hotel's interior.

art deco architecture in Napier is the Hotel Central in Dalton Street. It was designed in October 1931 by E.A. Williams for the Napier Brewery Company Limited. A reinforced concrete building, it originally had seven shops on the ground floor along with private and public bars, with guest accommodation on the floor above. Rectangular in plan, the hotel has long, low lines with the section around the main entrance on Dalton Street given greater prominence. This central section is slightly projected while the shop entrances on the ground floor with their metal-framed windows are inset. These plate glass shop windows have leadlights above and terrazzo work below. Above canopy level the windows, some with balconies, have had their top corners bevelled off to form a half octagon. This is repeated over the ornate openings above the main entrance. Here elaborate plaster infills incorporating both sunrise and zigzag motifs are a particular feature. The whole composition is drawn together by a continuous plaster frieze around the top of the facade. Inside, the art deco theme was continued with a stunning lobby lined with native timbers and imitation ashlar work. A staircase leads off this to the lounge and other rooms above, which are mostly in their original state. The building is a complete expression of art deco design and decoration and clearly illustrates the 'totality' of the style. It is also an important example of a style, principally imported from America, which was superbly adapted to fit happily into a New Zealand provincial city.

Although art deco style buildings are most numerous in Napier, many examples of Spanish Mission style architecture were also built. The best of these are the Criterion and Provincial Hotels and the former Gaiety Deluxe Cinema in Dickens Street. There are also plainer versions of the style, many of which were designed by the local architectural firm of Finch and Westerholm. The United Friendly Societies Dispensary building in Emerson Street was a typical example until its unfortunate demolition in 1986. It was designed by Finch and Westerholm for the Hawke's Bay United Friendly Societies in December 1931 and described in the *Hawke's Bay Herald* as an 'attractive Spanish design'. A standard, two-storeyed building, it had 127-mm-thick concrete walls tied together underground with reinforced concrete beams. There were two shops on the ground floor separated by a canopy from the plastered facade above. This had token Spanish detailing around the first floor and at parapet level. A Roman-tiled section of roof broke into the facade adding to its over-all Mediterranean character. The building was an excellent solution to the problem of imposing style on a simple, reinforced concrete structure. It was also economical to construct, costing about £1800. The U.F.S. building and others like it which survive such as the Ringlands, C.E. Rogers and Harstons buildings were not art deco, a fact sometimes lost sight of when Napier is described as an art deco city. However, their scale and form enabled them to slot easily into the prevailing art deco townscape.

The concrete facades of the new buildings were painted in a variety of colours. The Hotel Central, for example, was originally painted in a buff colour with some ornamental details picked out in black for effect. This colour scheme tied in with those chosen for other buildings in the city. The most popular colours were yellow, brown, pink, green and white. How modern, even foreign, these brightly painted buildings must have looked to the locals, who nevertheless seemed prepared to accept them: 'However, if the colours harmonize and are not too glaringly bright, the general opinion appears to be that the effect will be quite pleasing' (*Hawke's Bay Herald*, 22 January 1932). Doubtless Napier people

▲ *The facade of the Spanish Mission style U.F.S. Dispensary, designed in 1931 by Finch and Westerholm, with palm trees behind, exemplified the spirit of rebuilt Napier as 'a new place in the sun'. The building was, sadly, demolished in 1986.*

▼ *In times of economic stringency not all the grandiose plans for the rebuilding of Napier came to fruition. This entertainment centre was envisaged by Louis Hay for Marine Parade but was never built. The watercolour is held in the office of a Napier architect.*

were aware of the compatibility of these colours with the warm Hawke's Bay climate and the city's seaside location.

Today the green areas of Tiffen Park and Memorial and Clive squares with their tall palm trees provide perfect backdrops for Napier's art deco townscape. These squares housed Tin Town, a collection of corrugated iron buildings used as a temporary shopping centre during the reconstruction of the city centre. At the other end of the town Marine Parade and its associated leisure facilities provide a smooth transition between the city centre and the blue waters of the Pacific.

Interspersed among this antipodean environment are other buildings which are neither art deco nor Spanish Mission. These include buildings which survived the earthquake and a number built afterwards to the designs of J.A. Louis Hay. This important architect, whose work deserves separate study, also looked to America for inspiration but to the work of Louis Sullivan and Frank Lloyd Wright rather than to art deco. Perhaps best described as 'stripped classical' in style, his buildings, while they have features in common with art deco, should be viewed as the products of a more independent imagination. Probably the closest Louis Hay ever came to art deco is a watercolour for an entertainment centre which was to span Marine Parade at the point where the T. and G. building now stands. Unfortunately this remarkable structure was never built. It was one dream too fantastic ever to succeed. The pot pourri of non-art-deco buildings adds colour and texture to the two-storeyed townscape of central Napier, contributing to its distinct identity.

Napier is a unique place, shaped by a particular set of circumstances. In many ways the city's buildings represent a search for national identity, paralleled in the fine arts and literature of the 1930s and 1940s. Never before had New Zealand architects and planners turned *en masse* to America for guidance. In so doing they helped sever old colonial ties with Britain in favour of a new role as an independent Pacific nation.

In recent years a new appreciation of art deco has emerged. Separated from the 1930s by 50 years of history and World War II, people now look back on the period with renewed interest. Examples of the style have become collectables; nostalgic reminders of the zany inter-war years bought at antique auctions and set in fashionable neo-deco interiors. The growing awareness of the unique nature of central Napier is part of this new appreciation. However, just as we are beginning to understand and admire the city's special character, redevelopment plans have emerged to threaten the uniformity of its townscape. Already some important buildings have been lost. Today, more than ever, we have a duty to preserve and enhance this historic place as a monument to those who strove to build a better and brighter city: 'a new place in the sun'.

Further Reading

Campbell, M.D.N. *The Story of Napier 1874-1974* (Napier 1975)

Conly, G. *The Shock of '31. The Hawke's Bay Earthquake* (Wellington 1980)

Ives, H. *The Art Deco Architecture of Napier* (Napier 1982)

Glossary of Maori Words and Terms

It will be a happy day for New Zealand when it is no longer necessary, in a book such as this, to include a glossary of Maori words and terms. But until such words and terms are the familiar part of New Zealand English they should be, the meanings of words and terms that may be unfamiliar to some readers are given below. Meanings are also given, as a courtesy to overseas readers of the book, for words and terms which will be known to most New Zealand readers. Words whose meanings are given in or are obvious from the text are not included in this glossary. Several of the words listed have more than one meaning. Only those meanings relevant to the use of the word in this book are given in this glossary.

amo   upright support of the lower end of a maihi (*q.v.*)

ariki nui   chief of a leading line

haka   dance

hangi   earth oven, or its contents

hapu   clan, extended family group

harakeke   (New Zealand) flax

heke   rafters (of a meeting house)

hinaki   eel trap

huata   a weapon (spear)

hui   meeting, gathering

kai moana   sea food

kainga   settlement, village (unfortified)

kai takata (tangata)   human flesh, as food

kauta   cooking shed

Kohanga Reo   'language nest'; modern movement to teach the Maori language to infants

korupe   outer facing of a door lintel

koruru   figure on a gable (of a meeting house)

kowhaiwhai   painted scroll decoration

mahingakai   food resource

maihi   facing boards on the gable of a meeting house

makutu   the casting of spells; incantation

mana   prestige, standing

manaia   a grotesque beaked figure used as a motif in carving

manuhiri   guests, visitors

marae   the space in front of a house, an area important in tribal ritual and assembly

moko   tattoo

oriori   chant, song

pa   fortification, fortified village

pao   song

papakainga   home village, 'home base' of a hapu

pare   carved slab over the door of a whare (*q.v.*)

pataka   storehouse

patu   a weapon (club)

piupiu   a garment consisting of a heavy fringe attached to a waistband

poi   a light ball with a string attached used in certain dances or action songs

poupou   upright slabs forming (part of) the walls of a house

pouwhenua   a weapon (spear)

raupo   bullrush

raparapa   projecting portion of a maihi (*q.v.*)

runanga   assembly, tribal gathering

taiaha   a weapon (spear)

tangata whenua   'the people of the land'; the 'locals'; the people belonging to a particular place

tangi   funeral ceremony

taniko   ornamental border (of a mat)

tekoteko   carved figure (on the gable of a house)

tewhatewha   a weapon (axe)

Te Waipounamu   the South Island of New Zealand

tohunga   priest, expert

urupa   burial ground, graveyard

utu   revenge, payment

waiata   song

wananga   learning, lore

whakapapa   genealogy, lines of descent

whare   house, dwelling

wharepuni   sleeping house; the principal house of a kainga (*q.v.*)

whare whakairo   a carved house

wiwi   rushes

Acknowledgments

Adams: Pukekaraka
Father M. Mulcahy S.M. and Brother G. Hogg S.M., both of Wellington, for information and access to the Marist Archives. Father T. Laffey S.M., of Otaki, for access to records. Mrs T. Rikihana and Mrs M. Johnson, both of Otaki, for information.

Adams: Rangiaowhia
Mrs Te Aue Davis and associates, Waikato, for oral information. Father E.R. Simmons, of Auckland, for access to the Catholic Diocesan Archives.

Taumutu
Most of the information for this chapter came from conversation over many years with and from the papers of the late Riki Te Mairaki Taiaroa Ellison, to whose memory the chapter is dedicated.

Ria: Manutuke
Roger Neich, Sir Robert de Z. Hall and David Simmons, for information and assistance with writing the chapter.

Crawford: Timaru
Mr B.L. Evans, of Feilding, for the use of information from his 1938 M.A. thesis 'A History of the Wheat Industry in New Zealand'. Mr S.W. McRae and Mr R.B. Sherris of the Timaru Milling Company, for information.

Lambert: Benhar
McSkimming Industries Ltd for access to company files. Past employees of McSkimming Industries for information given in interviews.

Hanrahan: Ashburton
Mr R. Crum and Mr M. Beauvais, both of Ashburton, for information.

Fill: Christchurch
Mrs P. Wilson, of Christchurch, for assistance with research.

Cattell: Napier
Mr G.K. Natusch, of Napier, and the staff of the Hawke's Bay Art Gallery and Museum for information and assistance with research.

Biographical Notes

Patricia Adams was born in Hastings of families with Hawke's Bay, East Coast and Wellington connections. She has been a Wellingtonian since 1950. After attending Victoria University of Wellington, where she gained a B.A. in history and English, she joined the Public Service. She is now employed as Research Officer for the Historic Places Trust and has written numerous articles on historic places in New Zealand and on the work of the Trust.

Neil Begg of Dunedin, has, with his brother A.C. Begg, written several books dealing with the first days of European exploration of New Zealand. They have been particularly interested in the mountains and sounds of Fiordland. Dr Begg was for many years Director of Medical Services of the Plunket Society. He has served the Historic Places Trust, first as a member of the board for 10 years, and then as Chairman since 1978.

John Cattell was born in Christchurch. He graduated with a B.A. in art history and geography from Canterbury University and with an M.A. in art history from Auckland University. In 1982 he was appointed to the staff of the Historic Places Trust as Secretary to the Buildings Classification Committee. He has contributed a number of articles on New Zealand architectural history to the Trust's journal.

Ian Church was born in Devonport in 1941 but grew up in Port Chalmers and was educated at Otago Boys' High School and Otago University, from which he graduated with honours in history. Following 20 years of secondary teaching, he became Archivist at the Wanganui Regional Museum in 1983. He is a member of the Wanganui Regional Committee of the Trust and President of the Whanganui Historical Society.

Wynne Colgan was born in Auckland and educated at Auckland Grammar School, the University of Auckland and the New Zealand Library School. For a number of years before his retirement he was Auckland's Deputy City Librarian. He has written a history of the Auckland Public Library and co-authored a history of the Auckland Grammar School. He is a member of the Auckland Regional Committee of the Historic Places Trust and was elected to the Trust's board in 1981.

Noel Crawford, married with five children, is a third-generation farmer at Cannington in South Canterbury. Involvement with Young Farmers Clubs led to his being awarded a study exchange to the United Kingdom in 1964 and he has been active in other community organisations since then. He is Chairman of the South Canterbury Regional Committee of the Historic Places Trust and author of *The Station Years*, which shared the J.M. Sherrard award for regional histories in 1982.

Janet Davidson was born in Lower Hutt. Studying anthropology at the University of Auckland initiated her interest in Auckland's volcanic cones. She has undertaken archaeological research in the tropical Pacific and, as the first E. Earle Vaile Archaeologist at the Auckland Institute and Museum, in the Auckland Province. She now lives in Dunedin and is associated with the Anthropology Department, University of Otago. She is married to a fellow archaeologist, Foss Leach, and has one daughter.

Barbara Fill was born in Wellington in 1955. She moved to Auckland ten years later and attended Epsom Girls' Grammar School. She graduated from Auckland Teachers College in 1978 and completed a B.A. in social anthropology at Auckland University in 1981. She became interested in social history while studying towards an M.A. She has worked as researcher and writer for the Wellington Regional Committee of the Historic Places Trust but is now freelancing.

Mark Hanger graduated from the University of Otago with a B.Sc. in botany in 1978. An abrupt change in direction saw him carrying out historical research for the New Zealand Forest Service on the timber industry in Southland. He was employed for 6 years by the Lands and Survey Department as a research/publicity officer, working predominantly with the Otago Goldfields Park. Recently he has helped form a specialist natural and cultural history educational tour company, Southern Heritage Tours.

Michael Hanrahan, married with three sons, was educated at St Kevin's College, Oamaru. He now farms at Dromore near Ashburton. From being unable to stand history at school, he is now deeply interested in local history and the history of the everyday lives of ordinary people. He edits *Vintage Farming*, a magazine for those interested in the preservation of all types of vintage machinery. His interest in old buildings focuses on small, obscure buildings that wouldn't normally be noticed.

Gail Lambert is honorary curator of ceramics with the Taranaki Museum in New Plymouth which is her home. She was born in Napier and educated in Wanganui. She nursed in Wellington and Christchurch before moving to New Plymouth in 1972, where she developed her passion for New Zealand history and pottery. She is on the board of the Historic Places Trust. Her publications include *Peter Wilson: Colonial Surgeon* and *An Illustrated History of Taranaki*, which she co-authored with her husband.

Jack Lee after 5 years at Takapuna Grammar School was discharged onto the labour market in the depths of the Depression. He went north and worked for about 10 years in Northland at a variety of rural pursuits. He finally joined the Public Works Department on engineering survey work. In 1942 he returned to Auckland to work successively for the Auckland City Council, the Railways Department, the Metropolitan Drainage Board and the Auckland Regional Authority. He is author of a recently published history '...*I Have Named it the Bay of Islands*'.

Beverley McCulloch trained as a school teacher. She gained an M.Sc. in geology from Canterbury University and worked for a period as artist for the Botany Division, Department of Scientific and Industrial Research. She is at present Liaison Officer at the Canterbury Museum. A long-standing member of the New Zealand Archaeological Association, she has done much archaeological work in the Kaikoura area.

Jim McKenzie, born in Paekakariki in 1961, was educated at Kapiti College and Victoria University, from which he graduated B.A. in geography and history. While employed by the Historic Places Trust as a researcher for just over 2 years, he was particularly involved in the Trust's historic areas programme. He researched and wrote the original report on the South Lambton Quay Conservation Area. He is at present living overseas.

Sheila Natusch was born in Invercargill in 1926, the daughter of R.H. Traill and his wife Dorothy whose mother was the artist Emily Moffett. She is a great-granddaughter of J.F.H. Wohlers. Her primary school days and later holidays were spent on Stewart Island where her father was ranger and naturalist. After a few years' teaching she married a fellow tramper, G.G. Natusch. She has illustrated and written several books about native plants, animals and geology and also written larger historical and biographical studies.

Darcy Ria of Manutuke retired in 1982 after serving for 40 years as an officer of the Department of Maori Affairs. Most of his time with the department was spent as Maori Welfare Officer then more recently Community Officer in Gisborne. He saw service overseas during World War II with the Maori Battalion. He considers himself otherwise 'just an ordinary sort of bloke'.

John Wilson, editor of this volume, is a Canterbury historian and journalist. He studied history at Canterbury University and at Harvard University, from which he graduated Ph.D. On his return to New Zealand in 1974 he became a journalist on the staff of *The Press*, Christchurch. He was the first Publications Officer of the Historic Places Trust, 1982-84, and continues to edit the Trust's quarterly magazine from his 120-year-old farmhouse at Springston on the Canterbury Plains.

Brian Wood has had a long-standing interest in the historic places of the West Coast. He was born in Westport and received his primary and secondary education there. He graduated in history from Canterbury University. He became a member of the Westland Regional Committee of the Historic Places Trust in 1971 and served as its chairman 1976-81. He contributed two chapters on the West Coast to *Historic Buildings of New Zealand: South Island* and has researched the Brunner mine site for the Trust.

Index

NOTES: The numbers in regular type refer to the text and the numbers in italics to the pictures and their captions. The names on the maps are not listed in this index. The titles of books and newspapers and the names of vessels are italicised. The names of Maori people are listed alphabetically by surname only when the name clearly conforms to European Christian name(s)/surname usage. They are otherwise listed alphabetically as they read in the text.